Intuition in Psychotherapy
and Counselling

Intuition in Psychotherapy and Counselling

RACHEL CHARLES BA(HONS), MPHIL(PSYCHOLOGY)LONDON
BACP Senior Accredited Practitioner (UKRC Reg.)
Integrative Psychotherapist, Suffolk

W
WHURR PUBLISHERS
LONDON AND PHILADELPHIA

© 2004 Rachel Charles
First published 2004
by Whurr Publishers Ltd
19b Compton Terrace
London N1 2UN England and
325 Chestnut Street, Philadelphia PA 19106 USA

British Library Cataloguing in Publication Data

A catalogue record for this book
is available from the British Library.

ISBN 1 86156 417 1

Typeset by Adrian McLaughlin, a@microguides.net
Printed and bound in the UK by Athenæum Press Ltd, Gateshead, Tyne & Wear.

Contents

Foreword

The development of this publication owes much to the fact that Rachel Charles is a published author with considerable clinical experience. The combination of privileging both theory and practice in the context of this study means that the book engages with issues that affect the therapeutic alliance. It is not surprising, therefore, that Rachel Charles has chosen to devote a full chapter to what she terms 'interpersonal perception within the session'. It is known that debates surrounding the concept of counter-transference, such as 'whether or not a therapist can experience a client's unconsciously denied affect', throw up questions that touch upon the role of intuitive perception in relation to clinical interpretation, and in this light a study of intuition as a clinical concern is much needed. In the first instance this publication provides an extensive analysis of the meaning of intuition culturally, philosophically and psychologically, while at the same time offering a discrete clinical focus, primarily maintained by the qualitative research aspect in which actual therapists' experiences and views are profiled and evaluated.

The author points out a difficulty that the psychotherapy professions face, maintaining that, although therapists and counsellors appear to value intuition as a necessary aspect of their work, this contrasts with what seems to be a 'dearth' of scholarly attention to the subject. It is Rachel Charles' interest in this contradiction that has inspired the in-depth research and critical analysis that the book exhibits. What this means is that the problematic is addressed: namely, that psychotherapists or counsellors can claim to be using intuition as the process by which they interpret the needs of a client yet, paradoxically, they demonstrate a striking inability to explain the nature of the phenomenon in either clinical or theoretical terms.

Many within the profession would maintain that a study of intuition in relation to the psychotherapeutic encounter could be unviable without considerable attention to the work of Carl Jung, for it is within Jung's thesis of psychological typology that the intuitive individual is profiled. That is to say Jung establishes that some individuals prioritise intuition as their 'superior function' of consciousness, which indicates that they have a propensity to experience the world through intuitive process. This suggests that certain individuals have a more immediate access to intuition than to the other psychological functions, perhaps indicating that they are more 'naturally' intuitive. These are the kind of issues that Rachel Charles investigates. Her rigorous study of the 'intuitive type', and Jungian typology as a whole, means that her discussion is extensive, both in respect of historical analysis and psychological implication.

What is exciting about this publication is that Rachel Charles raises a number of key questions including: can individuals be trained to enhance their intuitive capacity? One of the ways that this issue is approached is specifically to address nonverbal cues that can be unconsciously, intuitively perceived within sessions. It is here that the material of perception is studied and the therapist's 'decoding ability' of bodily cues is discussed. Fundamental problems are illuminated, for example: how much of clinical perception is actually intuition and how much is simply inference? The author does not avoid the complexities of concerns such as these.

Further questions come to the fore in relation to the training of psychotherapists and the supervision of clinical work. In the first place we could ask if 'intuitive types' become psychotherapists and counsellors precisely because of their typological predisposition. Moreover, if intuition is seen to play an essential role within the therapeutic alliance, the subject arises as to how clinical trainings operate to enculture intuitive process. The qualitative research presented here to help answer such questions is supported by the use of the Myers-Briggs Type Indicator as a testing instrument. A valuable aspect of this approach is that the author both investigates therapists' views of their own intuitive capacities while formally evaluating their typological propensity. The fact that Rachel Charles is professionally conversant with the MBTI ensures that the reader will gain certain insights into the intricacies of psychological assessment on the one hand, and can witness the specificity of the results on the other.

What becomes increasingly evident as the chapters unfold is that the author has left few stones unturned. In this way the publication certainly contributes beyond the confines of psychotherapeutic practice. Essentially it is a *tour de force* in that intuition has been further endorsed as a capacity that will always intrigue us. Indeed, many of the chapters serve to locate the reader within profound debate as to the vicissitudes of intuition. Thus, Rachel Charles has successfully accomplished both a broad and in-depth study of intuition that welds clinical investigation with theoretical analysis and critique.

Above all the author's intention here is not solely to validate her claims, nor to establish a specific position, rather the research is designed to ensure the reader's engagement with the issues. One strength of the book rests on the fact that in all of the attentions to intuition, whether theoretical, clinical or through qualitative research, an extensive bibliography is provided which emphasises the value of this publication as a resource for further research. Rachel Charles has offered a work that will ensure that psychotherapists and counsellors will not only benefit from its findings, but will most certainly enjoy the text for its academic rigour, clinical relevance, illumination and discernment.

Tessa Adams, FRSA, PhD
London, 2004

Acknowledgements

This project would never have been started had it not been for the enthusiasm in the first instance of my colleague, Margaret Davis, who convinced me not only to run a workshop on intuition, but to research and write about it. Special thanks are also due to Dr Tessa Adams, Jungian analyst, who spent a number of years as my academic supervisor at Goldmiths College guiding me through an extremely complex topic. Later encouragement came from Dr Chris French of the psychology department. Much ongoing support and inspiration came from Professor Petruska Clarkson and members of our group at Physis, including Peter Gleeson, Maureen Luden, Angela Hall, Barbara Dale, Joan Kendall, Rev. Dr Len Kofler and Dr Riccardo Draghi-Lorenz. Other kind colleagues to thank are Chris Hart, Anne Baeppler, Margaret Field, Barney Smith and Lyz Mole, all of whom have given generously of their time and experience, either by discussing aspects of the subject, participating in studies, or reading draft chapters and giving me helpful feedback. Dr Paul Rogers, Karen Baillie and Elvina Gilbert have also researched in the area of intuition and have freely loaned me their theses and dissertations. Professor Brian Thorne made some very valuable suggestions for the book when it was in its early stages, and as a result the work has been both enlarged and enriched.

For reasons of confidentiality, most case examples in the book do not represent specific individuals, but are rather composites of my working experience. However, where details could not easily be changed, I am greatly indebted to those clients and supervisees who have generously granted me permission to incorporate some brief descriptions taken from sessions.

I would also like to acknowledge the helpful assistance of the psychotherapy and counselling training departments of the following institutes: Belfast Cognitive Therapy Centre, Birmingham University, Coleg Sir Gar, Havering College of FE & HE, Institute of Psychosynthesis,

Inter-Psyche, Life-Force, London Bible College, New School of Psychotherapy and Counselling, St Martin's College, Sussex Downs College,
University of East Anglia, University of East London, West Nottingham-
shire College of FE and Wiltshire College.

Finally I would like to offer warm appreciation to my husband, John,
who has solved difficult computer problems and tolerated my long
absences during the thousands of hours of research and writing during
the creation of this book.

Preface

In the spring of 1996, I was invited to run a workshop on the subject of intuition at a local training centre for counsellors. It was affiliated to the Westminster Pastoral Foundation and the orientation was therefore largely psychodynamic, with its emphasis on childhood experiences and unconscious origins of present problems. It was intriguing to contemplate why I in particular had been chosen for this task by such a school. No specific explanation was forthcoming except that the general impression seemed to be that I was an intuitive sort of person, and, moreover, that the earlier part of my professional training had been within the transpersonal framework. There therefore seemed to be a link between the spiritual and the intuitive. Was there some truth in this? Did this mean that because I had learnt about psychosynthesis, prior to studying the integrative approach, that I was in some way more intuitive in my work than other therapists? In any case, what did this faculty consist of within a therapeutic setting and how useful was it?

My curiosity was aroused and I set about talking informally to colleagues, asking initially if they thought of themselves as intuitive. Most replied in the affirmative and were eager to discuss the subject. It was clear that they valued this quality highly, but much less clear was an explanation as to its nature. Situations were described whereby an intuition prevented some impending disaster, and an assortment of phrases such as 'sixth sense', 'tuning in', a 'hunch' or 'gut feeling' were forthcoming. It was noticeable, however, that people struggled for words that would adequately describe the experience of intuition, particularly within the context of counselling and psychotherapy. There was something elusive about it. Among my colleagues, there was therefore a discrepancy between their enthusiasm for the subject and their ability to explain its nature.

While I could be sure of a good attendance at my workshop due to the popularity of the subject, useful contributions from participants might well be patchy because of vagueness concerning the process involved. This meant that I myself needed to research intuition as in-depth as possible within the time available. I surmised that there could be a strong connection between unconscious messages picked up by the therapist from the patient, that is reactive counter-transference, and intuition and I therefore started by trawling through the psychoanalytic literature. Most striking was an almost complete absence of any reference to intuition within the clinical context. The most notable exception was Carl Gustav Jung, founder of analytical psychology, who gave intuition a central place within his typology, although he was ambivalent about its use within psychotherapy. Here, at least, was a theoretical foundation for my workshop. Further study of Roberto Assagioli's writings indicated to me that intuition was a faculty that could be developed. Drawing on my experience of psychosynthesis, I therefore devised some exercises involving meditation and visualization, movement and art to assist with this process.

The workshop was a success and many participants were considerably moved by their experiences and insights. My own imagination was now fired, but I was left with the frustration of an unfinished task. I wanted to know more and to contribute more to counselling practice. Here, surely, was the basis for a thesis. I was therefore delighted to be accepted by Goldsmiths College of London University to pursue an MPhil degree. The aims of the project were to discover the essential features of intuition as an aspect of human functioning, to provide a vocabulary for its comprehension and to study its role within the context of counselling and psychotherapy. I anticipated that this knowledge would provide a basis for specific recommendations for professional training and practice.

To begin with, an intensive survey of existing literature was put in hand, including the significant contributions from philosophers and mystics. As with psychoanalysis, psychology produced few really useful studies that applied directly to the therapeutic situation. I therefore investigated some reasons for this dearth of information. Where there was some relevant psychological theory, it became necessary to extrapolate from this to the clinical settings of counselling and psychotherapy.

The review of the literature concerning the process of intuition revealed that it is allo-logical, global and empathic, and largely unconscious. These findings are presented here in the anticipation that they will help therapists to understand in detail what may happen in sessions. Most interesting was my discovery from experimental psychology that nonverbal messages have been shown to dominate interpersonal communication. Since their cues are gathered intuitively, it would appear to be an advantage for a therapist to be an intuitive type. The characteristics of such a type are therefore discussed in detail in this book.

Some studies suggested that psychotherapists are no better than controls in detecting unconscious communications and in making clinical judgements. This may point to a deficit in training procedures, which is a concern. While the nature of intuition can be largely explained, the evidence implies that it cannot be taught directly as a skill that anyone can learn. Nevertheless, the literature supports my own view that it can be enhanced and developed. Ways in which this might be achieved are fully explored.

As far as Jung's writings were concerned, it was anticipated that a significant relationship would be found between his theory of intuition and the employment of this phenomenon in clinical practice. An in-depth critique of Jung's work followed, a résumé of which is given in this book. Fundamental to Jung's theory is his definition of intuition. This in particular was subject to my scrutiny and a comparison is made with the psychological and psychoanalytic findings of the literature review. Jung makes many assertions regarding the phenomenon of intuition, but supports these mostly with examples from philosophy, religious and literary works, rather than from the practice of psychotherapy. Because of this void, I set in motion qualitative studies to examine the nature of therapists' experiences of intuition within their work, how it manifested itself and what the results were in terms of its impact on sessions. Although my hypothesis concerning Jung's work was mostly confirmed, some of his concepts were not supported by my findings, indicating that his assertions need to be assessed with care.

The research made it possible to fulfil two of my main objectives, which were to make specific recommendations for the cultivation and teaching of intuition for the benefit of the professions of counselling and psychotherapy. However, it needs to be pointed out that, due to limitations of time and funds, it was only possible to implement three qualitative studies, and my findings should therefore be thought of as preliminary. The research is also restricted to intuition within the therapist, not the client. The results are nevertheless important in that they are breaking entirely new ground and therefore make an original contribution to the understanding of this particular aspect of the process and practice of counselling and psychotherapy.

While I was compiling this book, several colleagues were curious to know which perspective I was taking. Was it written from a person-centred, psychodynamic or transpersonal viewpoint, they asked, or even existential or psychoanalytic? There was a sense of competition, as if each wanted his or her own orientation to be promoted as the most intuitive. On my offering the explanation that it was in fact a phenomenological enquiry, which endeavoured to take an objective stance, there was a puzzled response, a disbelief even that it was possible to construct a book concerning psychotherapy or counselling that was not based on some pre-existing model. This suggests that we professionals have become so used to defending our own particular corners, our pet ways of working and underlying belief systems, that we find it increasingly difficult to be open-minded about what others have to contribute. There also seemed to be a presumption that, since I was a woman writer, the book would in some way be an addition to feminist literature. Clearly, the idea of 'female intuition' is still embedded in the popular psyche, despite research demonstrating that there is only a modest difference between women and men in this regard.

The book arose from a research project, which was fundamentally athe-oretical in stance. Indeed, part of the objective was to construct new the-ory, as well as build on the old, where indeed such literature existed. This has been achieved by weighing the existing evidence as to the nature of intuition, from whatever source it could be found, and then comparing this with the results of the original research set up for the project. The work has involved collecting together in one place all the salient notions concerning intuition, where relevant to counselling and psychotherapy, an overview not previously attempted.

However objective one may set out to be, I am aware that it is I who have asked the questions which have driven the research. Other individu-als may have posed different questions. Moreover, over the years I have developed and adopted my own integrative way of working. No doubt this will come across in the book, particularly where examples are given which are based on my own clinical experience. At the same time, the intention has been to reflect the best that various approaches have to offer. The reality is that we all need to use our intuition to build worth-while therapeutic relationships. Indeed, this book will demonstrate that we cannot do our work without it.

CHAPTER 1

The neglect of intuition

At the outset of this project, it seemed important to discover what research already existed on the topic of intuition, before collecting together my own thoughts and, most importantly, prior to setting up some qualitative studies to provide fresh information. I had anticipated that there must be a certain body of writings on the process and application of the phenomenon, and that these would form the basis for my own enquiries. I would then be able to allocate myself a place among those researchers and the work would become a cooperative, rather than a solitary, venture. As I sifted through the psychological abstracts, however, it was with a growing degree of nervousness that I began to realize that there was no specialist group of scholars devoting themselves to the subject and advancing knowledge in the field. In particular very few papers were available that dealt specifically with my own area of interest, that is clinical intuition within the contexts of counselling and psychotherapy. While those that did exist offered a small starting point, it became increasingly clear that I would also have to investigate the work from related disciplines and then perhaps extrapolate to the process of therapy. This seemed to be a daunting task, because it meant bringing together ideas from different areas in a coherent way. At the same time, I had a sense of excitement at embarking upon such a new and challenging venture. Here was the opportunity to make a truly original contribution, that held within it the possibility of being of real value to practitioners. Yet I was astonished at the dearth of existing literature and left with a curiosity as to why the subject of intuition had been so neglected.

My first instincts with any major project are to go to dictionaries and encyclopaedias to search out existing definitions and descriptions. Since there was on my bookshelf the *Penguin Dictionary of Psychology* (Drever, 1952), this seemed to be a good enough place to start, even though by now it was somewhat dog-eared with use. Perhaps it might at least offer some clues. According to this author, intuition is 'immediate perception or judgement without any conscious mental steps in preparation'. It occurred to me that if indeed the intuitive process is largely unconscious,

1

then this leaves us with the uncertainty of not understanding how or why we know what we know. This could well account for the apparent confusion among the therapists with whom I had spoken, as to the precise nature of intuition. Suddenly one is aware of some kind of knowledge being available, but the stages whereby this or that conclusion was reached remain quite obscure. This leaves one with the impression that the process of intuition is mysterious indeed.

An example immediately sprang to mind from my own practice. I recalled the first interview with a young woman, with whom I had been working for some time. That initial encounter left me with the distinct feeling that she had suffered some severe trauma at a time in the past, probably in childhood. Moreover, I anticipated that the work would be long and slow, and my notes at the time incorporated these thoughts. Yet she had said nothing about any such troubling event. On the contrary, she appeared on the surface to be bright and open, with clear blue eyes and an engaging smile. Our talk was mainly about finding ways of improving her relationship with her son. Why, then, should I be left with such a notion? I could only describe it as a 'hunch'.

When, however, I subsequently considered our meeting in minute detail, I could recall the tiniest of hints at some deeper difficulty. Whenever we touched on an emotional area, even if fleetingly, there was a slight hesitation and subtle change in the expression around her eyes, which I could only describe as 'guarded'. She also had the habit of holding two fingers over her lips, which seemed to indicate that some kind of editing process was going on. At least, that was my interpretation. At the time I said nothing of these reflections, but simply noted them for future reference. It was many months before she was able to reveal to me something of the terrible cruelty that had occurred to her, and we were able gently to explore those sensitive regions and the impact on her present life. In retrospect, then, it is perhaps sometimes possible to perceive some of the small clues that provide the basis for an intuition, although at the time much information seems to be taken in at a subconscious level. If this is the case, then how is it feasible to examine this process?

Despite the fact that my Penguin dictionary also described intuition as 'a popular rather than scientific term', I decided to consult the psychological literature to find out what, if any, experimental studies had been conducted. These, perhaps, might throw some light on the unconscious processes involved. Dr Malcolm Westcott stood out as having taken the subject seriously and his book *Toward a Contemporary Psychology of Intuition* (1968) not only places the phenomenon in a historical context, but also examines it both theoretically and empirically. He regards as noteworthy less than a dozen studies carried out over the course of the previous 50 years. A survey of *Psychological Abstracts* for the years 1931 to 1941 produced only 20 references to intuition, and between 1941 and 1967 less than that same number. Moreover, most of these discussed philosophical issues, although some made practical recommendations for its use within varying contexts, ranging from judicial proceedings to art criticism. He does, however, point to a revival of interest in the processes of creativity during the 1950s and '60s by educationalists, and intuition features here.

By 1978 the situation had not improved, when another psychologist, Tony Bastick, initiated an exhaustive computer-aided search (1982, pp. 6–7). Of the 2,692,000 articles, reports and theses inspected from the five most likely sources (*ERIC* from 1966, *BIOSIS Previews* from 1972, *ISMEC* from 1973, *Psychological Abstracts* from 1967, and *Comprehensive Dissertations Abstracts* from 1861) only 91 contained the word 'intuition' in the title or as a description, and of these, a mere 24 were actual studies into the subject. My own searches were equally disheartening: just the occasional paper from varying disciplines looking at, for example, memory and intuition (Wippich, 1994), implicit learning (Lieberman, 2000), its educational applications (Brown, 1993), or its role in discovery (Bowers et al., 1990). It was notable that several writers bemoaned the lack of consistent research. After reviewing the existing literature, R.C. Frick in his study of intuition and inference declared: 'In general, few writers go beyond an almost wistful contemplation of this mysterious trait and what potentially dramatic properties it may have. The few attempts to seek it out, to define and measure it, have up to this time met with only moderate success' (1970, p. 2). Twelve years later, Tony Bastick was voicing a similar sentiment in his book *Intuition: How We Think and Act*, declaring that the 'hole' caused by the lack of studies into such a key concept was becoming an increasing embarrassment, and that the need for empirical research was crucial (1982, p. 7). Partly in response to this state of affairs the Academy of Consciousness Studies was set up at Princeton University in 1994 with the aim of taking a cross-disciplinary look at mental processes, including that of intuition, through the clarity of the intellect (Davis-Floyd and Arvidson, 1997). Yet even here the research described was of little help to my own investigation, none of it dealing with psychotherapy.

Considering that intuition has been called 'one of the most important cognitive faculties of man' by Nobel prize-winner Konrad Lorenz (1951), it is remarkable that it has received so little serious investigative attention in the past. After all, there is no lack of available material. Most people appear to have the ability to intuit. There must therefore be plenty of opportunity to study the process, for there is a lot of the 'raw material' about, whether this consists merely of everyday 'gut feelings' about a course of action to take, or the scientist's awesome moments of creative inspiration, as a result of which the boundaries of knowledge are pushed forward yet again.

One reason for the shunning of the term by psychologists may be that it had become associated, in the popular imagination, with the paranormal, which, despite serious research by the Koestler Foundation, among others, is generally regarded with suspicion. There are grounds for such an attitude, as some investigations into certain psychic phenomena have exposed fraudulent features. For example, analytical psychologist Carl Gustav Jung studied a 'Miss S.W.' (in fact a young cousin of his named Hélène Preiswerk), who had earned a reputation as a medium. Jung recorded her séances during 1899 and 1900 and these became the basis of his student dissertation (CW 1, pp. 3–88). While her 'somnambulistic states' were initially of psychological interest, these 'attacks' later faded and she was caught hiding small objects in her dress and otherwise cheating, after which Jung discontinued the study. Other investigations into the paranormal have been inconclusive. The psychoanalyst, J. Eisenbud, examined telepathy in the clinical context, but could find no substance in the notion that such a process might assist in the treatment of patients (1946).

Another possible explanation for the lack of research into this faculty is that it is too emotionally loaded, making objectivity difficult. It is associated with spiritual experiences of the most sublime kind on the one hand and basic instincts on the other. Westcott writes: 'The term, the concept, the fact or fiction of intuition – all carry emotional overtones, regardless of the persuasion of the writer or the context of the writing. These emotional overtones range from contemplative delight to livid disgust' (1968, pp. 1–2). The psychologist G.W. Allport also considered this to be a problem: 'The terminology "intuition" is often avoided in psychology as it is a term carrying excess emotional freight' (1965, p. 545). These quotations indicate that both the word 'intuition' itself and the concept behind it are not well disposed to objective analysis, because the emotional implications are such that they may invalidate any findings. Such an attitude would preclude the study of many other concepts, including inspiration, imagination and even creativity, all of which are generally considered to carry emotional content. Supported by much research Bastick took the opposite approach and accepted the emotional aspect as an intrinsic part of the phenomenon: 'Our theory is simply that we emotionally encode information. Our thoughts and behaviours are the decoded versions of this information which, associated by their contiguous common feelings, tend to be recalled when we re-experience these emotions' (1982, p. 354).

Most people seem to have personal associations with intuition and subjective experiences may have seemed magical, or at the other extreme derisory, because rational procedures were not in evidence. While it can be appreciated that experimental psychologists may find the word awkward, qualitative researchers take into account the interaction between observer and observed, realizing that total objectivity is an impossibility. Any emotional overtones entering the research are brought into awareness and may be used as additional information. Indeed, as far as this present book is concerned, personal process will be incorporated into the empirical studies and made explicit.

The negative attitudes towards the concept have led to a further predicament: in eschewing the term 'intuition', psychologists have introduced other phrases thought to be more 'scientific', which appear to describe certain characteristics of this aptitude, such as 'unconscious concept acquisition', 'preverbal concept formation', 'social perception' or 'implicit learning'. This means that the phenomenon is rarely considered as a whole, but rather particular facets may be found scattered across the literature.

The linking of intuition with unreliable 'hunches' in popular language has posed another problem. While these may be surprisingly accurate, they may also be misleading – and this is an aspect that will be studied further in this book. Whatever the reasons, most psychologists appear to have avoided the word. The closest term which they have adopted is 'insight'. Bastick debates the difference between the two terms and concludes that the theoretical usage of the word intuition is 'much older and more widespread' than that of insight, but that the latter term is more often linked with operational usage in experimental psychology and can therefore be regarded as 'more scientific' (1982, pp. 29–32, 35–50). The difficulty with this view is that psychology has concentrated only on the properties of intuition or insight that can be subjected to experimental analysis, with the main focus on their application in problem-solving. Bastick chooses to use the two terms interchangeably on the basis that this shortcoming is a methodological one, rather than a conceptual difference. However, in his book he does point out some conceptual differences, particularly with regard to theoretical applications, so this appears to be an inconsistency in his work. In psychotherapy it is notable that there are differences in usage: the word 'intuition' generally refers to the process within the therapist; this may facilitate the awakening of 'insight' in the client, whereby symptoms can be better understood.

There are other reasons why intuition has been so neglected. In early classical and philosophical writings there is a lack of any precise term at all for the intuitive process, although descriptions of particular mental states convey experiences associated with intuition, with a way of knowing that is not via the intellect. Indeed, the earliest connections with the subject are mystical or religious in character and take the form of some kind of communication from god to person, resulting in a revelation or prophecy, or alternatively a warning or monition. Socrates gives a very clear account of his own experiences of a daemon or 'prophetic voice' that advises on courses of action (Plato, in Tredennick and Tarrant, 1954). Because there was no concept of unconscious processes at that time, intuitions were projected out on to supernatural beings. Nevertheless, such writings provide valuable insights into important aspects of the concept and guidance as to its origins. These therefore deserve exploration and are included in Chapters 8 and 9.

Taking a look at more recent history, another reason may have been the pre-eminence of behaviourism, which from the 1920s for several decades was a major influence on psychological thought. Put simply, the aim here was that, given the stimulus, one would be able to predict the response. This overriding approach created difficulties for researchers wishing to carry out experiments within a different theoretical framework. In particular there was an ongoing controversy concerning perception and the process of learning between the Gestalt psychologists and the S-R associationists, who focused on the strength of an association between stimulus and response. The S-R theorists declared that learning was a step-by-step inductive process based on trial and error, whereas Gestalt psychologists promoted the idea that whole forms were the basic units of perception. It was the organization of these that resulted in insight. The deadlock that came about through this altercation seems to have caused a scarcity of literature on the related subject of intuition, which is similar in a number of respects, such as the seeing of connections and a sense of emerging patterns.

D. Cohen (1978), writing within an educational context, places the responsibility for this situation on the personalities of some of the theorists. After interviewing 13 prominent psychologists involved in the dispute, he reveals an 'evangelistic egoism' and a reluctance to recognize the work of colleagues who take a different viewpoint, or to deal dispassionately with criticisms. It is true that some of these psychologists took a strong position, for example, Professor B.F. Skinner, who, following the standpoint of John Broadus Watson (1924), rejected the concept of 'mind' altogether because it had no basis in physical science. As for artistic creation, he considered that this was controlled entirely by the contingencies of reinforcement (1969). However, it is unreasonable to dismiss a human attribute as non-existent just because it cannot easily be subjected to laboratory testing or statistical analysis.

The dearth of serious studies into intuition among psychoanalysts seems particularly remarkable, bearing in mind that it is a generally held view among practising psychotherapists that the use of this function is invaluable for the collection of clinical data. Freud only mentions it in passing, and even then in derogatory terms: 'Intuition and divination ...

may safely be reckoned as illusions, the fulfilment of wish impulses' (SE XXII, p. 159). I can only surmise that, like empathy (shown by Bastick to be a feature of intuition, 1982), it has been underestimated or taken for granted, along with the assumption that it can be neither taught nor learned and that a therapist either has an aptitude for this kind of inner knowing or does not have it (Greenson, 1960). There are a few exceptions, the most notable being, of course, Carl Jung, who valued the phenomenon highly and featured it in his typology (CW 6, 1923/1971). For this reason Jung's writings will be emphasized in this present enquiry. At a later date, Theodor Reik examined his own way of working with psychoanalysis, concluding that, despite Freud's assertions, the method was intuitive rather than scientific. His experiences are lucidly and honestly described in *Listening with the Third Ear* (1948/1975), and provide a valuable resource for my own researches. Psychiatrist Eric Berne is another exception and reference will therefore be made to the series of papers that he wrote on the subject (1977).

My own view as regards the neglect of serious study of the phenomenon during recent decades has to do with a broader issue, that of the pre-eminence given to the 'outer way of knowing' (knowledge from observation and experience) as opposed to the 'inner way of knowing' (ideas, principles and truths as seen in the inward light of the mind) during our present predominantly scientific era. Writing in the 1880s, the Reverend James McCosh identified these two 'schools of mind' from his philosophical investigations into intuition, each at that time still 'struggling for mastery' (1882, p. 4), despite the fact that Auguste Comte in developing his philosophy of positivism had already placed empirical, scientific knowledge at the pinnacle of his 'stages of knowing' (1830–42). During the twentieth century technological successes gave prominence to the analytic, conscious forms of intelligence, namely logic and reason. From a philosophical perspective, logical positivism has been a major influence, which has rejected the assertions of metaphysics in favour of verifiable cognitive statements.

Few seem to remember that some of the greatest scientific breakthroughs have stemmed from an intuitive flash, including the relativity theory of Einstein, although those who have experienced this state do acknowledge its importance, declaring even that reason is merely the servant of intuition. The mathematician Henri Poincaré took this stance: 'We believe that in our reasonings we no longer appeal to intuition; the philosophers will tell us that this is an illusion. Pure logic could never lead us to anything but tautologies; it could create nothing new; not from it alone can any science issue' (1929/1969, p. 208). It is clear from this statement that the creative mental leap that leads to scientific discovery depends upon the intuitive process.

Carl Jung ascribes the apparent lack of interest in intuition to fear:

> Through our feelings we experience the known, but our intuitions point to things that are unknown and hidden – that by their very nature are secret. If ever they become conscious, they are intentionally kept back and concealed, for which reason they have been regarded from earliest times as mysterious, uncanny and deceptive. They are hidden from the scrutiny of man, and he also hides himself from them out of *deisidaemonia*. He protects himself with the shield of science and the armour of reason. His enlightenment is born of fear; in the daytime he believes in an ordered cosmos, and he tries to maintain this faith against the fear of chaos that besets him by night. (Jung, 1933/1961, p. 187)

As an experienced psychiatrist, his view is that the prevailing belief in science and trust in reason, so characteristic of twentieth-century Western attitudes, masks the fear of chaos lying within the depths of the individual psyche. As long as people are dealing with the known and rational, they feel safe. To investigate something as nebulous as intuition, however, means probing beneath the surface, with the attendant risk of revealing something frightening or unpalatable. However, as an important part of human mental functioning, it cannot be excluded.

Theodor Reik makes the interesting observation that repression and denial greatly restrict our capacity for perceiving the minute signals that people send out (1948/1975, p. 137). Perhaps they also inhibit our willingness to analyze the perceptive process by which intuitions are reached.

* * * *

The experience of tackling this initial research was somewhat like encountering a complex maze. Promising leads would appear, inviting me to follow with enthusiasm, one reference pointing me in the direction of another. All along the way I would be considering how this route might take me towards better understanding of the central issue. More often than not I would find that I needed to turn a different corner from the one anticipated. Even then, after much scurrying about, the realization would dawn that I was approaching yet another dead end. Despite this, several paths had taken me close to 'home' and these were sufficient to encourage me to continue the exploration.

So what had I learnt so far? In addition to the possible reasons for the absence of research into intuition, it was becoming clear to me that it is a process that happens largely out of awareness, leaving us mystified as to how we arrived at a certain piece of knowledge. Indications at this stage were that intuitions may be both accurate and useful, but this is not always the case. I took this as a note of warning about relying unduly on them in an unquestioning way.

Having by now read much around the subject, I was beginning to have a feel for the historical context and how the ascendancy of logic and reason had left intuition in a subordinate position. Particularly extraordinary had been the disregard of this important process by early psychoanalysts in their efforts to make the practice of their profession conform to scientific principles. Only a handful of practitioners were sufficiently courageous not to follow this trend. Equally, the few psychologists who chose to study intuition experimentally had to resist abiding by the prevailing theories. Yet I was beginning to see that, although small in quantity, there were a few sources in existence that offered an auspicious starting-point for my own enquiries.

CHAPTER 2
Beyond reason

Since so little has apparently been written about intuition, how then is it possible to discover from the literature something about its nature? Fortunately, two major sources had come to light during my searches, which consider its constituents in some depth. The first is Carl Jung's book on psychological types (CW 6), offering an extended definition of intuition (paras 770–2), and the second is Tony Bastick's comprehensive volume *Intuition: How We Think and Act* (1982), which includes a list of properties. Each author approaches the subject from an entirely different perspective, but it struck me that this could be an advantage, since the one could be assessed against the other. Although neither of these texts is supported by empirical evidence from the clinical situation, it is nevertheless possible to learn something about the main constituents of intuition.

For some time I had been trying to track down Theodor Reik's work, but without success. One day, when leafing through a catalogue, the title *Listening With the Third Ear* suddenly came to my notice. By strange good fortune the last edition had been reprinted in paperback. It is a subjective account of work with patients, which, surprisingly, monitors the intuitive rather than analytic process. The text was absorbing, and I quickly realized that this would help to supply at least some of the case material that the other two sources lacked.

Jung's typological theories, of which intuition forms a part, were moulded over a long period of time and based on his professional and personal observations of people, together with a scrutiny of his own individual psyche. He thought of himself as a scientist and stated specifically that he was offering to readers a 'critical psychology' (CW 6, p. xv). However, some reviewers have found his work insufficiently rigorous and certain commentators have been witheringly censorious. Some orthodox psychoanalysts have been particularly harsh. Edward Glover, for example, alludes to Jung's writings as 'a mish-mash of Oriental philosophy with a bowdlerized psycho-biology' (1950, p. 134). It has to be said that Jung's statements are supported by examples from literature and philosophical and religious writings rather than from case material, and they need therefore to be considered with care. In particular, intuition receives little attention by way of sound psychological investigation to substantiate the views presented. However, Jung was ahead of his time in pointing out the shortcomings of the empirical method: 'A fact never exists only as it is in itself, but also as we see it' (CW 6, p. 303). In other words, the object observed can at best only be interpreted by the observer, and, moreover, the observer inevitably affects the observed, all of which has been a recent debate in research methodology. Jung wanted subjective empiricism, that is, observation of the self, to be regarded as just as valid as objective scientific research, but this brought him into conflict with scientists of the time. Despite the various criticisms, Jung makes some insightful assertions about intuition, which are of considerable benefit here.

At the other extreme is Tony Bastick, a psychologist, who constructs a theory of intuition based on contemporary knowledge of unconscious processes and how the brain works. Unlike Jung, he has a turgid and laborious writing style, illustrated with complex diagrams, which make his ideas difficult to assimilate. As already mentioned, he also equates insight with intuition, concepts which are not precisely synonymous. He is, however, clear about the properties of intuition and lists 20 as significant. Of these, I have selected the ones that have a direct bearing on the process that occurs within the therapist.

Derivation of *intuition*

Let us follow Jung's example first of all, and have a look at the derivation of the word 'intuition'. This should give us a feel for the origin of the concept. To open his definition (CW 6, para. 770), Jung refers to the Latin *intueri*, which he translates in his original German text as *anschauen*. The English version of his work by H.G. Baynes (1923) gives the meaning 'to look at or into', which is not exactly equivalent to the word chosen by Jung; indeed some shades of meaning are lost. Nor does it match the derivation supplied by the *Oxford English Dictionary* (Simpson and Weiner, 1989), which interprets *intueri* as to 'look upon', 'consider', 'contemplate'. *Cassell's German Dictionary* (Breul, 1909), in print at the time of the writing of *Psychologische Typen*, gives 'to look at' or 'contemplate', followed by the adjective *anschauend*, 'intuitive', 'contemplative' as in *anschauende Erkenntnis* or 'intuitive knowledge'. The English words given for the adjective or adverb *anschaulich* are 'perceptual', 'intuitively evident' or 'clear'. Held within the verb *anschauen*, therefore, are the related meanings associated with contemplation, perception, clarity and something intuitively evident, all missing from the rather superficial translation 'to look at or into'. The 'looking' therefore refers to an inner sight or vision, a mental apprehension, a process of perceiving, rather than something seen with the eyes.

Jung's definition does, however, incorporate both the 'into' and the 'at' in the sense that intuition may be either subjective or objective, the first being 'perception of unconscious psychic data originating in the subject', the second 'perception of data dependent on subliminal perceptions of the object and on the feelings and thoughts they evoke' (CW 6, para. 771). From the first of these two statements it is clear that the 'looking into' refers to the subjective kind of intuition, the looking into oneself and having access, through a perceptive process, to information held within the psyche but not previously available to conscious awareness. The second, which refers to the 'looking at', concerns the way in which perception of something or someone outside of oneself is arrived at through the taking in of information at a subliminal level, combined with the conscious awareness of the thoughts and feelings which this may arouse.

The introspection involved in examining oneself comes naturally to introverted types, who may have a temperamental advantage over extraverts in this respect. There is more about this in Chapter 4. Moment-by-moment self-awareness can be crucial to progress within the clinical situation, because the therapist's personal responses can offer vital information concerning the client. For example, in a recent session, I found myself becoming increasingly tired and, yes, even bored as I listened to my client's situation at home. This is most unusual for me, as I find people absorbing and it is rare that I find myself flagging. Most importantly I knew that I had had a good night's sleep and there seemed to be no reason why I should feel that way. The suspicion therefore entered my mind that the boredom might be hers rather than mine. I asked her if she found life tedious. At first she looked surprised and denied it: 'How could I, with such a wonderful daughter to care for?' But it gradually came out that she found the routine of domesticity dull. After eventually finding herself a challenging job, the dynamics of the sessions changed completely. With that client it was very easy to become involved in her story and to respond on that level, but that resulted in little forward movement. It was only when I used my inner response as information that useful progress was made. Within the context of psychotherapy this is sometimes referred to as 'reactive counter-transference' (Clarkson, 1995, p. 89). This is investigated in further detail in Chapter 7.

Equally, heightened perception of the object, in this case a person, can provide useful clues, which will aid intuitive understanding. Having moved into a new consulting room, which has its door at the bottom of some stairs, it was only after a number of sessions that I began to realize how much information was available from the sound of the footfalls.

Their dynamics, whether loud or soft, and pace, fast or slow, told me not only something of the mood of the person, but also the physical health. At first that information had been absorbed subliminally, but after focusing on it, much useful material became available to awareness.

Guy Claxton in his book *Hare Brain Tortoise Mind* (1997) dismisses Jung's concepts on the ground that he 'held to a view of intuition as a way of seeing *into* the unconscious, rather than as a product *of* it'. As an experimental psychologist, Claxton classifies intuition as a faculty that emanates from the unconscious. He continues: 'Jung's psychology ... now looks rather coarse in the light of our better, more empirically based, understanding of the way in which the unconscious itself generates intuitions' (p. 234). While Jung did indeed consider that intuition was, at least in part, a way of perceiving the contents held within the psyche, a looking into the unconscious as described above, or to use his own words 'perception of unconscious contents' (CW 6, para. 899), the implication from his writings is that he also saw it as a product of it, at any rate a part of the unconscious able to perceive data outside the self. This is particularly so with reference to the extraverted attitude: 'In the extraverted attitude, intuition as the function of unconscious perception is wholly directed to external objects' (para. 610). It seems from this that personal temperament may have a bearing on how one experiences intuition and whether the focus is mainly internal or external (see also Chapter 4).

As for contemplation, this is a process which has rather gone out of fashion in our fast-moving high-tech. world. Who today has time for quiet reflection, particularly those counsellors who work within the confines of a doctor's surgery or an agency, where waiting lists are long and sessions are necessarily limited? Nevertheless, this can be an important part of the intuitive process, and space is given to this subject in the chapter on spirituality.

In paragraph 951 Jung also adds that intuition is 'perception via the unconscious', in other words a method of perceiving that employs the unconscious, which is not the same as just looking into it. Furthermore, in continuing his definition in paragraph 770, he states that intuition 'mediates perceptions in an *unconscious way*' (his emphasis). He sees it therefore as a perceptive process that can also find the links between the perceptions, but without awareness that such mediation is taking place.

It is clear from these quotations that Jung did not hold exclusively to the view that intuition was a way of seeing into the unconscious; this was just a part of its purpose.

Looking at my own practice, I can see how often this making of connections takes place. A few weeks ago when with a client I spontaneously picked up a holiday brochure, which had been sent to me, offering workshops on a variety of subjects. On giving it to him, I had no idea that the week he would choose to book would have such a transformative effect. However, I did have an inkling that something there would be right for him. None of this was logically thought through. Connections had been made, out of awareness, with his loneliness and his longing for recognition, his need for self-expression and an outlet for his creativity, and some means by which he would at last give himself permission to have some fun. Combined with this was a sense that the timing would now be exactly right for him. It was. After this experience he was able to give up being in the position of victim, and began to take responsibility for building a new life for himself.

So far, then, to summarize the connection with its Latin origins, intuition is an inner form of looking, a perceptive process that may involve contemplation and clarity. Jung regards it as (1) a form of perception that employs the unconscious; (2) a means of accessing unconscious information held within the psyche; (3) a way of taking in information at a subliminal level about an external object (or person); (4) a process by which the links between perceptions are unconsciously found. The two types of intuition, subjective and objective, can be seen to be allied to the Latin derivation.

Subliminal perception

This discussion leads to the question of unconscious perception. There are many statements in Jung's writing concerning intuition which are based on the assumption that subliminal perception exists, that the function of intuition has the power to perceive unconscious contents and that it can find the connections between the perceptions via an unconscious process.

If this process of intuiting is unconscious, then how can we know it exists, let alone what it consists of? Jung admits that 'its nature is very difficult to grasp' (CW 6, para. 610). It seems to be possible, sometimes, to track unconscious connections in retrospect, as the above case shows, and one can of course infer its nature from the results of its processes. Many phenomena in our universe cannot be consciously perceived by the five senses, but we know of their existence nevertheless by observing how they influence surrounding procedures and objects. For example, although we cannot see radio waves, we know they exist simply by tuning in to a chosen station and listening to the transmission. Similarly, although we cannot observe unconscious processes themselves, we can see and hear how people's behaviour, feelings, conscious thoughts and perceptions are being altered by some invisible influences.

Freud had noticed how slips of the tongue, bungled actions, the mislaying of objects and so forth (usually referred to as 'parapraxes') had a hidden meaning and claimed that they occurred when a conscious intention was inhibited by an unconscious one (SE VI). Psychotherapists are familiar with such dynamics, for example resistance to the process of therapy, perhaps evident in the late arrival of a client, or the 'forgetting' of sessions, or the revelation of some important information during the last few minutes, when there is no time left to address the subject in depth. When the client is challenged, it invariably becomes evident that an unconscious mechanism is protecting him or her from facing some uncomfortable truths.

As far as psychoanalytic theory is concerned, the concept of the unconscious is central to it. Yet Freud did not 'discover' it, as is sometimes believed (Ellenberger, 1970). He was, however, the first person to investigate methodically the function of the unconscious in both normal and abnormal mental life. As a young psychiatrist, Jung also carried out psychological research into unconscious mechanisms, in particular the repression of painful or difficult experiences, through his word association tests. He noticed that patients were unduly slow in responding to certain stimulus words, or could find no associative answer at all. After further work with the patients, it became clear that such disturbances were linked to psychic conflicts or wounds (Jung, 1963/1995, p. 170).

Indeed, awareness of unconscious processes has a long history traceable to Galen (c. AD 130–200). Whyte (1962/1967) explores this in considerable depth, so it is necessary to give only a brief summary here. Galen, founder of experimental physiology, is credited with the acknowledgement that we make unconscious inferences from perceptions (Siebeck, 1884, p.195). Subsequently the subject appeared in different guises. The philosopher and theologian St Thomas Aquinas (1225?–74) reflected upon the products of the 'soul' as the source of certain functions that proceeded without conscious direction: 'I do not observe my soul apart from its acts. There are thus processes in the soul of which we are not immediately aware' (Gilbey, 1951, no. 292).

Jung made an in-depth study of the Swiss physician Paracelsus (1493–1541), mainly remembered for his recognition of the ways in which the mind and emotions contribute to disease. Study of his patients led him to realize that invisible influences were resulting in physiological changes. Such forces he believed were both biological and spiritual in nature (CW 15, p. 94).

The English Platonist, John Norris (1632–1704), gave a brief but lucid description of unconscious perception when he stated simply, 'We may have ideas of which we are not conscious.' He therefore understood that the mind could operate creatively without intervention from the knowing self. Further consideration in his 'Cursory Reflections' (1690) of the elusive nature of ideas shows that he realized that it is possible to be aware of the effect that ideas can have, without actually being able to discern them as such: 'There may be an impression of ideas without any actual perception of them' (in Whyte, 1962/1967, p. 96). Having an 'impression' of someone or something is often a way of recognizing that intuition is at work (see Chapter 10).

It was Leibniz (1646–1716), however, who gave a much fuller account of what he regarded as unconscious mental activity. He considered that human cerebral life was unquantifiable because it is so extensive and continues mainly below the threshold of awareness, with just a few perceptions rising to the surface: 'Our clear concepts are like islands which arise above the ocean of obscure ones' (1765/1981, Bk II).

There was a cluster of attention to the unconscious in the eighteenth century, notably in the work of Kant (1724–1804), who reflects a similar position to that of Leibniz. Those perceptions of which we are not directly aware he referred to as 'dark', while the others, of which we have full awareness, he called 'clear'. The area of 'dark' perceptions he considered to be 'immeasurable', while the 'clear' ones 'in contrast cover infinitely few points which lie open to consciousness' (1798/1978, p. 18). That relatively few points could be so illuminated led him to marvel at the nature of the mind.

It was left to Johann Gottlieb Fichte (1762–1814), however, to come up with the term 'the Unconscious' which he equated with the perceptive processes. Here lay the fundamental foundation of awareness, from which arose the experience of continuous consciousness within the framework of time. 'The apperceptive faculty of the mind is an activity which contains the ultimate basis of all consciousness, but never itself comes to consciousness' (1802, p. 161).

By the end of the eighteenth century evidence of unconscious perception had been clearly articulated by inference from its products. The man who was to have a direct influence on Freud's teachers in Vienna, however, was Sir William Hamilton, whose systematic enquiries into the nature of mental processes led to the formation of a British school of thinkers and physicians, generally referred to as the 'monists' because they viewed the patient as a body–mind unity. Experience taught them that it was erroneous to draw a dividing line between organic and psychical forces.

I.H. Fichte (1796–1879), a psychologist and son of the philosopher quoted above, came up with the concept of the 'preconscious' existence of ideas, a 'middle condition of the mind' in which consciousness lies in embryo, 'in a merely potential state', carrying nevertheless the characteristic of intelligence, although not yet expressed. Anticipating Jung, he saw the unconscious as 'rich' and containing 'hidden treasures', the place where creative ideas were gestated (Fichte in Whyte 1962/1967, p. 159).

It was Frederic Myers, who, towards the end of the nineteenth century, finally incorporated the unconscious into the notion of the self, describing it as the 'subliminal self'. This indicates an acceptance of unconscious processes as an essential part of one's being (1892, pp. 333–403).

With the development of psychology as a separate discipline, an interest arose in examining unconscious perception under controlled conditions. Some of these studies are described in Bornstein and Pittman (1992), several of which pre-date Jung's theory of typology; no doubt he was aware of these. For instance in 1898 B. Sidis carried out an experiment in which subjects were asked to state the number or letter written on a card which was held just too far away for it to be seen. When the subjects complained that they could make out nothing at all or could see only a blur, they were asked to guess and were correct significantly more often than by chance. The conclusion Sidis came to was that we have within us 'a secondary subwaking self' that perceives things that the primary waking self is unable to discern. It is interesting that the idea of a secondary self appears here within the context of experimental psychology. This is an area which is explored in detail in Chapter 8.

From the weight of attention in history to the unconscious, it is appropriate for Jung to maintain the assumption that unconscious perception does in fact exist. It monitors our bodily movements, and takes in information that interacts with our reservoir of ideas and emotions which in turn may affect our mood and behaviour, whether or not we are aware of these influences.

The 'infantile and primitive' aspects of intuition

It is important to realize that the words 'infantile' and 'primitive' in Jung's texts are not in any way intended to be pejorative, but rather are meant to be literal, that is, as earlier in time in a developmental or evolutionary sense. Thus, when he states in his definition that 'intuition is a characteristic of infantile and primitive psychology' (CW 6, para. 772), he means that this function evolved early in human history. This is paralleled in the developing child: intuitive and instinctive behaviour is therefore evident at the outset in small babies, while deliberate, rational thinking develops at a later stage along with language. Yet, as Jung stresses in his typology, the intuitive aspects remain of great importance throughout life, often not appreciated by modern Western societies which tend to place too much emphasis on the rational mode.

Jung undertook a considerable amount of fieldwork among undeveloped societies with the purpose of understanding more about the unconscious in himself and in Western people in general, and to see more clearly the primitive residues in the modern psyche. His discoveries informed much of his thinking, especially as regards religious rites and ceremonies, and the use of symbol and myth. In his autobiography, he wrote:

> I unconsciously wanted to find that part of my personality which had become invisible under the influence and pressure of being European. This part stands in unconscious opposition to myself, and indeed I attempt to repress it ... The predominantly rationalistic European finds much that is human alien to him, and he prides himself on this without realising that this rationality is won at the expense of his vitality, and that the primitive part of his personality is consequently condemned to a more or less underground existence. (1963/1995, p. 273)

Here Jung appears to be opposing the rational, thinking part of himself with the irrational, more primitive aspect, which, like most sophisticated Europeans, he is reluctant to acknowledge. The result, however, is a serious loss of vigour.

Psychologist Guy Claxton gives a vivid account of the sort of intelligence that is wired in to the entire animal kingdom, including human beings, with the purpose of aiding survival. Just as a spider weaves its web, manoeuvres its prey or freezes if the air moves in a disturbing way, so a baby may smile hopefully at its mother or turn its head away from a looming object (1997, pp. 16–17). These genetically given reactions may not be sufficient, however, if there is change in the environment. Thus, a spider may still freeze even if dangerously visible in a white bathtub, or a baby may turn its head away even though the object looming is in fact a harmless balloon. The next developmental stage is know-how, remembering useful patterns so that they can guide future actions. A baby will soon learn from experience the difference between a balloon and a face, will quickly distinguish between its parents' faces and react accordingly. Its brain is malleable, being formed not just from the built-in experiences of ancestors, but also from the idiosyncrasies of its own experiences. We find this listed in Tony Bastick's theory of intuition as property number 5: 'influenced by experience' (1982, p. 25).

The ensuing developmental stage evolves through curiosity, installed in many species as a basic drive. Actively exploring the environment and thereby learning more about it, often through play, extends competence and reduces uncertainty. No conscious intention, no deliberation is needed for any of this; acquisition of know-how happens spontaneously. Moreover, much of it evolves prior to language, or, in the case of many animals, without the language of words at all. Claxton thus justifies his statement that 'knowing, at root, is implicit, practical, intuitive' (p. 19). Bastick lists this as property number 13: 'innate, instinctive knowledge or ability'. Unfortunately, we in the West seem to have forgotten about this earlier form of knowing.

Like Jung, Claxton stresses the gravity of relying too heavily upon reason. Of our own contemporary Western society he declares that 'we have been inadvertently trapped in a single mode of mind that is characterised by information-gathering, intellect and impatience'. As a consequence we are extremely clever at solving the sort of problems that require analysis and technological expertise. We then attempt to respond to human predicaments using these same approaches, which are often wholly inappropriate. Indeed, we have so neglected the intelligent unconscious (or 'undermind' as Claxton calls it), that we cannot remember what it was for, or even that we have access to such a thing. If we think of it at all, it is as something 'wild and unruly that threatens our reason and control' and that exists in 'the dangerous Freudian dungeon of the mind' (p. 7). Counsellors and psychotherapists, therefore, whose working terrain is that of human difficulties, need to have the courage to face the more primitive aspects of themselves and be willing to respond intuitively.

Theodor Reik stresses the lack of concern for reason or for rules of behaviour in the unconscious and it is these factors which represent its archaic and primitive character. Moreover, it has the ability to tolerate contradictions and can glide easily from one realm to another (1948/1975, p. 454). In attempting to understand the complexity of a distressed human being, as in psychotherapy, it is of course an advantage to be able to withstand apparently incompatible elements and, as will be seen from the discussion in Chapter 4, this is a characteristic of the intuitive type. It nevertheless demands a willingness to let go of the logical, verbal mode and move into the unconscious terrain, an area which some people may find challenging or even frightening. The more that a therapist can become familiar with his or her own unconscious, therefore, the more he or she will feel sufficiently confident to use it as a resource.

It was Darwin of course who had shocked Victorian society by demonstrating that humans, like animals, had evolved to adapt to existing conditions in the environment (1859/1968). This meant that many of our reactions were instinctive and already built into our nervous systems, rather than being the product of education by society. Thus the views of many influential Western philosophers were brought into question, in particular the empiricists who believed that all knowledge came from experience. John Locke, for example, had stated that the mind was 'white paper void of all characters, without any ideas'. He asked: 'How comes it to be furnished? ... Whence has all the materials of reason and knowledge?' His own reply was 'in one word, from experience' (1689/1997, II.i.2).

Freud had been profoundly influenced by Darwin's theories. Darwin had noticed that when he took his small son to the zoo, he was afraid of the large animals despite having not seen them previously. He surmised that such childhood fears were inbuilt as a protection against possible predators. Freud picked up on this idea and postulated that certain childhood difficulties, such as neurotic phobias, were inborn (SE XII, pp. 313–26). It is now widely accepted by psychologists that many phobias have a genetic origin, for example arachnophobia (fear of spiders) or claustrophobia (fear of confined spaces). The behaviourists took an opposite view, however. John B. Watson argued that human nature was completely malleable, and therefore greatly affected by the environment: 'Give me a dozen healthy infants,' he wrote, 'well formed, and my own specified world to bring them up in, and I'll guarantee to take any one at random and train him to be any type of specialist I might – doctor, lawyer, artist, merchant, chief, and, yes, even beggar man and thief!' (1924, p. 104).

It is important to identify where Jung's ideas lie in relation to the nature vs. nurture debate. He acknowledges Darwin's influence on Freud, but declares that his own intellect was more deeply affected by the philosophers of the eighteenth and early nineteenth centuries (1963/1995, p. 184). Indeed he seemed diffident about expounding his ideas concerning childhood development, perhaps not wishing to trespass on Freud's territory. Jung saw parental influence differently from Freud, taking into account the subjective impressions of the child, the 'imago' (*die Imago*) of the parent carried in the individual's psyche: 'In the analytical treatment of unconscious products it is essential that the imago should not be assumed to be identical with the object' (CW 6, para. 812). The emphasis here is on the internal state of the subject and may include unconscious fantasies.

Generally, Jung saw personality development as a synthesis of inherited factors with environmental conditioning. He conceived of the innate components in terms of 'archetypes', or primordial images that were similar throughout human history and among different societies, and were products of the collective unconscious. They become most observable through the behaviour of humans at times of universal experience, such as birth, marriage and death. As such they form a kind of matrix for our humanness. Since we all contain these archetypes within our individual psyches, it is through this means that we can communicate most directly, without words and thoughts. This constitutes a total knowing of the other and can rightly be called intuitive. In therapy such immediate perception is often referred to more prosaically as being 'in tune' with the client as one unconscious communicates directly with the other. At a more elevated level, the experience might be described as mystical. Examples are presented in the studies of Chapters 5 and 10 and from the anecdotal evidence of Chapter 9.

Yet the archetypes themselves need some kind of medium through which they may be expressed. Arising from this archaic layer of the psyche, therefore, are symbolic images which are charged with meaning. They need a mediating factor in order that they may be understood and it is intuition which has this role. 'Intuition', writes Jung, 'counterbalances the powerful sense impressions of the child and the primitive by mediating perceptions of mythological images, the precursors of ideas' (CW 6, para. 772). Jung uses the term 'idea' 'to express the *meaning* of a primordial image' (CW 6, para. 732). He goes on: 'In so far, however, as an idea is the formulated meaning of a primordial image by which it was represented symbolically, its essence is not just something derived or developed, but, psychologically speaking, exists *a priori*, as a given possibility for thought-combinations in general.' This concept is in the Platonic tradition, by which the prototype of all things exists initially in the minds of the gods.

Thus, an intuitive understanding or insight may result from mythological imagery, which appears spontaneously and with a natural vitality in that it 'seems to strive for its own realisation' (CW 6, para. 736). Rational elaboration may turn such insights into ideas, subject to environmental conditions and the spirit of the time.

There are many well-substantiated stories that testify to the importance of imagery as a precursor to ideas that have revolutionized science. One such came in the form of a dream, which resulted in a brilliant discovery. Friedrich August von Kekulé, professor of chemistry in Ghent, was dozing in front of the fire one afternoon in 1865, when a vision of long rows of atoms came to him:

> all twining and twisting in snakelike motion. But look! What was that? One of the snakes had seized hold of its own tail, and the form whirled mockingly before my eyes. As if by a flash of lightning I awoke ... Let us learn to dream, gentlemen. (Quoted in Koestler, 1964/1989, p. 118)

The vision of the snake biting its own tail gave Kekulé the clue to his ground-breaking proposal that the molecules of certain organic compounds are closed chains or rings. This is a classic example of a mythological image leading to an intuitive revelation.

Albert Einstein's description of his own creative process follows similar lines:

> The words of the language as they are written or spoken do not seem to play any role in my mechanism of thought. The psychical entities which seem to serve as elements of thought are certain signs and more or less clear images ... [These elements take part in] a rather vague play ... in which they can be voluntarily reproduced and combined ... This combinatory play seems to be the essential feature in productive thought, before there is any

connection with logical construction in words or other kinds of sign which can be communicated to others. (Einstein in Hadamard, 1945, pp. 142–3)

It is clear from this quotation that it is not words which initiate the creative process, but rather 'psychical entities' and images. These precede the ideas and thoughts that can, at a later date, be transmitted to other people in a comprehensible fashion. Here Jung and Einstein are in agreement.

It is also notable that Einstein uses the words 'combinatory play', a process that might well be regarded as 'infantile', play usually being ascribed to the province of childhood and regarded by developmental psychologists as a necessary part of learning. By implication this supports Jung's idea that intuition is evident very early in childhood, before the development of rational thought. A small number of experimental studies with children, reviewed by de Sanctis (1928), suggests that they are superior to adults in making intuitive assessments of time, mass and form. The results evidently justified de Sanctis in making the statement that intuitive cognition 'is not only more rapid, but also more accurate in children than in the individual who possesses the complete development of common logical thought' (p. 25). This seems to imply that the development of logic and reason leads to the suppression of the spontaneous intuitive mode.

One avenue for reconnection with the intuitive function, therefore, is a return to the thought-forms of children through the instigation of play. It is notable that intuitive and creative types do this instinctively (see Chapter 4). Jung recommended the use of drawing and model-making to awaken the imagination and as a way of being in touch with the symbolic language of the unconscious. He explored his own inner child through an elaborate building game, constructing miniature cottages, a castle and a church on the shore of the lake where he lived, which released a whole stream of meaningful fantasies. He describes in his autobiography how he used to paint a picture or hew a sculpture whenever he came up against 'a blank wall'. Each such creative act seemed to be a *rite d'entrée* for the work that ensued (1963/1995, pp. 197–9). By following this example, professional therapists can keep open the channels to the intuitive source. Equally, the introduction of art therapy into sessions can encourage the client to reconnect with unconscious material, which may prove invaluable.

Dreams may also often feature in psychotherapy sessions. The task then is to derive meaning from the symbols, which in turn may help the client towards self-understanding. Freud considered that analysis of his own dreams gave him deep insights into the nature of his emotional life and that of others, and that the introduction of this procedure marked a turning point in psychoanalysis, creating a 'depth psychology' (SE XXII, p. 7). Jung equally believed this technique to be a most important means of opening up avenues to the unconscious (1984/1995, p. 3). A client may bring a dream because the recollection leaves some kind of impression that needs resolution. Reik gives an honest description of the process of disentangling the meaning of one of his own dreams, in which he stands before judges accused of murder. The hidden wish gradually becomes clear over the course of time as he makes connections between the dream symbols and his external life: he wants to prove himself right to the critics who have slated certain aspects of a book he has recently had published (1948/1975, pp. 38–43). The meaning that emerges provides an important insight into his character. This kind of intuitive knowledge cannot be forced. As Reik demonstrates, patience is sometimes needed to allow time for all the pieces of the puzzle to fall into place.

It has to be said, however, that the mediating process of intuition does not necessarily involve symbols that are 'mythological', as Jung seems to imply, in the sense of traditional myths and fairytales. While Kekulé's famous snake image could indeed be described as a classical mythological image, many symbols from dreams and reveries involve scenes from contemporary life. Perhaps Jung would argue that we have created images that are symbolic of the myths of our time.

Equally, intuitions may not be entirely 'primitive' or 'infantile', bearing in mind that they may be the result of making connections with knowledge held in the memory, perhaps involving mature experiences or sophisticated art forms. The importance of such associations in therapy is further explored in Chapter 10.

The 'irrational' nature of intuition

The question to be explored now is Jung's description of intuition in his definition as an 'irrational function of perception' (CW 6, para. 770). Before comparing this statement with other findings, it is first of all necessary to determine what Jung means by 'irrational'. He explains that the term does not denote something contrary to reason, but rather 'something *beyond* reason' ('*im Sinne des Ausservernunftigen*') or, more literally, *outside* reason, 'something, therefore, not grounded on reason'. He includes in this concept elementary facts, such as the earth having a moon, or chlorine being an element. He points out that intuition is not directed in the way that the functions of thinking and feeling are, but is immediate perception that may happen by chance, without being subject to the laws of reason. The definition given in *Chambers Twenty-First Century Dictionary* (Robinson and Davidson, 1999) also gives this impression: 'the power of the mind by which it immediately perceives the truth of things, without reasoning or analysis'. As for the question of the truthfulness of intuition, this is another issue, which is dealt with else-where in the book.

Jung has stated, therefore, that intuitions are products of the mind which are not logically thought out. Here, at least, there is considerable agreement among writers from various disciplines. An American psychologist, Alexander Guiora, in comparing intuition with inference, explains that the former depends upon 'allological principles', a form of comprehending in which the external cues are inadequate for logical judgement, yet prediction is made through 'the mediation of idiosyncratic associations' (1965, p. 782). Once again there is the idea of different elements combining in some novel way. Inference, however, is characterized by conclusions derived from a given set of data or premises 'in compliance with the rules of Aristotelian logic'. So a judgement would be arrived at on the basis of thinking something through logically. Moreover, the steps by which the conclusion was reached would be known.

It is difficult to assess what proportion of the therapist's process is logical and how much happens out of awareness, but clearly both aspects are necessary and may sometimes be working in conjunction with each other. If a client sits in front of me who has suffered a breakdown due to work-related stress, then it is reasonable for me to infer that she needs to begin to say 'no' to the amount of work coming her way. Moreover, I will show her how to relax deeply, will prescribe frequent rests and, when ready to return to work, ensure that she has proper breaks for coffee, tea and lunch. We will also look at how better to manage her time. These processes are logical and conscious. In parallel with this, it is likely that my intuition will be prompting me that, for example, the stress is not purely due to work, but also has some origins with family demands and expectations. I may pick this up from the tone of voice in reference to her son, or a little laugh when describing her husband. After gentle questioning I then discover that those at home rarely finish anything, so that clothes will be put in the washing machine, but not hung out to dry, half a dinner will be produced (if at all), with meat but no vegetables, or one wall will be painted but not the next. Always the supposition is that she will finish everything. Then I will switch into logical mode again, deducing that she needs to ask for practical help and make specific requests so that jobs are finished. In such a session, intuition and reason work creatively alongside each other for the benefit of the client.

Eureka!

Most counsellors and psychotherapists will be familiar with that enlightening moment when, after feeling 'stuck' with a client, or sensing that something important is missing, suddenly the connections are made and they will exclaim 'Ah, that's it!' At last the solution is there. A supervisee described just such an experience to me. Both she and her client had been puzzled about his cross-dressing behaviour, neither able to understand the origin of this need, which was troubling him deeply and causing feelings of shame. He always pursued this activity in secret when his wife was out. Use of reason and the application of theory suggested that it was to do with the loss of his mother in childhood, but my supervisee's intuition had told her not to offer this interpretation. Later the answer came to her: he needed to dress in his wife's clothes quite simply because he missed her desperately when she was out at work. Yes, that was it! The relief to the client on realizing that he was not abnormal was huge. It later transpired that a previous counsellor had said that his behaviour must be due to his relationship with his mother. Unfortunately this had served only to increase his feelings of shame. In this case intuition proved to be more helpful to the client than psychodynamic theory.

Numerous scientists, mathematicians and inventors have attested to the non-rational aspects of intuition, some of whom have described their experiences of breakthrough insights. This is commonly referred to as the 'Eureka effect', first experienced by Archimedes when he discovered how to measure the volume of an intricately fashioned crown. None of his geometrical formulae could help him. Only when he climbed into his bath did he notice that his body displaced the same volume of water, which could of course easily be measured, at which he shouted 'Eureka!' This sudden insight, rather than logical reasoning, had given him the answer to his problem. As Arthur Koestler points out in *The Act of Creation*, the problem of the volume of the crown belonged to one set of mental associations to do with mathematical formulae, and taking a bath belonged to a totally different set of associations concerning personal cleanliness. It was only when these two matrices unexpectedly met in the unconscious that the solution arose into awareness, presenting itself as an intuitive insight. Koestler calls this process 'bisociation' (1964/1989, p. 107).

This event occurs most obviously in psychotherapy when, for example, an association is made between a well-known figure, or character from a book or play, and the client in question, which provides the clue to the understanding of the case. Reik relates several such experiences, one of which involved the interpretation of what appeared to be a brief and obscure dream, which consisted only of the following: he says to his sister, 'Ha-ha, a nickel is more than a dime.' The patient could offer no associations, just that he was left with the feeling that he had cracked a huge joke. What was so funny? Neither he nor Reik could offer an answer. Some background information came to mind, however, that the man was supporting his sister financially. Then the character of Hamlet surfaced in

Reik's mind as a thought-fragment, followed by the scene in which the prince makes fun of his two courtiers, Rosencrantz and Guildenstern, to reveal their hypocrisy. Later it emerged that the sister always pretended that the money she requested was quite small, whereas in reality her demands were becoming increasingly onerous. It was then that Reik was sure of the interpretation: his patient was telling his sister, in sarcastic fashion, that he could no longer withstand the situation (1948/1975, pp. 188–90).

One of the pioneers of experimental psychology, Wilhelm Wundt, wrote as early as 1862:

> Our mind is so fortunately equipped, that it brings us the most important bases for our thoughts without our having the least knowledge of this work of elaboration. Only the results of it become conscious. This unconscious mind is for us like an unknown being who creates and produces for us, and finally throws the ripe fruits in our lap. (Quoted in Whyte, 1962/1967, p. 160)

Wundt was clearly convinced that a great deal of activity went on in the unconscious, resulting in creative production of some kind at a later date. His theory was examined by Henri Poincaré, eminent scientist, who, in 1913, gave examples from his own experiences in his essay 'Mathematical Creation'. He concluded:

> Most striking at first is this appearance of sudden illumination, a manifest sign of long, unconscious prior work. The role of this unconscious work in mathematical invention appears to me incontestable. (Poincaré in Ghiselin, 1952, p. 38)

Jung describes the contents of intuition as having the character of being 'given'. They appear of their own accord, rather than being consciously produced, as in the rational thinking process. Reik (1948/1975) writes about this experience within the context of psychoanalysis (pp. 193–7). He claims that the most important problems are solved not by logic, but by intuition:

> [The analyst] arrives at his deepest insights neither by searching for a conclusion nor by jumping to one. The best way is for him to wait until a conclusion jumps to him. It is at this moment when a longer or shorter suspense is lifted, when he has this special and psychologically significant, 'Oh, that's it!' – experience (pp. 192–3).

This denotes a kind of passivity, a waiting period, before the conclusion arrives without any apparent assistance.

There are a great many reports from the arts about this characteristic, often described as 'inspiration'. The Early English composer, William

Byrd, referred to it as 'a mysterious hidden power' and that the most fitting strains in his music occurred 'of their own accord' (in Maine, 1933, p. 117). He noted that they offered themselves to him copiously even when his own mind was 'sluggish and inactive'. In this description, he thus distinguishes between consciously directed thought, and ideas that arrive by themselves. Cézanne, the French artist, also appeared to suspend rational thought when painting, playing rather with the different hues until recognizable images appeared: 'I take colours and they become objects without my thinking about them' (in Haftman, 1954, p. 137). In a lecture, A.E. Housman talked about his individual experience of poetic inspiration as 'less an active than a passive and involuntary process' (1933, p. 49). He was clear that the intellect was not the means by which great poetry was created, and, moreover, that it might actually hinder its production. Nor, he comments, could reason be trusted to recognize poetry after it had been produced.

Certain behavioural psychologists have disagreed with Wundt and Jung, saying that invention and discovery by this so-called intuitive process are merely due to chance. For instance, Charles Nicolle in his *Biologie de l'Invention* of 1932 claimed that discovery was 'an accident' (in Hadamard 1945, pp. 18–19). There is certainly evidence that chance may assist in discovery. In writing about the reality of the psychoanalytic experience, Reik (1948/1975) admits that there is less of classification and formulation than of uncertainty and chance occurrences: 'Lucky breaks and unfortunate mistakes, the combination of trial and error, suspense and surprise – everything that makes psychoanalysis an intellectual adventure' (p. 198). He describes a case that centred around a dream, in which the patient sees himself on board a ship with his father (p. 266). The patient asks: 'Does mother know that you are leaving?' His father cries and admits that he has forgotten to tell her, so they decide to telephone. They arrive at Lands End. The patient had no associations with any part of this dream. Reik unexpectedly asked him if he knew the play *Outward Bound*, at which his patient expressed astonishment, because he had thought of this same play just a few seconds before. Although there are certain parallels between the dream and the theme of the play, it was pure chance that they had both seen it. Subsequently a meaningful interpretation could be made concerning the recent death of the patient's father and the unconscious fear of his own death.

It can be appreciated, of course, that 'accidents' may increase the opportunity for creative and unusual connections to be made. Ernst Kris (1939) qualifies this idea by suggesting that what appears to be chance is in fact 'an observation impregnated with previous preconscious experiences' (p. 383). Yet the lucky occurrence has in some way to fit with those experiences in order for an intuition to be formed.

* * * *

At this point in my research it was clear to me that a wide consensus of opinion existed among philosophers, scientists and artists as well as psychologists to support Jung's view that intuition is not a rational process. Yet it can be pivotal in understanding human dilemmas. Helping to solve life's problems, as in counselling and psychotherapy, may often involve non-analytic procedures. We may have to draw on that instinctive and direct knowing that occurs when one human meets another. Know-how that was learnt implicitly, perhaps even before words were available to us, can be a further resource, along with the expertise on human affairs gathered through personal experience, often nonverbally. Several elements may need to combine before understanding materialises. Unconscious analogies and sheer luck together with preconscious information may all play a part in making the connections necessary for an intuition to emerge.

This was only part of the picture, however. There was more to be discovered about the nature of intuition.

CHAPTER 3

Whole and complete

When considering the theme of this chapter, I suddenly had in my mind's eye the image of a kaleidoscope. As I shook and turned the instrument, the colours and shapes shifted and mingled until a meaningful new pattern emerged. In my imagination, I felt awestruck by the way in which the many differing elements had come together to form such a symmetrical and beautiful whole. Moreover, I could not have foreseen what shape might emerge from the various parts.

This seemed to me to be a colourful representation of Jung's notion that intuition is a holistic form of perception. In his definition he declares: 'In intuition a content presents itself whole and complete, without our being able to explain or discover how this content came into existence' (CW 6, para. 770). There are two important aspects to this statement: the first concerns the moment when the intuition reaches consciousness and presents itself as a complete construction, providing in that instant a total understanding of the subject in question; the second refers to the quality of intuition which is sometimes described as 'mysterious', because the person cannot recall the process by which this new comprehension was reached.

Tony Bastick (1982) uses a somewhat different term for 'whole and complete' content, namely 'global knowledge'. He lists it as property number 15 (p. 25) and considers this feature to be so important that he devotes an entire chapter to it. He makes many references to the literature, from philosophical writings, such as Locke's view of intuition as holistic perception (1690/1997) to Poincaré's observations of intuitive mathematicians (p. 236). The common factor was that whatever was essential and new in their creations came to them without premeditation and as a virtually ready-made whole. However, much of Bastick's discussion concerns the global nature of the intuitive process, rather than the presentation of a complete content. This involves in particular receptivity to peripheral cues both within oneself and outside in the environment, with parallel processing as opposed to serial, and with the ability to discern the form of a whole from its parts.

So what does this mean in the clinical situation? The therapist, by implication, must be in a receptive state, willing to monitor personal responses to whatever is happening in relation to the client, at the same time taking in subtle cues from the client's body posture, gestures, tone of voice, pacing of language and so on. Moreover, any information thus gleaned has to be combined with known facts concerning past history and present circumstances. The term 'parallel processing' indicates that all such clues need to be sifted through and evaluated more or less simultaneously until, as they move and recombine, just as in the kaleidoscope, a new concept presents itself. Thus, the parts have created a new order, a new whole. One cannot tell in advance, however, what this new concept might be. Bastick's position is summarized in the following statement: 'The wholeness of intuition lies in the interaction of internal and external perception and the continuing integration of the information with the internal affective cognitive contexts' (1982, p. 187). Thus, whatever the therapist carries on the inside in terms of feelings, body responses and thoughts, is combined with information reaching him or her from the client, which in turn will affect the light and shade of the thoughts and feelings in the therapist, and so on, until a meaningful concept emerges. All of this happens unconsciously, or only just below the threshold of conscious awareness, preconsciously (property no. 3).

Bastick's 'Theory of Intuitive Thought' is based on the idea that much information is emotionally encoded (property no. 2): 'emotional involvement is central to all aspects of intuition' (p. 84). By the word 'emotion' he means feelings as experienced in the body. He refers to experiments which have measured physiological arousal during the intuitive process and concludes that it is an interactive mind–body phenomenon. He describes the feeling of tension before any solution arises and the relief or even excitement when it appears. Moreover, he sees the intuitive type of person as emotionally sensitive and variable, and as empathic. (The participation of empathy is further discussed in Chapter 7.)

Within Tony Bastick's theory, therefore, emotions are involved with thoughts (p. 84). This is a somewhat different position from Jung's, because feelings, sensations and the intellect are presented as essentially interlinked and fundamental to the intuitive process. In his typology, Jung had opposed the psychological function of intuition to the other perceptive function, that of sensation, on the basis that the individual cannot be open to one while focusing on the other. Isabel Myers, who based her Type Indicator on Jung's (see Chapter 4), compares this to trying to listen to two radio stations on the same wavelength (Myers and Myers, 1980/1993, p. 174): one cannot hear the intuitions while the senses are ringing loudly in the ears. This opposition of sensation with intuition is seen as a real problem by many commentators, however. Psychiatrist and analyst, Dr Anthony Storr, for example, states that the ability to pick up cues from the environment at a subliminal level requires 'a sensory apparatus of a high order which registers reality accurately' (Storr, 1973, p. 77). As we have seen, Bastick goes even further by emphasizing the interactive feedback nature of intuition, which involves bodily sensations as well as feelings and thoughts. Yet, in paragraph 771 of *Psychological Types* Jung does admit that there may be some sensory involvement, at least in 'concrete' intuition, which is concerned with the reality of things, as distinct from 'abstract' intuition which has to do with ideas. Bastick writes about the many simultaneous changes throughout the body which influence the cognitive associations and perceptions, which in turn continue to change the state of the body. It is this which is central to the global nature of intuition. This is quite distinct from analytic thought, which follows a linear pattern, each word, phrase, sentence being produced one after another, rather than all at once. The intertwining of cognitive, bodily and affective states, rather than their separation, is thus at the core of the intuitive process, according to Bastick's theory.

Nevertheless, the degree of involvement of the other functions in intuition has been disputed. In describing his technique for the use of intuition, Roberto Assagioli, founder of psychosynthesis (1965/1975), reminds the student to eliminate temporarily from the field of consciousness all other functions, which may interrupt the process. Undisciplined thoughts, emotional reactions and bodily distractions are likely to intrude, so that the entrance or the recognition of intuitions becomes 'impossible or difficult' (1965/1975, p. 219). As such, he is following Eastern meditation practice, in which the mind has to be stilled. The student's aim should be to carry out a 'psychological cleansing' of the field of consciousness. This is followed by a quiet waiting to allow the intuition to enter. Such an approach can be regarded as a spiritual practice and is therefore discussed in depth in Chapter 9. It could be that in calming the internal chatter the therapist has access to intuitive information which might not otherwise be perceived. This practice may be of particular value at an interval after a session, rather than during it, by which time much unconscious processing will already be complete.

Jung states elsewhere in his definition of intuition (CW 6, para. 770) that its peculiarity 'is that it is neither sense perception, nor feeling, nor intellectual inference, although it may also appear in these forms'. The meaning here is not immediately obvious, particularly as this statement appears to contradict the definition of a psychological 'function', which, according to Jung, 'remains the same in principle under varying conditions' (CW 6, para. 731). How can intuition, as a psychological function, stay the same and also sometimes appear in the guise of one of the three other functions? There seems to be confusion in this aspect of his theory. While Bastick's investigation provides a full description of the intuitive process, it still leaves the question unanswered as to the exact form in which it arrives. Jung implies that it may appear as a feeling, a thought or a bodily sensation, but gives no examples. Having opposed sensation with intuition in his typology, he then, in the definition under discussion, admits that sensation may be involved after all, in particular, as already mentioned, with the 'concrete' form.

While precise descriptions of the form of intuitions seem to be elusive, the debate does suggest that there are various types. As has been seen, Jung also refers to 'subjective' or 'objective' intuitions (CW 6, para. 771). By the second type he means data dependent on subliminal perceptions of the object. However, this second type also apparently includes a subjective aspect: the feelings and thoughts evoked by perception of the object. So are the other functions involved after all? This part of Jung's definition implies that intuitions arrive in the form of 'data'. How then are such data 'whole and complete'? As always, the problem with Jung's theory is the lack of empirical material.

The question as to the exact form or forms in which intuitions arise, at least in psychotherapy, is further explored in Chapter 10 of this book, which offers examples based on therapists' experiences in sessions. The study conducted for that chapter demonstrates that there are at least 13 types of intuition within the clinical context. Jung is right in that some do indeed appear as a feeling, thought or bodily sensation, but others may take the form of an impression, a joke or a visual image, which he does not mention. One of my supervisees related how, during a session with a male client, she suddenly had a strong image of the man bearing 'sandwich' boards inscribed with the words 'Don't touch'. This led to some pivotal work about his difficult feelings in relation to women. Many layers of meaning were attached to this single image, almost like a shorthand for the central difficulty. In this case the counsellor trusted the intuition and took it as a signpost towards the next step in the therapy.

Eugene Gendlin, instigator of the technique of focusing (1978/1981), is very clear that intuitions form in the body to produce a complete 'felt sense'. In describing the process, he asks the student or client to pick a single problem to focus on. Without going into the problem, the person is then required to recall it in its entirety and notice what happens within the body. Gendlin continues: 'Sense all of that, the sense of the whole thing, the murky discomfort or the unclear body-sense of it.' The next step is to focus on the quality of the felt sense and invite a single word, phrase or image to come to mind, described as the 'handle'. This is compared with the felt sense to ensure that a good match is found. The individual then asks: 'What is it, about the whole problem, that makes me so ...?' (pp. 173–4). The emphasis is not just on the problem as a whole, but also on the wisdom supplied by the body as a total felt sense.

Myers and Myers (1980/1993) take up a topic only mentioned in passing by Jung, and that is the intuitive's ability to sense the possibilities in whatever captures his or her attention: 'Those people who prefer intuition are so engrossed in pursuing the possibilities ... that they seldom look very intently at the actualities' (p. 2). They do not, however, explore the way in which this interest in the possibilities increases the opportunity for global processing. While I was with a client recently, who was worried about the state of her marriage, a game of cricket came to mind: each time I bowled a ball to her, she batted it away. I would try again and bowl her another, which she also batted away, and so on. This left me with a feeling of frustration at not being able to connect with her and find a way in. At the same time I had the impression that this is what she did at home with her husband, that his approaches were made light of, joked about, so that he would eventually give up and choose to spend time with his beloved motorbike rather than with his family. He had begun to talk about moving abroad. Despite my client's fears that he would leave her, I was holding for her the possibility that their marriage might be repaired. After describing the cricket image to her, she began to take responsibility for the part she played in unconsciously driving her husband away. The reparation work could now begin. The cricket game not only demonstrated to me what she did, but also the possibility that the ball could be batted back to me rather than away, offering the opportunity for genuine rapport. This one image held within it past, present and future and it took no effort at all to comprehend its meaning. The more the possibilities are sensed, the more the links can be made between apparently disparate phenomena. This in turn increases the likelihood of producing a novel and complete entity. If the therapist is to have access to intuition, therefore, keeping an open mind and being aware of the possibilities as well as tuning in to peripheral cues are important aspects of global processing.

Psychoanalyst Richard Board (1958) writes about the 'intuitive synthesis of associative material, welling up from the creative unconscious of the analyst' (p. 233), and how 'a new organization' takes place (p. 236). This he compares with the characteristics of Gestalt phenomena in which there is a sudden reassemblage of elements. This configuration, this whole form, is more than the sum of its parts. Indeed, the aim of Gestalt therapy is the harmonization of the various elements, including the incorporation of potential, so that people may become fully themselves. As Professor Clarkson points out, the Gestalt approach is deliberately 'right-brained', and characterized by the use of metaphor, imagery and movement, on the principle that this allows past and present experiences to be better understood and integrated (1989, pp. 1–2). The method is therefore fundamentally intuitive. While Fritz Perls, originator of Gestalt therapy, rejected analysis and an over-intellectual approach, modern

Gestaltists guide clients towards complete integration of body, feelings and mind within the social context. Sensitivity and awareness are deliberately encouraged in the therapist so that he/she can more easily tune in to the entire climate of a client's being and environment. Petruska Clarkson emphasizes the wholeness of the Gestalt system, and how 'all the symbols and words, and cadences and shapes, interweave in a tapestry vibrating with life and tragedy and humour' (1989, p. vi).

Taking a more scientific approach, psychologist Peter Andersen, who is a specialist in nonverbal communication, agrees that intuition has to do with the absorption of the whole picture and the seeking of Gestalt patterns: 'It is likely that multichanneled gestalt impressions are the basis of human intuition. Conversely, single-channeled, discrete verbal messages are the basis of logic' (1999, p. 23). Moreover, nonverbal messages, so often the basis of human interaction, are frequently encoded as complete entities, often made up of many smaller signals. Try being cross with someone and using your facial expression only, without wagging a finger or using a loud voice! Equally, what is it like to show love purely with words, but without the warm tone, the smile, and without any gestures? Anyone who experiments with examples such as these is unlikely to succeed in putting their message across.

Assagioli (1965/1975) also considers that the complete nature of intuition has to do with the synthesizing, the bringing together and the integration of the various parts to create the whole: 'It is a synthetic function in the sense that it apprehends the totality of a given situation or psychological reality' (p. 217). This making of connections to form an intelligible whole is a prominent feature in the process of psychotherapy, which not only contributes to the therapist's understanding of the case, but may also result in client insight.

In this respect, Bastick concedes that a rich background of knowledge and experience is needed and complete immersion in it (1982, p. 174). Most psychotherapists acknowledge the importance of the gathering of information concerning the client in the early stages of therapy, and free association is often the tool for this in the psychoanalytic situation. A period of incubation may also be necessary before any insights emerge. This indicates that interpretations should perhaps not be offered too quickly.

Within Bastick's Theory of Intuitive Knowledge the incubation period allows the drifting through 'emotional sets' so that different connections may be made. He offers the view that information is encoded into these sets, which are formed through kinaesthetic sensations along with affective and cognitive components (p.78). This involves the association of ideas with experiences. On p. 209 he comments on how free associations can be used to map the content and combinations of these. Guiora et al. (1965), in a preliminary statement concerning intuition within a clinical

setting, remark upon 'the idiosyncratic association aspect' of the phenomenon (p. 215). Free association allows novel combinations of
emotional sets, increasing the global, non-linear nature of the process
and therefore the likelihood of intuitive, non-analytic perception.
Bastick's research gives added substance to the psychoanalytic technique
of free association, useful to both the patient and analyst in arriving at
intuitive understanding.

Being unable to explain how one arrives at an intuition is well documented in the psychological literature. Indeed, Westcott (1968) remarks
upon the agreement among independent commentators concerning this
feature. It is the obscurity of the steps by which one arrives at an intuition
that most intrigues him. Experimental psychologists have used this aspect
in studies of intuition, deliberately imposing conditions that limit the
information available to subjects, so that they are unable to use conscious,
logical thinking. The reason for the inexplicable nature of the intuitive
process is, of course, because it occurs below the threshold of awareness.
As Jung rightly points out: 'It is the function that mediates perceptions in
an *unconscious way*' (CW 6, para. 770). This processing out of awareness
may be made up of countless impressions of the client and his or her history, combined with many other factors relating, for example, to the
professional and personal experiences of the psychotherapist.

Theodor Reik (1948/1975) considers that intuition is the result of the
joint assimilation of both conscious and unconscious perceptions, with
the emphasis on the latter. This combination and the way in which the
mind has made the connections can only be seen in retrospect, if at all:
'In truth, we are incapable of dissecting into all its component parts the
process by which we recognize psychological fact' (p. 132). Could it be
that this type of dissection has rarely been attempted, on the assumption
that it would be a fruitless task? Yet in his book Reik is able to trace some
of the steps by which he arrived at certain interpretations, although when
they first occurred to him, he could not explain why. One case that he
recalls revolves around a furious quarrel between a young man (Reik's
patient) and his girlfriend, who had been feeling unwell, had complained
of being too thin and that she needed to put on flesh. Reik's intuition
immediately told him that the latent meaning of the quarrel really concerned a child, rather than the girl's appearance, yet there was nothing in
the session that pointed to such an interpretation. Subsequently he
remembered that the girl had had an abortion some eighteen months earlier. He could then see that this information, held somewhere out of
current awareness, had combined unconsciously with the phrase 'put on
flesh', which together had prompted the idea of pregnancy.

Some qualification needs to be made to Jung's definition here, therefore. Rather than being totally inexplicable, it seems that it may

occasionally be possible to recall at least some of the fragments that contributed to the whole form, thereby resulting in an intuition.

It is interesting to consider what might restrict the parallel processing needed for an intuition. Tony Bastick, in discussing its global nature, found that anxiety was an inhibiting factor, by interrupting the numerous simultaneous interactive feedback systems taking place in the body (p. 215). He refers to fifty papers which have studied the negative effects of anxiety on memory and learning, particularly where novel responses were concerned. He concludes that stress causes 'functional fixedness' and the inhibition of the combination of emotional sets (p. 233). This would suggest that in order to have access to intuition, a therapist needs to be in a relaxed state and not suffering from stress. Looking after oneself is of crucial importance therefore. I sometimes offer to my supervisees the concept of 'healthy selfishness' on the basis that if they are not feeling rested and well nourished, with energy to spare, then it is unlikely that they can be fully present to someone else. Therapists need to be alert in order to pick up those subtle cues that may contribute to an important intuition.

The question of subjective certainty

The experience of the completeness of intuition often carries with it a feeling of rightness and conviction. This is particularly present in the 'Eureka' moment, when the intuition reaches consciousness, and the person may exclaim 'Yes, that's it!' I had an extraordinary intuition one day when completing my notes concerning a worried and nervous client, who had suffered panic attacks accompanied by terror of dying. Before guiding him through some relaxation exercises, I had suggested that he take some deep breaths to help settle himself, but this had been difficult. He complained that this did nothing for him. While writing the words 'deep breath', I had unconsciously left out the end of the first word and the beginning of the second and found myself putting down instead 'death'. I stopped in astonishment and, in that moment, realized that it was not death that so frightened him, but fear of living life to the full. That was it! Although I had no proof, nor even corroboration from the client himself, I was absolutely sure that the intuition was accurate. Subsequently we began to find ways of releasing his repressed creativity and the panic gradually subsided.

Words of caution need to be made about linking the feeling of certainty, often experienced in intuitive moments, with truth. In his definition Jung does not claim intrinsic accuracy, but highlights the subjective experience of intuition, that carries with it a sense of conviction. This, however, implies a correctness. Here he has been influenced by the philosophical writings of Spinoza and Bergson, acknowledged in his book, who considered intuition to be the highest form of knowledge (CW 6, para. 770). Despite this, Bergson stated in his *Creative Evolution*: 'Dialectic is necessary to put intuition to the proof, necessary also in order that intuition should break itself up into concepts and so be propagated to other men ...' (1913, p. 251). Thus intuition is only the basis of knowledge, which then has to be tested with logic and reason, and transformed into intelligible language before being broadcast to others.

Philosophers might argue that it is unsound to say that intuition may be incorrect. If the product is inaccurate, then this means it was not an intuition at all but just a bad guess. This refers to a specific way in which the term is used, and that is in reference to self-evident propositions that can be seen to be true (non-inferentially) once one fully understands them. Russell states that 'It is often held that all and only self-evident propositions are knowable through intuition, which is here identified with a certain kind of intellectual or rational insight' (Russell in Audi, 1995, p. 382). However, intuition in psychotherapy is a multi-faceted process, not exclusively concerned with self-evident propositions, so the cautions mentioned in various texts need to be taken seriously.

Jung compares the certainty experienced in an intuition with that in sensation, the main difference being that the latter rests on physical foundations. He declares that the certainty of intuition rests on a 'definite state of psychic "alertness" of whose origin the subject is unconscious' (CW 6, para. 770). It is not at all clear what he means by this, as he offers no further explanation. It can only be surmised that he is referring to an inner state of alertness to the cues which may be picked up subliminally from the environment, or from within oneself. However, it is difficult to see how accuracy can rest on 'alertness'.

In terms of the clinical setting, the therapist always has the option to check any intuitively based interpretations with the client. In paragraph 772 of CW 6 Jung remarks that many intuitions can afterwards be broken down into their component parts and rationalized, in the way that Bergson recommended. Precisely how intuitions are verified during psychotherapy is investigated in the study described in Chapter 10, which reveals that there are at least six ways, some not purely cognitive.

Assagioli comments on individuals who are too prone to be impressed by hunches, and do not have sufficient cognitive ability to distinguish between true and false intuitions. He recommends the development of the other functions, so that intuition can be used in cooperation with them (1965/1975, p. 222). It would seem to be in the interest of counsellors and psychotherapists to heed this advice.

Tony Bastick (1982) stresses the subjective aspect of correctness (property no. 10, p. 25) which cannot of course be equated with objective accuracy. His list of properties therefore also incorporates: 'Intuition need not be correct' (no. 9). The sense of accuracy can be very powerful, so therapists and counsellors need to be aware of the possibility that such a feeling may be misleading, before acting on information received in this way.

* * * *

At this point in my searches, I felt I had acquired a sound understanding of the main properties of intuition. Having studied its irrational nature, I had then looked at the holistic aspect, how the processing is global rather than linear, and that it arrives in consciousness as a complete construct in one of a variety of forms. Since the processing happens out of awareness, the steps are usually obscure, but sometimes it is possible to see a number of connections in retrospect. The weight of evidence seemed to lie with Tony Bastick, rather than with Jung, in that it is an interactive mind/body phenomenon, dependent upon complex feedback systems that happen in conjunction with one another.

Here and there allusions had been made to the qualities that allow a person to be more open to intuition. The question that then persisted in my mind was: 'Are some people more naturally intuitive than others?' This was the area that now fascinated me and I decided that it would become the subject of the next chapter.

CHAPTER 4

The intuitive type of therapist

As soon as the word 'type' is mentioned in reference to character, I am aware of my own reluctance to put people into any kind of a box. Humans are so very complex, can they really be categorized in a meaningful way? Yet I myself had been referred to as an intuitive sort of person when asked to run that workshop, so what was it that others had seen in me? I seemed to have earned a reputation for being able to tune in to people and sum up situations fairly quickly, no doubt fostered of necessity during my earlier years of working in business. Then there was a perceived sensitivity linked to my musicality, and love of dance and drama. In the past I recalled having been referred to as 'mysterious' or as being a bit 'other-worldly' (not an asset in business!), although I never thought of myself in those terms and was surprised by such comments.

When I was discussing intuitive types with a Jungian analyst, she suggested that I study the Myers-Briggs Type Indicator (MBTI)[1], which is based on Jung's typology, and which gives intuition a prominent role. I found myself drawn to this, because of its positive approach, and because it sets out not to type-cast, but rather to offer just an indication of character so that people are better able to understand themselves and others and see why they behave in the ways that they do.

Jung's typology

Because Jung's concepts are so helpful to this enquiry, it is worth giving here a brief résumé of the structure of his typology, so that readers can appreciate how intuition is located. Considering the diversity of human personality, Jung set himself a seemingly impossible task to devise a model that would incorporate its innumerable variations and combinations of characteristics. Yet the structure he finally arrived at is, in principle, straightforward, being based on the concept of introversion and extraversion. It is important to understand that these terms refer to the way in which a person's psychic energy moves: either in an outward direction towards the external world, or else inwardly towards one's inner being. These two different attitudes are not meant to characterize behaviour, but rather the structure of consciousness. Jung had evidently arrived at them after examining a great many cases, although unfortunately we are given no clear examples from his clinical work. However, the distinction between the two attitudes has found widespread assent, not least by H.J. Eysenck (1952), the well-known psychologist, who confirmed their existence in human personality using carefully controlled quantitative studies. Although there are other ways in which personality can be analyzed and described, Eysenck acknowledges the usefulness of the concepts: 'these are the only two which have been found again and again by many different investigators, using many different methods, and it may perhaps be agreed that these two dimensions are the most important ones in describing human behaviour and conduct' (1965, p. 60).

Yet Jung admits that it is only possible to distinguish between the extraverted and introverted personalities if those concerned are reasonably well differentiated, in other words if they clearly prefer one mode of operating to the other, as manifested through their behaviour, mannerisms, actions and so forth. It is obvious that most individuals combine extraversion and introversion in their approach to life, but Jung noted that each person has a preference for one or other attitude over the other.

The question that is raised is whether people have a genetic predisposition to extraversion and introversion, or whether these factors are the result of environment and conditioning. Jung, while acknowledging the importance of parental guidance, considered not just introversion and extraversion, but type in general to be inborn: 'the decisive factor must be looked for in the disposition of the child' (CW 6, para. 560). This is the theoretical standpoint taken up by the Myers-Briggs Type Indicator, in which type is compared to the spontaneous inclination to write with either the left or the right hand: 'The hypothesis is that type is inborn, an innate predisposition like right- or left-handedness' (Myers and Myers 1980/1993, p. 168). This does not mean that right-handed people are unable to use their left hand (or vice versa), just that it feels more awkward. If type is innate, then there are important implications for therapists, as different types are likely to be drawn to this or that theoretical orientation, and to approach the work and respond to clients in diverse ways. You can read more of these points later.

The remainder of Jung's typological model has been variously received within the psychological community. The theory is constructed around the question: which basic functions of consciousness are necessary if an internal or external object or factual situation is to be fully grasped? Jung selected four, namely thinking, feeling, sensation and intuition, but offers no *a priori* reason for this particular choice. He simply points out that he arrived at these functions after many years of experience as a psychiatrist and analyst. Here again, he produces no empirical evidence, but expects us to take him at his word. He distinguishes between the four in this manner:

> The essential function of sensation is to establish that something exists, thinking tells us what it means, feeling what its value is, and intuition surmises whence it comes and whither it goes. (CW 6, para. 983)

Each can be introverted or extraverted, forming eight types. A psychological 'function' Jung defines as 'a particular form of psychic activity that remains the same in principle under varying conditions' (CW 6, para. 731). Fantasy, for example, would be excluded as a basic function because it can manifest itself in any one of the given four.

The four functions are divided into two categories, the 'rational' and the 'irrational'. He classifies the perceptive functions of sensation and intuition as 'irrational', not to denote that they are contrary to reason, but rather that they are beyond reason, as described in Chapter 2. Thinking and feeling he regards as 'rational' because they are 'discriminative'. While it is possible to agree that thinking and feeling are two different ways of forming judgements, it is open to debate as to whether feeling can be regarded as 'rational'. Jung seems to have an ideal human state in mind, saying that thinking and feeling 'function most perfectly when they are in the fullest possible accord with the laws of reason' (CW 6, para. 787). Equally, intuition and sensation 'find fulfilment in the absolute perception of the flux of events'. These functions, therefore, appear to have pure and impure forms, according to the amount of contamination present from one of the other modes. Just as extraversion is opposed to introversion, Jung also saw intuition opposed to sensation (the two perceptive functions), and thinking to feeling (two ways of making judgements). The question of opposition has a philosophical basis which appealed to Jung and is discussed in detail in his book on psychological types (CW 6) and examined further in my thesis (written under my married name: Fulcher, 2002). In principle, he considered that the very concept of energy implied polarity, positive and negative, basic to the vitalistic current of life.

The typological model that Jung offers is thus cruciform in structure with the rational functions placed at right-angles to the irrational, and with the primary function placed at the top. The type depicted in the figure below is predominantly intuitive, with its opposite, sensation, in the inferior or least differentiated position, and thinking in the supportive auxiliary role opposed by feeling. If the dominant function is introverted, then its opposite is extraverted and vice versa.

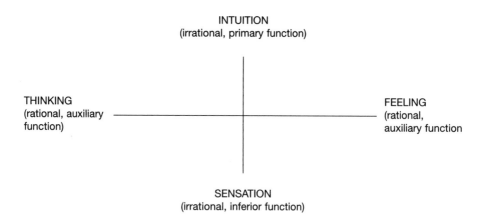

INTUITION
(irrational, primary function)

THINKING
(rational, auxiliary
function)

FEELING
(rational,
auxiliary function

SENSATION
(irrational, inferior function)

The person illustrated by this diagram is therefore likely to be highly intuitive, with a sound intellect by way of support. He or she may be somewhat aloof from tangible reality with sensation in the inferior position. The person may also have some difficulty in expressing feelings, being more at ease with the intellect. Jung sees this type as having 'philosophical intuition systematizing its vision into comprehensible thought by means of a powerful intellect', in my view a portrayal of his own orientation towards consciousness (CW 6, para. 669).

It is particularly interesting that Jung was not the originator of the intuitive type. It is credited to Mary Moltzer, who was a student of Jung and co-translator of his paper 'The Theory of Psychoanalysis' (1913). It is possible that during the earlier years of his work on the typology Jung had difficulty being objective about this particular type because he was so identified with it. Moreover, it was women who were popularly regarded as more intuitive than men, evident in the phrase 'feminine intuition'. Could he, as a man and a professed scientist, acknowledge that he had intuition as the primary function rather than thinking? Yet, since the prevailing Western culture has favoured thinking as the dominant mode of the two, it is to Jung's credit that he was ultimately able to give equal credence to intuition in his typology, thereby offering support to those people who felt out of step with the times.

The Myers-Briggs Type Indicator®

While Jung was developing these theories, an American woman, Katharine Briggs, had also concluded, quite independently, that it was possible to classify people according to their preferred way of operating and some of her types matched Jung's. She entered into correspondence with him after publication of *Psychologischen Typen* in English in 1923. She subsequently adopted his main theories in a modified form to provide a framework for her own concepts, and then elaborated them, with the aim of creating a psychometric testing instrument that was of practical value to people. The horrors of the two world wars inspired her and her daughter, Isabel Myers, to find ways of encouraging people to tolerate and understand each other better. They realized that conflict often arose because of the differences in perception and the bases on which judgements are formed. The way forward seemed to be for people to comprehend their own way of operating and to appreciate that others use their minds differently, but that all have something of value to offer.

During many years of research, an item pool was gradually built up by Isabel Myers, descriptive of different behaviours and attitudes. This eventually formed the basis of an in-depth questionnaire. Despite extensive testing, the MBTI® was not published until 1962 and only gained widespread recognition in 1975, by which time it was seen as a valuable tool for measuring personality, with many applications in education, personnel, counselling, religious and other contexts.[1]

Briggs and Myers agreed with Jung that a dominant process was necessary: in order for any one function to reach full development it needed special attention to the temporary exclusion of the others. However, Myers emphasized the importance of the auxiliary function, which, when cultivated to a reasonable degree, acted as a necessary support. She described an extreme perceptive type with no judgement as 'all sail and no rudder' and an extreme judging type with no perception as 'all form and no content' (1980, p. 11). Thus a fourth pair was added to Jung's three. This was based on how people prefer to orientate themselves to the external world, that is whether they primarily use a judging process (thinking or feeling) or a perceiving process (sensing or intuition) in the extraverted attitude.

Because of the emphasis on the auxiliary and its incorporation into the fundamental design of the MBTI, each of Jung's original eight types are divided into two. For example, the introverted thinker becomes the introverted thinker with sensing, or the introverted thinker with intuition. This, along with the judging-perceiving preference, completes the type table, as illustrated in Myers and Myers 1980/1993, p. 29.

The MBTI is based on a 95-item forced-choice questionnaire which determines the preferences (i.e. the person selects the statement or word that applies to him or her from sets of pairs). These are then scored. According to the highest score in each pair of opposites (introverted or extraverted, sensing or intuition, thinking or feeling, judging or perceiving), the person can be classified in one of 16 different ways. The individual is then encouraged to read the description of their type and to decide whether or not it fits.

If we are using the MBTI as a source of information concerning the process of intuition, then we need to know how reliable it is. If, therefore, a person is tested again for type, the result should be the same on repetition. We also need to be sure that it is valid and does what it sets out to do, and that the classifications do reflect people's preferred way of operating as regards (a) how they take in information (intuition or sensing) and (b) how they form judgements and make decisions based on that information (thinking or feeling). The interested reader is referred to the MBTI *Manual* (Myers and McCaulley, 1985) which gives details of a number of studies, which do indeed show that the MBTI has a good standard of reliability and validity. However, it needs to be borne in mind that Isabel Myers always emphasized that it is only an indicator, and, moreover, people's preferences may change over time.

Having studied something of the MBTI, I was intrigued to discover whether I was indeed the intuitive person as perceived by my colleagues. I came out as an INTJ, that is, introverted intuition as the dominant function, with extraverted thinking by way of support.[2] The description seemed to fit remarkably well, having 'a clear vision of future possibilities' and the 'organization and drive' to implement my ideas. I am also drawn to 'complex challenges' and 'readily synthesise complicated theoretical and abstract matters' – yes, indeed, as the present project demonstrates! INTJs 'value knowledge highly' and 'expect competence of themselves and others' (Myers, 1987/1994, p. 12). While this means that tasks are usually done to a high standard, it may also result in internal pressure and stress – a problem which I am acutely aware of.

According to this model, then, there are eight intuitive types, but there are certain characteristics common to all.[3] When taking in information, intuitives tend to focus on the big picture rather than the small details that particularly interest the sensing types. They are adept at seeing the connections and relationships between facts and instinctively see the patterns in things. Intuitives are future-orientated and can quickly grasp at the possibilities and new ways of approaching something. They have a love of theories and the abstract, rather than the concrete and the practical as with sensing people, and are drawn to imaginative areas, with a deep trust in inspiration.

So what does this mean in the clinical situation? Therapists who focus on the big picture and are future-orientated will be good at seeing a person as a whole and will be able to hold for that client the vision of his or her potential. They are more likely to be attracted to humanistic and transpersonal models of working, rather than analytic, in which the emphasis is on what the client may become. Exploring future possibilities for that person is second nature to intuitives. Additionally, they are quick to sense the connections between a client's past and presenting issues, and are able to see the patterns which may be causing problems. Being drawn to the meaning of things, intuitives will probably prefer to work long-term and in depth, with the emphasis on self-development, leaving the practicalities of short-term work to sensing types. Creativity is a natural mode for intuitives, so they will enjoy bringing poetry, art and role-play into sessions. Extraverts, in particular are likely to introduce psychodrama or Gestalt techniques, in which the client is invited to identify with and imagine becoming different aspects of his or her self, or with different members of the family. They can also be great motivators. Symbolism and imagery are the intuitives' first language, and they are therefore likely to be accomplished at guided visualizations and the interpretation of dreams. The main disadvantages in being an intuitive type of therapist are that, in the search for meaning, he or she may overlook realistic, practical solutions, and they may also find it difficult to plan and give structure to sessions, being inclined rather to go with the flow. This is particularly so for intuitive feelers (NFs), who prefer to make decisions via the feeling rather than the thinking function, and also for perceptive types (Ps) who are not well disposed towards scheduling. Moreover, being confident of their insights, it is important that they always check these out with clients, as confidence is not necessarily synonymous with accuracy.

Creativity and play

Although approaching the subject from a completely different perspective through the incorporation of experimental psychology, some agreement with Jung's typology can be found in Tony Bastick's discussion. A cognitive style emerges which is typical of the intuitive type. Intuitives are predominantly divergent thinkers, as opposed to convergent, able to evoke a wide variety of remote and original associations from the same word (1982, p. 315) and enjoying the mingling of contradictory ideas (p. 188). Very often visual images, metaphor, simile and analogy are combined with organized thought processes (pp. 190, 191). This encourages novel associations which can lead to some new understanding. This is very different from convergent, analytic thinkers, who tend to reject the aid of the imagination. Intuitives have a propensity for primary-process thinking, enjoying fantasy, hypnogogic reverie and dream images. It can be seen from this that Tony Bastick's assessment of the intuitive's thought processes parallels that of Isabel Myers, with the emphasis on the imagination rather than logical analysis.

A proficient therapist can assist with the inducement of hypnogogic reverie in the client through the use of guided imagery, a technique practised by professionals trained in transpersonal methodologies and originally developed by the French psychotherapist Desoille in the 1940s. The client is encouraged initially to relax deeply, after which the therapist accompanies him or her on a fantasy journey, facilitating the process through the use of skilful questioning. Desoille considered that this promoted the evoking of archetypes, as defined by Carl Jung, which in turn put the client in touch with the collective unconscious. John Rowan reports: 'Desoille believed that this entry into the world of the collective unconscious was one of the most powerful change agencies in psychotherapy' (1993b, p. 69). The reason for this is that the client is able to set his or her personal conflicts into an impersonal and collective background through the guided imagery. In this manner it becomes possible to uncover the roots of the conflict within the personal self, rather than via the transference as in psychoanalysis. Assagioli offers a classic example of this process, which is well worth recording here. The client presented a symbol of an octopus in the depths of the sea, which threatened to engulf him. With encouragement from the therapist, he imagined rising up towards the surface along with the octopus, which then became transformed into the face of his mother. At this point the patient was able to experience how engulfing and possessive his mother was, threatening his very identity. Further visualization involved ascending a mountain with his mother, and the higher they climbed, the more he could see her in a different light, as someone who had struggled with many problems. She no longer appeared menacing. Ultimately he was able to feel real compassion for her, which contributed towards a more rewarding affective life (1965/1975, pp. 212–13).

Visualization is a technique that I often use in my own practice and, while I can confirm from professional experience that archetypal images may well occur, the symbolism may also be personal to that particular client and therefore not necessarily an aspect of the collective unconscious. Intuition is needed to inform the therapist whether or not to guide the person into an archetypal domain. Just as some form of ascent seems to evoke the transpersonal, so does descent often symbolize entry into the personal unconscious. Whatever the mode of the imagery, insight often results, because the client has had access to material previously held out of awareness. A helpful figure, such as a wise being, can also be evoked, who may advise on a fruitful course of action. These are important aspects of transpersonal therapy, and belong within Chapters 8 and 9, where they are considered in detail. However, in order to be able to facilitate this process, the therapist needs to feel comfortable with the language of symbolism and intuitives are more likely than sensing types to find such an approach congenial.

One of the characteristics of primary-process thinking was termed 'condensation' by Freud, whereby two or more ideas or images are fused, a mechanism particularly noticeable in dreams (SE IV). When written down, a dream usually appears to be quite brief and may fill less than half a page, but the thoughts and meanings that can lie behind it could occupy many times that space. The therapist needs to be prepared to accompany the client into that unknown terrain, with a sense of adventure and the willingness to explore unusual connections. Transpersonal therapists, rather than offering an interpretation to a dream, may invite the client to re-enter it in imagination and re-experience the symbols, uncovering their meaning from the inside. The psychologist H.R. Pollio (1974) described intuitive thought as a 'primary process ideally suited to breaking down patterns of usual thought'. He continues: 'an individual who can occasionally "dip down" into such thinking, and not get lost in its labyrinth, is precisely that person who might be able to come up with a new insight' (pp. 152–3).

Often a client may be stuck with a particular belief system or customary pattern of thinking and be unable to find a way out of it. It is then up to the therapist to assist with the discovery of a new approach to the problem concerned. For example, a client who is unhappy at work may feel unable to find more congenial employment because of a limiting self-image that is associated in his mind with a rather mundane, poorly paid position. He is unable to imagine anything better for himself. I worked with just such a client recently. By employing drawing and Gestalt techniques, we uncovered a flamboyant aspect of his personality which was deeply repressed. As he became more familiar with this part of himself and gradually allowed it to be expressed, he began to realize that other, more interesting opportunities were open to him. Pollio connects this type of lateral thinking with the early stages of creativity (1974).

The implication here is that the therapist needs to be a creative type, or at least be willing to honour his or her inner resourcefulness in this respect. While Freud considered that psychoanalysis was a science, other writers view psychotherapy as a creative art form. Carl Rogers makes a comparison between painting a picture or composing a piece of music with 'creating new formings of one's own personality as in psychotherapy' (1961/1967, p. 349). He defines the creative process as 'the emergence in action of a novel relational product, growing out of the uniqueness of the individual on the one hand, and the materials, events, people, or circumstances of his life on the other' (p. 350). The mainspring of creativity seemed to him to be comparable to the curative force in psychotherapy, that is a person's natural tendency to actualize him- or herself, to fulfil those potentialities which may lie dormant. This may involve a wish to express oneself, to expand as a human being, to develop one's talents, to mature and become wiser. Yet so often this urge for growth becomes buried under many layers of psychological defences or stultified through fear. In my practice I have several times heard the statement, 'I'd rather not begin, because I'm so afraid of failing.' The therapist must then work creatively to supply that 'novel relational product' within the safe haven of the consulting room and facilitate the process whereby the client can begin to break through those defences and lead a more rewarding life. Of course it is important to look at the causes of those fears and this may involve logic and analysis, but such understanding may not of itself motivate the client towards change. It seems that unconscious contents are stored in the form of symbols rather than words and it is primary-process thinking rather than the logical, verbal mode that is needed in order to have access to that hidden store. Thus, opening the gateway to neglected aspects of oneself may only be possible through the use of the imagination.

The paediatrician Donald Winnicott made a connection between creativity and play and considered that psychotherapy took place in the overlap between the play area of the patient and that of the therapist:

> If the therapist cannot play, then he is not suitable for the work. If the patient cannot play, then something needs to be done to enable the patient to become able to play, after which psychotherapy may begin. The reason why it is essential is that it is in playing that the patient is being creative. (1971, p. 54)

As a paediatrician, he was of course making particular reference to his work with children, in which play was specifically used as a therapeutic tool. However, he considered that this mode of working applied equally to adults. It was through play that the child first learned to form a meaningful relationship, that is if the mother or carer responded in a positive way. Within the context of object-relations theory, the quality of this initial encounter contributes either constructively or negatively to the development of the personality. If the child suffers early damage, and is not played with, then this neglect is carried into adulthood in terms of emotional difficulties. In forming the reparative relationship through the therapeutic encounter, healing may often be achieved through the creative and formative play that the person never experienced in the first instance.

Cues for such work may often come from the client. If I sense that the individual wishes to stand up and move, then I join in, initially mirroring whatever the client expresses, reflecting back in both movement and words or sounds. On one such occasion, my client wanted to explore the baby part of herself, so we both entered into this in a spirit of fun. There was much cooing, gurgling and smiling as this baby expressed her contentedness. Everything seemed fresh and there was much pleasure in the sensuality of touch, especially when discovering the silkiness of a satin cushion, or the woolliness of the carpet. Then suddenly there was a change in atmosphere at the approach of her father. Happiness was replaced with heaviness. The client took on her father's posture, which was rigid and held-in. His breathing was shallow and he had a habit of sucking in his breath through his teeth, which the baby found frightening. Gradually we created a 'dance' between the movements of the baby and of the father and as we did this, my client understood why it was that she so often felt weighed down. Her aim then became to free up the baby part of herself so that she could become more spontaneous. It was through playing with movement in the form of a dance that she was able to arrive at this new understanding.

Bastick notes that intuitive types naturally find the solving of problems 'fun' and enter into the process in a playful spirit (p. 133). An aspect of his thesis is that humour involves 'recentring', or the change in the structure of the subjective relationships between the elements that are associated with an emotional set. To take the analogy of the kaleidoscope once more, it is as if it has been shaken afresh, the coloured pieces re-combine and a new pattern forms.

Theodor Reik writes fluently on the subject of psychoanalysis and wit (1948/1975, pp. 249–57), making the point that the process of condensation sometimes takes the form of a pun, which may later re-emerge in a dream. In order to be able to interpret such material, the analyst needs to have access to his or her own sense of humour. He offers the example of a patient who brought to the session a dream located in a Viennese hotel. The most striking feature was the appearance of the Austrian statesman Metternich, but what was he doing here? The patient could offer no associations until he and Reik began to play with the word, in the same way that children often do. They then realized that it sounded like the three short words 'met her nicht', an Anglo-German phrase which translates 'I did not meet her', offering the meaning that the patient was seeking. Here the mind has used the sound of the sentence to process the information, and the dream re-presents it in the figure of the statesman. Arthur Koestler describes how a comic effect is produced following the 'sudden bisociation of an idea or event with two habitually incompatible matrices, provided that the narrative ... carries the right kind of emotional tension' (1964/1989, p. 51). In Reik's example of the dream-pun, two contexts are linked by sound affinities. If he had not explored the dream in a spirit of play, the association would probably not have been made. Intuitive individuals enjoy such unusual connections and are more likely to approach client material with a sense of fun, when appropriate.

The high spatial ability among intuitive types is noted by a number of writers. The Austrian ethologist Konrad Lorenz comments: 'The person with relatively high spatial ability has a marked tendency to seek for and recognize regularities and patterns in his experience' (1951, p. 230). The seeking of patterns in the client's past history and current way of being can be central to the process of therapy. Such repetitive forms of behaviour may or may not be helpful to the individual, but their recognition at least offers a choice concerning the way forward. The emergence of a behaviour pattern is often described in terms of fitting together the pieces of a puzzle, until understanding results. Bateman and Holmes, in reporting a moment of insight, use this analogy: 'at a particular moment something the analyst says lifts the whole atmosphere and pieces of a jigsaw come together to form a complete picture' (1995, p. 176). A comment from the analyst may indeed be the final piece in that particular puzzle, although a therapist may also facilitate the process in ways other than exclusively through words. For example, I encouraged one client to do a drawing of her family of origin as she remembered it when a child. The aim was to show the relationships, degree of closeness or otherwise, between the different members. She drew herself as a baby, very enclosed in her mother's arms. On their left was the family dog and on their right her brother. Beyond him was their sister, looking miserable. Apart from this group was their father, very large, frowning and furious. I already knew the details of her current family relationships, in particular the distant and angry husband, and commented on the resemblance. She herself instantly saw how she had been instrumental in recreating the same situation, through the various choices she had made at different points in her life. And so the pattern had been repeated. Now that she could see her part in this family system, she could begin to replace it with something more rewarding.

Other characteristics

Malcolm Westcott found that there were other distinguishing features of intuitive types, including introspection, moodiness, intense involvement with the process, and unconventionality (1968, p. 43). It is not often appreciated by the general public that the hour spent in the consulting room does not represent the total time devoted to the job. Conscientious counsellors and psychotherapists may reflect on the case between sessions and may also consult a supervisor or colleague in confidence for additional input. Having a propensity for introspection is therefore an asset. Mulling over the material in this way gives the mind the opportunity to make those novel connections that can lead to insight.

Evidence was also produced by Westcott that intuitives are low information demanders. Perhaps they do not need a great deal of information on a conscious level, because they are so used to picking up relevant material subliminally and can trust in that process. No doubt this demands the intense involvement referred to. In a clinical situation, this implies focus and concentration when with a client and the monitoring of the therapeutic interaction. They thus watch themselves as well as the patient. Self-monitoring of emotional and bodily reactions is essential if one is to become aware of counter-transference responses, which can be so useful in supplying additional information about the client. Since there is always more to discover, this introspective practice is never at an end. Bastick remarks that the global nature of intuition is dependent upon the interaction of internal and external perception, awareness of what is happening in the environment as well as what is occurring with-in one's body and feelings. Different kinds of information may be absorbed subliminally, or there may be a rapid toing and froing of aware-ness from the client to oneself, intermingled with fleeting thoughts and impressions. Out of this mélange may rise clear notions that point the way forward.

Working at odd times in unusual settings offers a wide range of stimuli and provokes unique emotional contexts, according to Bastick (p. 205). While this may be appropriate for artistic production, such contexts may be unsuitable for therapy, possibly provoking anxiety in clients. Lomas recommends 'ordinariness' within the consulting room, so that the patient may feel safe (1994, p. 132). Equally, unusual clothes with bright colours and eccentric patterns may simply be a distraction. However, much of the rumination concerning the client's material may take place between sessions in a variety of settings. Important associations may be made, for example, when relaxing and reading a novel, in which there are certain parallels between the presenting issue of a client and the behav-iour of a character in the book. Further illustrations of this process appear in the diary studies of Chapter 10. Exploration of the unconscious is not regarded as a conventional activity, since it often means entering an 'uncivilized' terrain. Counsellors and psychotherapists may have to set aside social norms if they are truly to empathize with the inner experi-ences of clients, especially if these involve very dark material, or at the other extreme the highest transpersonal encounters.

An aspect of the unconventional which may be a helpful component within a therapist's personality is the avoidance of dogmatism. Intuitives are not interested in other people's rules and are little influenced by authority (Bastick, 1982, pp. 133 and 188). They depend primarily on their own experience, on their own system of evaluation, rather than on external opinions. They are thus likely to offer the client a fresh approach, in which theoretical considerations take a back seat. Seeing the person as a unique individual from a phenomenological perspective therefore comes naturally to intuitives, an attitude which can help the client to feel both well understood and special. This is particularly beneficial if he or she suffers from low self esteem – a common problem.

On the other hand, intuitives' dislike of rules has led to a certain amount of conflict within professional associations concerning the degree to which the practice of therapy should conform to set standards and regulations. Brian Thorne, writing within the context of person-centred therapy, expresses with eloquence his concern that too many requirements might interfere with the therapeutic relationship and lead to under-involvement on behalf of the counsellor (2002a, p. 17). Bearing in mind that much research shows the relationship between therapist and client to be the healing factor, rather than technique or theoretical orientation, this could be a real problem (Clarkson, 1995, p. 4). Additionally this same author sees statutory regulation as a threat to creativity, through the development of an exclusive 'club' whose members have all agreed to conform to a certain way of working (Thorne, 2002b, pp. 4–5). Such an outcome would indeed be anathema to intuitive types.

Helpful evaluation

Nevertheless it is necessary to form certain kinds of judgements, especially initially, in order to make a diagnosis and arrive at a decision as to whether or not the counselling we are offering is appropriate, and, if not, how else the client can be helped. It appears that some people are better at making these sort of judgements than others. The questions that arise, therefore, are how much intuition is a part of this process, whether intuitive types are more skilled than others at forming such judgements and, if so, why.

Philip Vernon of Harvard University (1933) set himself the task of studying individual differences in the ability to judge personality. He was careful to ensure that his series of 44 tests, designed to study the judgements of self and others, was carried out under as wide a variety of conditions as possible. His results confirmed former suggestions that general intelligence and artistic qualities are consistent characteristics in good judges of personality. He did not, however, discover any general trait of 'intuitive ability', but that may have been due to limitations in the studies. Vernon drew a practical conclusion that any person whose vocation depended on judging people 'should be both intelligent and artistically inclined' and probably also 'somewhat introverted'. Moreover, he found 'considerable individual differences in the "intuitive" abilities of different judges or raters' (p. 56). He agreed with Gross (1918) that accurate self-knowledge led to better judgement because it was more likely to insure against mistakes. Two findings by Vernon important for psychotherapy were that good judges of self were more intelligent and possessed a greater sense of humour than average, and that good judges of strangers were 'distinctly more artistic and intelligent than average'

(p. 57). The basis of the artistic assessment was the ability to appreciate art, literature and music.

Ronald Taft of the University of Western Australia (1955) provides a useful review of the studies relating to the ability to judge the emotional, personality and behavioural characteristics of others. In differentiating between analytic and non-analytic forms of judgements (the first involving mainly inference and the second global, empathic responses), he concluded that some people may be better at judging others on analytic tests, while others do better using an intuitive approach. Taft deduced that good judges show consistency in their ability to judge irrespective of the type of subject or the qualities being assessed. However, he noted that judgements were more accurate when there was a similarity between the cultural backgrounds of the judge and the subject, and to a lesser extent of age and sex. It may be that where such similarity exists, the judge is more able to select appropriate 'norms'.

In reviewing experiments concerning intuitive modes of judging, there were lower correlations between intelligence and accuracy of judgement. Taft thought it possible that accurate non-analytic judgements of others were more a function of good perceptual and judgemental attitudes rather than abstract intelligence.

Aesthetic or artistic ability correlates positively with successful judgements of people according to a number of studies examined by Taft in his paper of 1955. However, he concludes that the ability to judge others appears to be higher 'in those persons who have dramatic and artistic *interests* rather than *ability*' (p. 13). He proposes that further studies should be carried out on dramatic ability, which has a bearing on role-playing theory. There are, of course, forms of psychotherapy within the humanistic/existential school which specifically use dramatic re-enactment as a major constituent of the therapeutic process, notably psychodrama, as developed by J.L. Moreno (1946). It seems, however, that therapists from any orientation would do well to develop such interests. Drama has to do with human conflict in all its aspects and its resolution or otherwise. Much can be learnt about human nature from well-produced plays and films. These also provide a resource for the process of 'bisociation' already referred to and described in Chapter 10. It is not clear from Taft's review how artistic interests assist in the assessment of others. Clearly, an attraction to the fine arts will aid the development of the imagination and the perception of spatial relations and patterns. Perhaps it also denotes an absorption with other individuals and how they express themselves.

Taft asks an important question: Is a well-adjusted person less subject to projecting him- or herself into others than a poorly adjusted person and therefore able to judge the individual more accurately? Or, is a

poorly adjusted person who is also aware of his or her emotional difficulties therefore more sensitive to similar difficulties in others? Where
analytic judgements are concerned the literature appears to affirm the former, that is a positive relationship between accuracy and emotional
adjustment, but for intuitive judgements the evidence is contradictory.
The received wisdom among psychotherapists is that training should
include personal therapy for self-understanding. This is supported by several writers referred to in Taft's paper, who affirm that the acquiring of
self-knowledge and knowledge of others 'are indispensable to each other'
(p. 15). Psychoanalyst Peter Lomas comments: 'therapists will be required
to scrutinize, at the deepest level, the reasons for their own responses to
their patients and would therefore be well advised to submit themselves
to the experience of therapy' (1994, p. 5). It is essential that therapists are
clear about whether their responses within sessions have to do with their
own private experiences or whether they are intuitively picking up unconscious communications from the client. Self-knowledge would therefore
appear to be pivotal in the evaluation of intuitive information.

Emotional sensitivity

Rosalind Dymond, in her study of 1948, found that insight into other individuals depended upon the ability to take the role of others, that is on
empathy. This is the position adopted by Rogerian client-centred therapy,
which focuses on understanding the client as the client sees him- or herself. Dymond makes an important distinction between this process and
projection, in which one's own thoughts and feelings are attributed to the
other person. Her tests showed a wide range of individual differences in
empathic ability, some individuals showing more sensitivity in this respect
than others. This ability to see situations from the other person's point of
view appeared to result in more effective communication and comprehension, considered to be crucial for any therapist.

You will see from Chapter 7 that empathy is closely related to intuition.
The question that now arises is: are high-empathizers also high-intuiters
and low-empathizers low-intuiters? Bastick's research provides evidence
that the intuitive type of person is naturally empathic. His 'Theory of
Intuitive Thought' incorporates the idea that intuitive information is
accessed through appropriate feelings, which have been evoked 'mainly
subconsciously through empathy' (1982, p. 320). Emotional involvement
with people, objects and situations evoke feelings which are used for intuition. Since, according to Bastick, intuitive information is emotionally
encoded, it is necessary to experience concordant associated feelings in
order to recall that information. He explains that as the emotional state

drifts and changes, new elements associated with the new states are linked with the old elements, which can lead to original juxtapositions (p. 61). Not only must the intuitive type be empathic, therefore, he or she must also be emotionally variable and sensitive, aware of personal subjective processes and receptive to input from the environment. In the clinical situation, the therapist needs to be emotionally responsive to the client, so that the person feels understood. As the individual describes various situations, the therapist also has to be able to change feeling states with ease in order to track the emotional transitions of the client and his or her own responses, yet at the same time maintaining overall cognitive control. This is a complex task. H.R. Pollio (1974), a psychoanalyst, describes a session in which there appears to be a chaotic leap in the associations made by the analysand, who spoke firstly about her father, then, in an apparently unrelated way about a policeman, then again about the father (p. 152). Yet underlying the descriptions was categorization by a common emotional set, that is anxiety and authority. The therapist must listen not only to the surface narrative, but also to the emotional subtext in order to pick up important cues.

A salient aspect of primary-process thinking is that feelings are evoked via imagery. A metaphor, for example, such as 'Juliet is the sun' conjures up a subjective vision of a warm and vibrant woman; categorization is by common subjective associated feelings. In contrast, analytic thought categorizes by common consensus: 'Juliet is female'. This is a fact, which does not generally arouse sentiment. When images are shared between client and therapist, therefore, it is likely that there will be a mutual experience of emotional connectedness, which helps to affirm and strengthen the therapeutic alliance.

While emotional variability is a feature of the intuitive type, he or she must also be able to tolerate the discomfort of vagueness and ambiguity and the tension of not knowing, until a solution arises. Psychoanalyst Patrick Casement (1985/1990), in discussing unconscious communications from the patient, recommends that therapists persevere in their wish to understand 'even when they are experiencing the confusion or pain which some patients induce in them' until 'the unconscious purpose of these pressures becomes apparent' (p. 73). Ability to delay the appraisal of one's own ideas is a characteristic noted by psychotherapist F.V. Clark (1973), to allow time for the intuitive process to take place: during intuition 'the ego must stand aside in order to permit the experience. Interpretation and evaluation must be temporarily suspended or held in abeyance' (p. 162). Bastick suggests that curiosity, combined with the expectation of relief on reaching a solution, can act as a motivating force (1982, p. 164).

At the same time it needs to be remembered that Westcott observed that intuitive types are low information demanders (1968, p. 43). They are willing to take the risk of drawing conclusions from a small amount of data and have the confidence to do this. While this might be an asset in terms of forming hypotheses, there could be a danger of rushing in with untimely interventions. Intuitive types are therefore well advised to heed the recommendations offered by F.V. Clark.

How many counsellors prefer the intuitive function?

Since intuitive people appear to have characteristics which are suited to the profession of psychotherapy, it is interesting to note whether such types are indeed attracted to it. In a study of 1,803 counsellors which used the Myers-Briggs Type Indicator as the instrument, 45.81 per cent were found to be NFs, that is intuitives supported by the feeling function (Myers and McCaulley 1985, p. 257). Levin's study of psychotherapists (1978) showed a high 91 per cent preference for intuition (N) over sensing (S). Myers and Myers describe extraverted intuitive types at their best as being 'gifted with insight amounting to wisdom and with the power to inspire' and introverted intuitives as having, at their best, 'a fine insight into the deeper meanings of things and with a great deal of drive' (1980/1993 pp. 106 and 109), clearly admirable qualities for a counsellor or psychotherapist. It needs to be noted, however, that Myers emphasized positive qualities in her typology, even though it is based on Jung's model in which pejorative statements can be found. His opinion is that extraverted intuitives are totally lacking in judgement, that their 'consideration for the welfare of others is weak' and that they have 'little regard for their convictions and way of life' (CW 6, para. 613). He also considers that the type is more likely to be found among women. It is unclear how he draws such conclusions, since there is no reference to supporting material. These remarks are at variance with the experimental literature reviewed, except that Isabel Myers warns that if ENs do not find a rewarding outlet for their gifts, they can become abrasive and rebellious and lack direction (Myers 1987/1994).

The intuitive's profile

The intuitive type, as it emerges from the literature, can be summarized as follows. Such an individual is likely to be intelligent, with artistic interests, somewhat introverted, reflective and self-aware, with a good sense of humour. An intuitive is of necessity empathic, emotionally variable, sensitive and responsive to the environment. He or she can tolerate vagueness and ambiguity and delay the appraisal of his or her own ideas, being more inclined to have a personal system of evaluation rather than being guided by others' opinions. Intuitives avoid dogma and authoritarianism. They are divergent, creative thinkers, taking pleasure in a playful atmosphere and becoming intensely involved in the process. Curiosity may be a motivating force. There is a noticeable liking for metaphor, simile, analogy and imagery among intuitives and they are at ease with primary-process thinking, enjoying fantasy, reverie and dream-images. A high spatial ability is a marked characteristic, with the ability to see patterns in experience. Intuitive types are insightful with the confidence to draw conclusions from little data. They have a tendency to look for the bigger picture and are future-orientated, able to see what lies in potential.

Some drawbacks have also been noted, which intuitive types need to be aware of. In particular they may overlook significant small details and practical solutions, while time-keeping, planning, invoicing and record-keeping could be problem areas. When focusing on the future and the overall picture, elements from the past and present may be missed. Unless they have a strong thinking function by way of support, intuitives can be over-confident of their insights and neglect to check them out. They will probably find short-term work frustrating. Presenting themselves and their environment as rather unconventional may be alarming to some clients. Extraverted intuitives might find introspection difficult and thereby fail to grasp some salient points of the case.

While valuing their positive qualities, intuitives can also work towards greater integration by developing their sensing function, taking particular note of the details of cases and instigating an effective routine for their working life. Those who prefer the feeling function over thinking need to be careful about evaluating decisions, and may have to develop their verbal skills to ensure that explanations are clearly given. Intuitive thinkers will benefit from cultivating empathy, being certain to give sufficient personal response and encouragement to clients. All intuitives are likely to find saying 'no' very testing, if they sense that there are exciting possibilities for the future. They can thereby take on too much and over-stress themselves. A skilful supervisor can assist with these areas of self-awareness and growth. See also Chapter 12.

* * * *

A clear profile of the intuitive type of person had now emerged, at least from the theoretical writings, but I had the growing feeling that my head had been buried in books for far too long. Empirical material was now urgently needed. It was time to talk further with colleagues and begin to put in place some practical work.

Notes

1. The Myers-Briggs Type Indicator® and MBTI® are registered trademarks of Consulting Psychologists Press, Inc. The questionnaire is copyright, but if you wish to have your personality type assessed, contact the secretary at the British Association of Psychological Type (BAPT) at PO Box 404, Norwich MLO, Norfolk NR2 3WB, who will send you a list of qualified practitioners. See also Keirsey and Bates (1978/1984); this book suggests a way of assessing your own type.
2. Since introversion is coded as I, the letter N is used to denote intuition.
3. For descriptions of the different types, see Myers and Myers (1980/1993) and Myers (1987/1994).

CHAPTER 5
The focus group

In setting up my own studies, I would be able to compare existing theory concerning the process of intuition with the day-to-day work of practitioners. I was hopeful that my findings would demonstrate what the experience of intuition means to psychotherapists and what the implications are for clinical practice. Since the emphasis would be on description and discovery, rather than hypothesis testing and verification as in traditional scientific experimentation, it was obvious that qualitative methodology would be the most appropriate. The process would be inductive, allowing the theory to emerge from the data, following procedures laid down by Strauss and Corbin for the development of grounded theory (1998).

In considering which methods would be most likely to produce the required information, I investigated a number of possible procedures, some of which might involve the analysis of taped material. Enquiry concerning participation revealed reluctance among psychotherapists to record their sessions, not only for reasons of confidentiality, but also because tape recorders are considered to be a disturbing element, interfering with transference. This difficulty precluded a number of possible methods. Approaches which were feasible, however, were a focus group and the keeping of intuition diaries, and I considered that these would be likely to provide the in-depth, rich material required.[1] These would, however, require a testing instrument, and the Myers-Briggs Type Indicator (of which I am a qualified user) seemed to be eminently appropriate, providing a direct link with the typology of Jung. I chose the focus group in preference to individual interviews, anticipating that therapists' interaction with each other would be more likely to produce novel information, with less dependence upon my questions or other interventions as researcher.

The first study to be initiated was the focus group, followed by the therapists' diaries. I anticipated that the group members would raise new questions and leave others unanswered, given the semi-structured format. The diary study could therefore be designed with the purpose of eliciting further responses. (This is described in Chapter 10.) After completion of the data collection, all professionals involved were tested with the MBTI with the purpose of discovering their preferred psychological functions and their degree of intuitiveness. Central to this was the question of whether there was any relationship between individual responses and type; if so, this could be used as a check against possible bias.

As is customary in setting up a focus group, the participants were personally selected, on the expectation that these individuals would be able to provide data that were particularly relevant to this research (Krueger, 1994). Professionals known to myself were therefore invited. There was a number of other characteristics which were common to all. Most importantly, they needed to be fully accredited practising therapists with a minimum of five years' experience of one-to-one work. Supervision requirements according to their professional body should have been met, indicating a willingness to reflect on their practice. Additionally, I viewed them as mature professionals and anticipated that they would be stimulated by the discussion of the topic of intuition. Although I was not specifically intending to make a comparison between men and women, both sexes were invited. Of necessity they had to live within a twenty-five mile radius of the meeting place, and, as it happens, all participants were white and British.

My initial contact was by telephone. Each was informed that the topic under discussion was intuition and that the main purpose of the group was to collect together information concerning personal experiences of this phenomenon in clinical practice. Eight individuals were approached and of these, seven accepted. The date and time were agreed, approximately one month in advance, and a confirmatory letter followed. I suggested that the interval of time would enable them to reflect on their employment of intuition in their work.

At a later date, after the group discussion had been transcribed, the participants were invited to comment upon it and make any further observations if they so wished.

The group participants

The group consisted of five females and two males, summarized in Table 5.1, with first initial only used for identification, for reasons of confidentiality. The intention was to keep it fairly small, to enhance interaction and allow space for the less vocal people.

While all were registered practitioners with the British Association of Counselling and Psychotherapy (BACP) with the exception of one who belonged to the United Kingdom Council for Psychotherapy (UKCP), my

Table 5.1 Group participants

Initial	Gender	Age	Years practised	Orientation	Professional body	Type[a]
C	Male	51	7	Psychodynamic/psychosynthesis	BACP	ISTJ
G	Female	46	14	NLP/hypnotherapy	BACP	ENFP
A	Female	57	7	Psychosynthesis	BACP	ESTJ
M	Female	58	13	Psychodynamic/humanistic	BACP	ENFJ
B	Male	65	17	Person-centred	BACP	ENFP
L	Female	34	6	Psychoanalytic	UKCP	INFJ
T	Female	42	5	Integrative	BACP	ENTJ
Moderator/researcher:						
R	Female	56	10	Integrative/psychosynthesis	BACP	INTJ

[a] The meanings of the type codes are as follows:
ISTJ: introverted sensing with extraverted thinking; ENFP: extraverted intuition with introverted feeling; ESTJ: extraverted thinking with introverted sensing; ENFJ: extraverted feeling with introverted intuition; INFJ: introverted intuition with extraverted feeling; ENTJ: extraverted thinking with introverted intuition; INTJ: introverted intuition with extraverted thinking

initial concern was that there was a lack of homogeneity among their trainings and modes of practice. However, further reading and reflection suggested that this could be an advantage in this type of study, since the phenomenon being researched was presumed to be common to all, and furthermore, a variety of approaches could add to the richness of the material (Strauss and Corbin, 1998).

As moderator/researcher I made written notes during and immediately after the group session to record any observable nonverbal communications, and, where appropriate, made members' gestures explicit by incorporating a description of them into my responses. The following illustrates this:

R: (Laughs.) And you made this gesture with your hands.

L: Mmm.

R: Something rounded and global and sort of ...

L: Yes, because it was a body feeling for me as well ... something like this in me (repeats gesture).

R: ... A coming together? ... And you do this kind of rotating gesture ... all fitting together.

In this way aspects of body language became a part of the transcript.

The setting

It was made clear to participants that the evening would be divided into two sessions of approximately 50 minutes each. There would be an extended break with a buffet supper. The sociable atmosphere was deliberately encouraged, with the anticipation that this would facilitate the discussion (Krueger, 1994). Each session was tape-recorded, using two recorders placed apart, just in case one failed and to ensure that nothing was omitted. Group members sat comfortably in a circle together with myself as moderator/researcher, so that no hierarchy should be implied.

Role of the moderator/researcher

My overall aim as moderator was to elicit from the therapists firstly what they understood by the word 'intuition' and secondly to accumulate information concerning their experiences of this phenomenon within clinical practice and its impact on the progress of the work. I was also curious as to how much thought had been given to intuition in terms of both training and practice, and how far practitioners were aware of using it. My specific role was to act in a facilitating capacity, allowing the ideas and experiences of the group members to dominate the conversation, meanwhile remaining unobtrusive as far as my own thoughts and feelings were concerned. The framework was semi-structured, which meant keeping the main questions in mind, pulling the group back if responses strayed too far from these, yet at the same time remaining open to completely novel material should this arise.

Although the typological questionnaire was not completed until the end of the group discussion, I anticipated that some members would be more extravert in temperament and therefore more vocal, so it was necessary to address some questions directly to the quieter, more introspective people so that space was created for their views to be expressed also. Even so, it is obvious from the transcript that G., C. and M. took up far more of the time than A., B., L. and T. In particular B. and T. made only fleeting contributions, although they nominated themselves as extravert. Temperament apart, it appeared that some members had given deeper thought to the topic than others prior to the focus group meeting. For example, T. admitted that she had had no time 'to do any homework' or prepare herself.

Equally, I was aware that, as researcher, I was viewed in a special light by group members, which may have had an effect on their responses, resulting in an emphasis on their more positive thoughts and experiences. One member voiced this attitude by saying: 'But R. would find that a bad thing if we've all come here to say that intuition is rubbish. If we denigrated it.' They seemed to imagine therefore that negative responses would be unwelcome. This attitude needs to be taken into account when assessing results.

I inevitably brought certain expectations to the study. These were that the chosen therapists would have at least some experience of the use of intuition within their practices, and would be able to articulate it. Most striking, therefore, was the degree of difficulty experienced by the group participants in finding words that were sufficiently adequate. Some reasons for this will be considered below.

The analysis

Having carefully transcribed the group discussion from the tapes (see Appendix A for sample page), sometimes playing certain sections several times over to ensure accuracy, the raw data were then coded into concepts. I sorted these into categories and gave each a conceptual label for identification; separate cards were thus formed which listed the pertinent data, together with the page reference from the transcript and the initial of the person who had made the quotation. This process involved the splitting and amalgamating of some of the data groupings, and occasional alteration of conceptual labels, until each category was satisfactory, reflecting only the data. Links were noted with other categories and a definition formed by which the concepts were selected for inclusion (see Appendix B). In all there were 22 categories.

The next task was to examine the relationships between these and then sort them into overarching categories. It seemed first of all that certain conditions might favour or enhance the intuitive process, in terms of the personality and background of therapists and also their bodily and mental states during a session. Important features of intuition also emerged, without which, it was thought, the phenomenon could not take place. Further properties of the process were prominent in the discussion, as were particular subjective experiences. When considering what exactly intuition offered, creativity and some kind of knowing were the two products that came to mind. It was noticeable that intuition attracted various reactions, so that the responses and difficulties encountered formed the final overarching category. A summary is given in Table 5.2.

It was already becoming clear that, by asking an open question at the outset, namely 'What do you understand by the word "intuition"?', an opportunity had been created whereby the nature of this phenomenon could be discussed. A considerable amount of useful material was forthcoming about the intuitive process in general. Despite a specific request

Table 5.2 Overarching categories

Category	Card no.
1. Conditions that favour intuition	
Intuitive types	11
Relaxed or altered state	14
Development/training	15
Competence	2
2. Essential features of the intuitive process	
Not rational	9
Picking up clues/cues	3
Relationship or connection	10
Holistic	4
Validation	18
3. Other properties	
Innate, instinctive	8
Empathy	22
Congruence	16
Speed/immediacy	5
Sensory involvement	13
Adaptability	21
4. Subjective experiences	
An interruption	17
Psychic, spiritual	6
5. Products of intuition	
Some kind of knowing	1
Creativity	12
6. Reactions to intuition	
Difficulties	19
Social response	20
Descriptive language	7

from myself that we focus on the professional sphere during the second half of the group discussion, few specific examples of intuition in clinical practice arose. Equally, participants appeared to have difficulty in evaluating the degree to which intuition featured within their sessions. This was contrary to my expectations. However, I anticipated that the diaries would produce the necessary descriptions. With the exception of M. and, to a lesser degree, C. and L., therapists had apparently given little previous consideration to the phenomenon, although five out of the seven nominated themselves as intuitive in response to the MBTI questionnaire. Moreover, B. stated that intuition was highly valued in the professional arena, and there was no disagreement with this. There therefore seemed to be a mismatch between the perceived importance of intuition in psychotherapy and a real awareness of its constituents. Answers to my questions concerning trainings were more specific, providing a basis for further theoretical consideration.

The sorting of categories having been completed, the next step was to consider each category in turn and compare the data with existing theory. Lists of 'theoretical memos' were thus drawn up to provide a foundation for this process. The purpose here was to find support for statements made during the focus group, and conversely to give further weight to theoretical points discovered in the literature. Additionally, it was possible that ideas already put forward might be developed, or even that completely novel material might emerge.

Consideration of the categories

I will provide here a brief summary of the data forthcoming from the group within each of the six overarching categories. A comparison with other theories concerning that aspect of intuition will be incorporated into the discussion, together with any relevant points of interest.

1. Conditions that favour intuition

To take this first category, participants discussed intuitive types of people and particular states of mind that might be conducive to intuition, the influence of psychotherapy training and the question of competence at one's profession. There were therefore three main elements that emerged as most significant (see Figure 5.1).

The intuitive type has already been examined in some detail in Chapter 4, with sensitivity and responsiveness to the environment featuring on the list of attributes. It is reasonable to assume from this, therefore, that the comment made during the focus group that some people are more 'tuned in' to intuition than others has a real basis. It is interesting that A., whose MBTI type preference is for sensing rather than intuition, should make the point that 'grounded' types may be less intuitive. Since she had already described herself as a 'very grounded, very down-to-earth kind of person', this gives the impression that she was talking about her own experience. Indeed, she seemed unsure whether any of her skills as a therapist, such as picking up clues, could be called intuitive. This may simply be a question of language (category number 6). Myers and

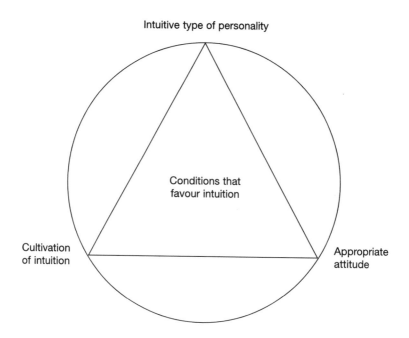

Figure 5.1 Favourable conditions.

McCaulley (1985) comment that 'in theory, helping people through psychological methods requires more intuitive than sensing skills, since intuition is concerned with the perception of patterns, recognition of inferred meanings, and intangible relationships' (p. 73). They quote Newman's study of 1979, which showed that N types scored significantly higher than Ss on ability to identify inferred meanings, and DiTiberio's of 1977 which found that Ns were higher for covert feeling messages.

Nevertheless, it needs to be pointed out that since S types form approximately 75 per cent of the general population (Myers and Myers 1980/1993, p. 58), many sensors may feature among clients. It is argued that such people are more likely to be interested in practical solutions to problems rather than depth of meanings or self-understanding. Intuitive therapists may need to adjust their counselling style with such clients. Mendelsohn and Geller (1963) reporting on students attending the Counseling Center of the University of California, Berkeley, found that those of different types from their counsellors attended for only a few sessions. Having a propensity for intuiting subtle messages, therefore, may not always be to the therapist's (or client's) advantage. Moreover, intuitive types may misassess the needs of sensing types, be vague about significant facts and be less inclined to help the client find practical solutions to problems. They may also be poor at routine tasks, such as payment and time-keeping. Psychotherapist M. Sabini enumerates, with honesty, some of the hazards of having the sensing function in the inferior position, including the forgetting of sessions (1988).

The association between highly gifted people and the process of intuition recurred in the focus group. Musicians and artists were thought to be intuitive and connections were made between inspiration, genius and intuition. While it is clearly not necessary for a therapist to be in any sense a genius, nevertheless, as already demonstrated in Chapter 4, there are striking parallels between the intuitive and creative processes, both of which are concerned with novel ideas, and the seeing of patterns and relationships. Although no new material was forthcoming from the participants during the group session in this respect, C. supplied some relevant material afterwards (see under category 4 below).

One of the most interesting questions to emerge from the focus group is whether women are in any way more 'gifted' than men at intuition. Women are clearly more attracted to counselling and psychotherapy as a profession than men, since their numbers are greater, but this may be for reasons such as social acceptability or the fact that women are more accustomed to the role of carer. The possibility was put forward by group members that women may be more skilled at social intuition and the suggestion made that some people may be more 'tuned in' to it than others. Examination of type tables produced by Myers and McCaulley (1985, pp. 50–1) shows no significant difference between males and females in the American population as far as a preference for intuition is concerned. However, researchers Graham and Ickes (1997) do offer evidence that women possess greater intuitive skills than men regarding emotional responding and nonverbal decoding ability. They ascribe this to differences in motivation, since it appears that men can learn to be as proficient as women, if they so wish.

It was noticeable that C.'s observations concerning meditation reflected the teaching of Roberto Assagioli. It was interesting to hear about its usefulness in clinical practice from someone trained in Assagioli's methods, apparently employed by C. on a daily basis to quieten himself by 'turning down the noise' of his own thoughts. The result of this practice was that he was able to be 'centred' and more open to the client. This can be taken as good advice to other T types, who will have a preference for being in logical rather than allological mode. Such centring was also practised by M. which enabled her to be more 'receptive'. G. also thought that meditation and peace and quietness were important for 'tuning in to intuition', a condition which she described as 'an altered state of consciousness'. This discussion reflected Assagioli's 'quiet waiting' for intuitions to enter awareness (1965/1975, p. 219). Agreement was voiced that these techniques were helpful in developing one's intuition, although practising it and trusting in the process were other important ingredients. Its usefulness depends on getting to know it and testing it out. This underscores Assagioli's concern that intuition can atrophy from inattention. The opinion among the majority of group members was that the practice of meditation was helpful to the intuitive process.

There was one note of dissent, however, from B., who considered that, from a person-centred perspective, attending and being with a client were focused rather than relaxed. L., a psychoanalyst, reported how she could be both relaxed and professional at the same time, being open to the client (a child) but simultaneously ensuring his safety. Assagioli describes a similar condition, an attitude of relaxation and quietness, but one which is not passive (1965/1975, p. 219). This has a bearing on some of the multiple and apparently contradictory levels with which the therapist needs to work at any given time, receptive yet watchful, touching in empathically yet also having access to the cognitive mode (see also Chapter 7).

The question was raised as to whether competence was a basis for intuition. This was linked with the ability to 'bring in more cues at a time' leading to a 'bigger picture' (G.), also greater relaxation and therefore 'expansion' (C.). While it can be appreciated that experience as a therapist can sometimes lead to greater skill in picking up clues and making sense of them, and that competent practitioners are more likely to be relaxed during a session, the evidence from studies is contradictory, as can be seen from Chapter 6. Here it is noted that if competence has increased the confidence of the therapist too much, then this may lead to less accurate clinical judgements. Moreover, trained psychologists are shown to be less successful at picking up bodily cues than others. Such studies indicate, perhaps, that experienced practitioners need to retain a sense of humility in their work. Further research in this area could be most illuminating.

As regards the possibility of enhancing one's intuitive faculty, it is notable that the development of the psychological functions is a central concept within the MBTI, to provide balance and harmony within the personality (Myers and Myers, 1980/1993, pp. 173–202). Psychologist Guy Claxton states of intuition: 'though it cannot be trained, taught or engineered, it can be cultivated by anyone' (1997, p. 14). Jung had already perceived that neurosis could set in if the environment did not support the child's natural propensities (CW 6, para. 560). Reasons for the lack of encouragement of intuition have been put forward in Chapter 1, and some of these were voiced again by the group participants, listed under 'Difficulties' on card 19 and considered again below.

Part of the purpose of this book is to raise awareness in the profession concerning the function of intuition, so that it can be consciously utilized for the benefit of clients. However, as one participant declared, 'You cannot decide to have an intuition; it happens to you', so how can it be 'practised'? As is becoming increasingly clear, you can augment the opportunities for its occurrence. Indeed, specific characteristics of the intuitive type can be consciously developed, as suggested by Patricia Hedges (1993, p. 141). For example, since intuitives are future-orientated, therapists can focus on the possibilities within a client's situation and find out what lies in potential. If there is an awareness of a 'hunch', this can be consciously followed up and perhaps formed into a hypothesis, which can be tested out with the client. Play and artistic creation can be incorporated into sessions in terms of drawing, modelling, movement, dramatic re-enactment and so forth. Symbols, myths and dreams all provide fertile ground for intuitive understanding.

It is a matter for concern that only a few psychotherapy institutes seem to incorporate intuition into their courses. There was no recollection among participants of intuition being taught at school and only two, both with a background of psychosynthesis, said that the process was explicitly included in their professional training. Some institutes were thought actively to discourage or suppress the intuitive process, through fear of loss of control in the session among novice therapists. Integrative and psychoanalytic approaches were said to 'allow' intuitions with the implication that they might be helpful. Further study into this area is incorporated into Chapter 11.

2. Essential features of the intuitive process

The second overarching category collects together the features considered by participants to be essential to the intuitive process. These include its irrational nature, a way of knowing that cannot be explained, the picking up of relevant clues or cues either consciously or subliminally, a connection or relationship between individual ingredients which produces novel information, a whole which is more than the sum of its parts, and the subsequent validation of the intuition. Figure 5.2 depicts the relationships between these elements.

There was unanimous agreement in the focus group that intuition is a non-rational, non-analytic way of using the mind, which added support to Jung's definition discussed in Chapter 2. The character of being 'given' (CW 6, para. 770) was expressed as: 'It's not about being informed, but guided' (B.), and 'It happens to you' (L.). C. was very clear about the distinction between the 'rational, concrete, linear and causal way of thinking' and intuition, which may come in the form of symbols, images or insights and which are not causal but are 'just there'. M. stated emphatically that it was not a cognitive process, since it was not possible to explain how you worked it out. Rationalization may come afterwards,

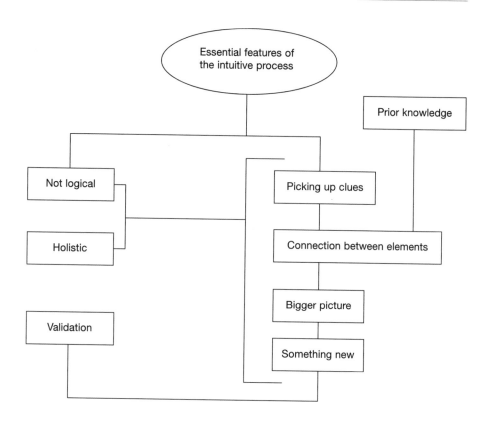

Figure 5.2 The intuitive process – key components.

however, when the intuition has reached consciousness. Jung had verbalized this more precisely: 'many intuitions can afterwards be broken down into their component elements and their origin thus brought into harmony with the laws of reason' (CW 6, para. 772). C. emphasized that you could stop the cognitive process through meditation.

When it came to discussing the picking up of clues, participants were unclear whether this process could be equated with intuition or whether it was simply a matter of keen observation, which they linked with the sensing function. This was confounded by the fact that training institutions and supervisors tended not to use the term 'intuitive' when such observations were made. What was not specifically stated in this aspect of the debate, however, was the importance of making links between clues or cues and other elements in order for an intuition to be formed. A. provided an example from her practice of how the picking up of cues could lead to a shift in the session. She had suggested a drawing to the client, but the fact that this individual was gazing elsewhere and demonstrating by her body language a lack of interest in the process, prompted A. to lead the work in a different direction. It was generally concluded that clues could be picked up either consciously or subliminally, or as A. expressed it perceptibly or imperceptibly, and that a sensory clue did not invalidate the intuition.

The topic of making connections was touched on initially, but considered in more depth later in the evening. L. described this as the coming together into 'a certain kind of relationship' everything thought or known about the client. M. thought that 'connecting' was a key word and that intuition could be described as 'connecting at a subliminal level', very often 'from outside to inside'. In other words, cues coming from the external environment are combined with inner thoughts and feelings, making new links. This mirrors Bastick's theory when he writes about the parallel processing of cues within and without (1982, p. 9). In C.'s opinion intuition 'cuts across different areas and is somehow connecting'. This word made several appearances, as did 'relationship'. These concepts seemed to be attached to the idea of 'tuning in', becoming 'more attuned' to what is going on, or being 'in tune' with another person. This implies an accord between the therapist and client, which enables those external and internal links to be more easily formed. Here again, meditation was thought to assist with the tuning in, which might be carried out before a session by way of preparation. Participants thought that being in tune was closely allied to empathy (see also Chapter 7).

L.'s hand gesture of two halves of a circle rotating and coming together to form a globe was most expressive of the holistic nature of intuition, which is Bastick's property number 15 (1982, p. 25). Therapists experienced this as 'seeing mind, body and spirit of the client in one go' (G.), as a 'gathering together' (A.), or as 'everything falling into place' (M. and G.). This process led to 'something rounded and global' (L.) that was 'more than the sum of the ingredients' (L.) and that resulted in the seeing of the 'bigger picture'. L. also talked about the physical impact of an intuition, which was experienced in her whole body. C.'s experience, however, was rather different in that the holism transcended boundaries, involving 'many different levels'. There is a real impression here of something new coming into being which is somehow beyond or more than the everyday detail. An element of the transpersonal appeared to be entering the discussion.

The falling or slotting into place was M.'s way of validating an intuition, which could be performed retrospectively. C., however, considered that an intuition was 'self-validating' in that there was 'a sort of a "yes" to it', which reflects Jung's statement that it carries an 'intrinsic certainty and conviction' (CW 6, para. 770). The point that subjective certainty does not guarantee veracity is debated more extensively in Chapter 10.

G. recognized an intuition from experience and that it should 'have a good feeling about it'. It is a concern that there was so little material in the group debate regarding validation, which gives the impression that therapists do not regularly go through a conscious process of testing out their intuitions as recommended by Assagioli.[2] However, type may be playing a part here, in that four of the seven participants had a preference for the feeling function over thinking.

3. Other properties

Other properties of intuition formed overarching category number 3. The group considered that intuition is to a certain extent innate, but participants made a distinction between this phenomenon and instinct, which they thought was more mechanical. Contrary to my expectations, empathy had only a brief airing. A new concept entered the debate with 'flow', which the group considered to be important, giving a flexibility to the session. Speed of processing and the suddenness with which an intuition appears generated agreement among the members, who had all experienced this, and many descriptions were forthcoming. They were also aware of the sensory components of the intuitive process, whether collected consciously or subliminally. There was some discussion about the different levels of intuition and its ability to fit into different frameworks or systems and the label given to this category was 'adaptability'.

Jung had made a strong case for the instinctive component of intuition, not in any sense to denigrate it, but rather as a necessary forerunner to the rational way of using the mind (see Chapter 2). In his definition he calls it 'a kind of instinctive apprehension' (CW 6, para. 770). It was interesting that G. made a link between intuition and survival, since this is an important aspect of Guy Claxton's thesis (1997). While reflexes are inborn, he emphasizes the amount of learning by experience that babies undergo pre-verbally, gradually turning strangeness into certainty. It is thus that intuitive know-how is built up, through experience, but without the words to describe it (1997, pp. 17–21). M.'s comments in the group that intuition is 'to some extent innate' and that it 'includes more than instinct' would therefore appear to be accurate in that there is an instinctive component, but also an unconsciously learned aspect. By applying Claxton's ideas, the implication is that 'know-how' or 'implicit learning', much of which is unconscious and nonverbal, is concerned with creating a repertoire of life-skills, and it is this that a therapist needs to draw on, or indeed anyone involved with working with people.

B. thought that the phrase 'gut instinct' was more acceptable as a phrase to males than 'intuition', which has female associations. When someone bases a decision or course of action on such 'instinct', they are really referring to an unconscious memory store of experience, which prompts the person to make that particular choice, usually without knowing why. The survival instinct may on occasion be crucial for psychotherapists and psychiatrists who work with psychotic or borderline cases and could therefore be at risk of attack.[3]

It was remarkable that the focus group produced so little on the subject of empathy, although a degree of involvement in the intuitive process was implied. The imagination was thought to be an important element in this process. M., who teaches counselling skills, gave an example of how she encourages students to employ imagination to assist in understanding a client's world from that person's standpoint. She saw this process as facilitating empathy and thereby the intuitive comprehension of another human being.

The word 'flow' had not so far featured in the literature on intuition, so its entry into the focus group was particularly notable. The general consensus was that theory, or having a pre-determined plan for a client, was unhelpful because the flow was thereby impeded. Forming theories and plans involves cognitive processes, and these would indeed hinder intuition, which, as has been seen, is a non-rational function of perception. The concept of 'flow' incorporates the idea of having a good rapport with the client, and being open to whatever he or she may spontaneously wish to bring to each session. Furthermore it can be associated with Carl Rogers' idea of 'fluidity' (1961/1967, p. 188), an existential way of living in which the self emerges from experience, rather than being forced into some pre-conceived structure. This involves an ability to adapt to ever-changing circumstances. Rogers had applied this to the evolving client, but it might just as well be applied to the therapist. When considering the intuitive type in Chapter 4, a characteristic that was noted was the avoidance of dogma and lack of interest in others' rules. While psychotherapists need to conform to professional codes of ethics and practice, there needs also to be scope for creative and original ways of working if intuition is to flourish.

'Congruence' was found by Rogers to be a prime condition of successful therapy, crucial to the therapeutic relationship (1961/1967, pp. 61–2) and a pre-condition for trust. By this he meant that the counsellor needed to be genuine and straightforward, true to him- or herself. It may well be that intuitions are more accessible, the more in touch with oneself that one is. Psychologist David Myers points out that people who are not self-aware are more prone to being overtaken by dysfunctional negative emotions, which are likely to block empathy and hence access to the intuitive source (2002, p. 35). Within the context of the focus group, however, the congruence seemed to refer to the interaction between therapist and client, once more reflecting the ability to 'tune in' to the other person.

Phrases used to depict the speed of intuitive processing included 'it's just there' (C.), 'you get there very quickly' (M.), 'suddenly it comes to you' (M.), an 'enlightened flash' (G.) or 'immediate recognition' (B.). This property appears to be commonly experienced. It is remarkable, therefore, that Jung does not incorporate it into his definition. In psychological studies of clinical judgements, speed has usually been associated with the idea of rapid inference (see Chapter 6). Bastick, however, ascribes it to parallel processing, the ability of the mind to deal with and make sense of a global field of knowledge, to which he devotes a whole chapter (1982). As such, speed is allied to holism (card 4).

Participants had no doubt that the senses were involved in intuition, because they were the only means by which it could reach awareness. The debate touched on the way in which memories are held in the body, and C. referred to the 'felt sense' of focusing, which was developed by Eugene Gendlin. There is more about this method of working in Chapters 3 and 8. L. reiterated how she experienced intuition with her whole body. There was resistance to the idea of any kind of a mind–body split, which was associated with destructiveness. Jung's typology, which opposes intuition and sensation, was found to be problematic in this respect, therefore. It needs to be pointed out, though, that the typology is really concerned with the favouring of one function over the other, and that everyone has access to all of them to a greater or lesser degree. However, an intuitive type will, according to Jung, have the function of sensation in the inferior, or least developed, position. This is very much at odds with the view that intuition actually requires sensation of a high order, voiced in the group by M. Indeed, Bastick found that intuitive types have a marked tendency to rely on body sensations as a source of information (1982, p. 133). It is interesting that the five intuitives in the group were equally aware of the important role of the body as were the two sensing types.

4. Subjective experiences

Two particular subjective experiences formed the fourth overarching category. The first was how intuition could arrive as some kind of interruption, and the second embraced the spiritual or psychic aspects of the phenomenon.

C. explained how, in a session, he may be following a particular line of thought, when something intrudes. This could be a body sense, an image or uninvited thought, and it demanded attention. He experienced this as 'uncomfortable and an irritant', because it prevented him from going where he was aiming for. This description seems to be somewhat at variance with the concept of 'flow' discussed above. However, C. continued that if he paid attention to this interruption, then the flow was increased.

In his feedback after the group meeting, he equated this with the process of painting, a subject which he has studied and practised extensively. In both he experiences an intermingling of thought processes with bodily sensations and feelings, in a kind of 'multi-layered web', keeping in touch with many subtle occurrences all at once. Sooner or later the web becomes entangled and 'stuckness' results. An intuition arrives in response to this and the result is a movement or shift reaching into a deeper engagement with the painting or client. In this respect he sees the process of painting and therapy as 'identical'. The parallel with creativity, already commented upon, is striking. This is a most interesting account of an intuitive process, which Bastick refers to more prosaically as 'overall impression' (1982, p. 61). He contrasts this with analytic thought, which is based on only two elements at a time rather than on all the elements in a field of knowledge.

Spiritual associations with intuition entered the group debate from time to time and seemed to form some kind of underlying preoccupation. Reference was made to psychic or clairvoyant ability, which were seen as quite different from learned knowledge. B. put this succinctly: 'It is not about being informed, but guided'. G. spoke of spiritual healers 'working with guides', at the same time making it clear that this was simply a question of language, a euphemism for knowledge that had an unexplained source. Nevertheless, the word 'guide' implies a helpful pointing of the way forward. The concept of forward movement also appears in A.'s language: 'It takes you beyond where you were.' It is of relevance here that students trained in psychosynthesis are encouraged to refer to themselves as 'guides' rather than 'counsellors' or 'therapists'. Gaining new ground through increased understanding is of course a necessary part of psychotherapy.

A. proposed two levels of intuition: everyday and transpersonal. A difference in quality can be discerned when comparing the inspiration of genius, the intense experiences of the mystics or the 'ultimates' of philosophers (see Chapter 9), with the sort of day-to-day intuitions involving personal relationships or mundane occurrences. Data from the diary study indicate that in psychotherapy it is the everyday kind that predominate, yet even apparently ordinary intuitions can have a considerable impact on the client and progress of the work (see Chapter 10).

5. Products of intuition

The products of intuition as conceived by the group constituted overarching category number 5, and were of two kinds: knowing and creativity.

At the outset of the discussion, 'knowing', or 'a deep knowing' were directly equated with intuition. By this was meant a knowledge that did not necessarily derive from one's own skills or experience, with the characteristic of bordering on a kind of 'psychic' or 'clairvoyant' ability. The ensuing debate indicated that the group members believed such knowledge to be contained within the person, rather than in any way being 'given' from some exterior source. The depth of the intuitive experience is commented upon by William James (1902/1982, p. 73): 'If you have intuitions at all, they come from a deeper level of your nature than the loquacious level which rationalism inhabits.' In taking a look at the mental life of a person, he saw that rationalism had the prestige, because it had the ability to challenge for proofs and argue with words, but he considered it to be, compared with intuition, 'relatively superficial'. In the context of his book, which examines religious experiences, intuition has a profundity with which reason cannot compete.

Some further characteristics of the 'knowing' experienced by group members were put forward, which, in addition to 'deep', was described as 'pure' (G.), 'a still voice within' (C.) and 'inner wisdom' (G.). The concept of purity was allied to the idea of everything falling into place, that the pieces were congruent with each other and therefore made a perfect fit, producing a knowledge that was self-evidently right.[4] This process seems to incorporate an emotional satisfaction, which involves aesthetics as well as the relief from the tension of an unresolved problem. Bastick provides considerable evidence of these emotional aspects of intuition and discusses them with authority (1982, pp. 84–138).

The 'still voice within' has spiritual connotations, the felt reality of a presence, a perception of what James refers to as '"something there", more deep and more general than any of the special or particular "senses"' (1902/1982, p. 58). This kind of voice is 'still', born of a tranquillity that has no need of words, providing a direct knowing. C. further described it as a 'knocking on my awareness' which demanded his attention. So, while being 'still' in character, it also seemed to be quite powerful, so much so that it could not be ignored. Such experiences are further deliberated in Chapters 8 and 9.

The group members considered that, in addition to knowledge, intuition could also produce something creative. Indeed, the literature debated in Chapter 4 makes strong links between intuition and the creative type of individual. Card 12 lists nine references associating intuition with scientific inventions and the creation of music and art. The involvement of the imagination through the use of dreams and imagery was mentioned as an important factor and some classic examples were provided, including Kekulé's experience (described in Chapter 2). Unfortunately, no illustrations of the use of dreams in psychotherapy were offered by the participants.[5] However, the overall implication was that the knowledge and insights gained from intuition could be used in an imaginative, inspired or novel way, not just to produce a work of art, but within the clinical context.

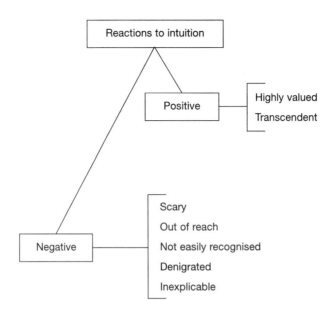

Figure 5.3 Positive and negative responses.

6. Reactions to intuition

These are summarized in diagrammatic form in Figure 5.3. Some of the difficulties associated with the concept of intuition, as put forward by the group (card 19), were redolent of those mentioned in the first chapter, when debating the lack of good literature. A.'s reactions are of particular interest here, because she describes the phenomenon as 'scary', which adds some substance to Jung's view that people are fearful of this aspect of themselves. However, her fear does not emanate from the chaos within, but from her perception of it as 'high-flown', implying something beyond her reach. As a practical, 'down-to-earth' person, according to her own description and MBTI profile, she wonders whether or not she could have such a faculty. Perhaps there is a case for encouraging sensing types within the profession to acknowledge their least preferred function, and understand that intuition is not beyond their reach.

Social responses to intuition were also thought to be problematic, since it is often associated with unintelligent females and is therefore denigrated. An 'intuitive therapist' was sometimes taken to mean a woman who is poorly trained and has little grasp of what she is doing.

The main problem with intuition, however, according to the group is that it is not straightforward or easily recognizable and can 'get muddled up with other things' (C.).

If therapists are confused about the nature of intuition, and the group indicated that they were, then research that explains and describes it with clarity is long overdue.

Summary of findings of the focus group study

So what did I learn from the group? As moderator/researcher, my own overall impression during the evening was of a struggle among participants to find words that could adequately describe the phenomenon of intuition. Sentences were often broken by pauses, 'mm' or 'er', and speech was frequently slow and measured. C. voiced this towards the end of the evening: 'the models, the words we've got to describe this experience are inadequate'. His comment prompted the idea of producing a model depicting important elements of the intuitive process, arising from this research (see Figure 5.4).

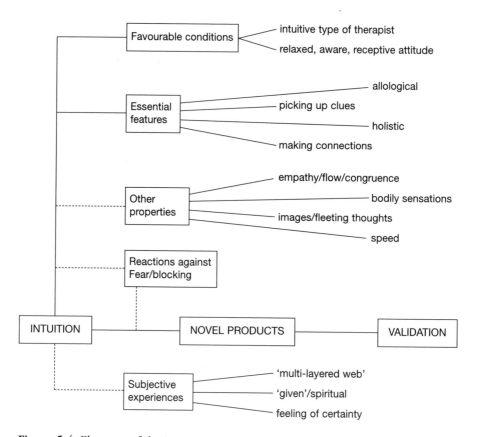

Figure 5.4 Elements of the intuitive process.

This figure demonstrates that the richest material emanated from the first question regarding therapists' subjective experiences of intuition, with the most lively components of the debate revolving around the varying aspects of the nature of this phenomenon. This makes clear that intuition is more likely to occur under certain conditions, which include the following: the personality of the therapist and the degree to which the intuitive mode is employed as a preferred function; the attitude of the therapist when with a client, described as relaxed but aware, centred yet open and receptive. Prominent are particular features, without which it is thought that intuition cannot arise, namely the allological and holistic aspects of the mental processing, the picking up of cues or clues (which may or may not be combined with pre-existing knowledge), the making of connections to produce something new, and the subsequent validation of the intuition. Other properties may be experienced as significant, such as the innate propensity of the function, the involvement of empathy, sensory input and the speed with which an intuition can apparently appear in consciousness. Intuition may also arrive unexpectedly, as an interruption, and may have the character of being 'given' or of offering guidance. There is a novel production, consisting of some kind of knowledge or creativity.

I was disappointed that so few specific examples from clinical practice were forthcoming, which meant that the second question concerning the implications of the use of intuition was left unresolved. Fortunately, however, the diary study provides rich material in this respect (Chapter 10).

As far as therapists' MBTI type and their responses were concerned, some correlation was noted, but this was too slight to draw any conclusions.

The mystical and spiritual elements seemed to intrigue group members and it was evident to me that they wanted to know more. For this reason I decided to explore the literature in greater depth and my findings form the bases of Chapters 8 and 9.

An important question that emerged during the debate, was whether intuition was in any way taught during professional trainings. Two of the five had had one extended seminar on the subject during a three-year psychosynthesis course, and mention was made of a lecture at the London Centre for Transpersonal Psychotherapy, but there was no knowledge of intuition being part of the curriculum of other institutions. There seemed to be a contradiction between its perceived importance within the profession and the attitude towards its use from training staff. The fact that different trainings are allied to specific theories, while intuition is atheoretical is problematic. Responses such as these from group members prompted me to set up a further study with the purpose of discovering precisely which colleges offer intuition as a subject area. The results are reported in Chapter 11. All in all, there was general agreement among participants that the usefulness of intuition within clinical practice was dependent upon becoming more familiar with the process and learning to trust it.

Notes

1. A more complete account of these studies is available in thesis format, lodged under my married name at the University of London (Fulcher, 2002).
2. There is clear evidence from the diary study that therapists do in fact verify their intuitions in a number of ways (see Chapter 10, category 7).
3. Data from the diary study, category 2, indicate that therapists are very alert to any kind of warning, not just as far as personal safety is concerned, but also for the care of the client.
4. The 'fit' of an intuition is shown in the diary study to be one way in which a therapist validates intuitive knowledge (see Chapter 10, category 7).
5. There is an example in Chapter 10 of the therapist's intuition assisting with the interpretation of a dream.

Chapter 6

Interpersonal perception in the session

What do most people expect when they come for the first time to a counselling or psychotherapy session? The assumption is that they will sit in a room with another person and talk about whatever is troubling them and that the therapist will listen and respond, also verbally. While some forms of therapy may deviate from this format, the interview is indeed the standard procedure, with speech taking the predominant role. At the same time it is generally accepted within the profession that nonverbal communication also plays a significant part. This raises some noteworthy questions with regard to intuition. How important are such communications, how do therapists read and understand these, and how accurate are their interpretations? Do counsellors and psychotherapists receive training in the comprehension of body language and, if so, does this improve their ability to pick up such cues? Are nonverbal communications recognizably the same from person to person, or do they differ with cultural conditioning? How many of their meanings are idiosyncratic and how much do they depend on the context in which they are expressed? It is remarkable that important questions such as these are so little discussed in the counselling literature.

Ray Birdwhistell, a psychologist who pioneered research into nonverbal communication, is of especial interest here because he made a number of studies of psychotherapy sessions. He focused particularly on subconscious bodily movements and examined their role, terming this approach 'kinesics' (1970). He came to the conclusion that much human communication is carried on at a subconscious level, and reckoned that a comparatively small percentage of meanings are embedded in the words actually spoken: 'no more than 30 to 35 percent of the social meaning of a conversation or interaction is carried by words' (p. 158). If this is so, then the emphasis on the discursive mode within sessions, often seen in theoretical writings, is misplaced. Moreover, it would appear that therapists have a difficult task in picking up and decoding the 65 to 70 per cent of messages which are nonverbal.

First impressions

Let us imagine meeting a client for the first time, and consider what opportunities present themselves for the therapist to draw on his or her intuition. First of all, is she on time, early or late, and what responses might this behaviour evoke in the therapist? While being aware of spurious interpretations, the client's attitude to time-keeping may say something about personal style within the social context and also degree of commitment to the work. Is the knock on the door loud or soft, prolonged or brief? What might this initial communication say about the client's feelings of acceptability, of how welcome, or otherwise, she might suppose herself to be? How does she enter the room? Timidly, peeping round the door first, or marching straight in? What about the way she walks and how do the shoes determine the character of the tread? Perhaps the steps are short and mincing with the weight of the body pushed forward by high heels, or maybe casual strides are made possible by down-to-earth trainers. Such indications can say how grounded the person is, or otherwise. Moreover, it is useful to be aware of any hints concerning energy levels and degree of health as compared with age.

It can be all too easy to stereotype a person's character where body build is concerned, but nevertheless independent research has supported Sheldon's findings regarding the three basic sorts: endomorph (round, soft and heavy), mesomorph (angular, muscular, athletic) and ectomorph (linear, thin, underweight) (1940). What impression does this person's body shape give you, how do you find yourself responding and what associations do you make? The most positive feelings are generally linked with people of the second type, who are perceived as strong and healthy and are generally chosen as leaders, while the first are often thought of as lazy or even stupid, unattractive (from a Western perspective) although jolly, and the last as nervous and frail, but also studious and intelligent. It is important to be aware of cultural as well as personal prejudices, as these can interfere with accurate intuitive decoding of nonverbal messages. Nevertheless some validity can be ascribed to Sheldon's types, if only because they can become self-fulfilling prophecies. If an overweight child is treated as slow and stupid, then she is more likely to become so. Consider also how the body of the client is held. Tension can indicate anxiety or hostility, a stooping posture someone weighed down by many burdens and/or a poor self-image, a head held high a superior attitude, and so on.

What about the nonverbal message behind the greeting? This might be conveyed by the pitch or tone of voice, the volume, or the pacing of the words, or a mixture of these elements. A flat monotone is often linked with depression, loudness or harshness with aggression, edginess with nervousness, breathiness with sexuality, a high pitch with excitability or childlike feelings. Accent will give information about social class. It is well worth turning the attention away from the words to tune in to the ways in which they are spoken.

You may have detected a scent or smell as the client comes into the room. This could be a light feminine perfume, unwashed body odour, or even the smell of furniture polish. Commenting on this last aroma recently with a client led to discovering that she has a real love of beautiful furniture and a long-repressed wish to learn how to make the pieces herself. Subsequent sessions were spent considering how she might free up her creativity and what the blocks were that intervened and made progress in this area so difficult for her. This useful work all stemmed from the detection of a faint aroma.

There is, of course, the question of a handshake. Some psychotherapists avoid any kind of touch, but this social convention can convey a considerable amount about the individual's attitude towards interpersonal relationships, and hence how the therapeutic alliance might develop. A cold, clammy hand can indicate that fear is present, while the fingertip grab may suggest low levels of self-confidence. Conversely, a wholehearted grasp can be experienced as warm and friendly, with a willingness to interact. Then there is the interpersonal distance to consider. Does the client stand far away, or does she walk towards you with an open posture? Her level of sociability may be evident from this body language.

Have you noticed the facial expression and what this might reveal about the client's feelings or social mask? Is there an engaging smile, a troubled frown, eyes wide with apprehension or even a sense of surprise or interest? How much will you incorporate such messages into your assessment of the work to come?

Dress is perhaps the most obvious statement of the person's sense of self and the impression she wishes to make. The clothes may reveal or conceal the body, be expensive and well cut or comfortably hand-knitted from the charity shop; colours can be flamboyant and denote an extravert personality, styles can be original and imaginative, or else sombre tones of grey, black and beige can indicate that the person wishes to blend into the background and not be noticed.

Positioning of the chairs has generally been pre-determined by the therapist, but it can be advantageous to suggest to the client that she move her chair so that she feels comfortable. Her choice can be revealing. Does she set it at an angle and sit in it with her body turned away, a leg and an arm forming barriers and gaze averted to reduce contact, or does she turn it towards you, offering the opportunity for good interpersonal communication?

This initial encounter has probably taken less than two minutes of the session time, verbal exchange has been minimal, yet the unspoken messages have been multifarious and continuous, so much so that it will have been impossible for the therapist to take all of them in on a conscious level. Indeed such an avalanche of information can cause the recipient to switch off and thereby to miss some important cues. It is therefore helpful for the therapist to be aware of this difficulty and consciously to increase awareness of subtle clues. Nevertheless, intuitive, unconscious processing will have been at work, leaving the counsellor with a distinct overall impression of the client, a valuable resource for making an initial assessment, and to draw upon as the work together unfolds. Indeed, it is likely that several examples of the different types of nonverbal body codes will already have presented themselves, in terms of facial expressions and gestures (kinesics), eye movements, eye contact and pupil dilation (oculesics), personal space (proxemics), scent (olfactics), tone of voice (vocalics) and possibly touch (haptics). Additionally, cultural messages will have been sent regarding physical appearance, social standing, attitude towards time and speed (chronemics) and gender orientation, not to mention the predominant emotional content and degree of willingness to engage.

Indeed, whenever people are together, nonverbal messages are being sent continuously. These may take the form of wordless emotional contact, may enhance and emphasize the verbal communications, may contradict what is spoken, or simply indicate pacing and timing of turn-taking by a nod of the head or a pause. As communication psychologist Peter Andersen affirms, it is impossible not to communicate something as long as there is a recipient: 'Attempts to create a blank expression are perceived by receivers as anger, sadness, or withdrawal' (1999, p. 20). Equally, a lack of gestures conveys some kind of meaning. For example, a person whose hands are completely still or folded may be regarded as calm and composed.

Psychoanalysis and covert messages

Remarkably, most of the traditional psychoanalytic literature gives body language passing mention only. Freud noted the 'chance actions' of patients when first lying on the couch, such as the young girl who pulled the hem of her dress down over her ankles. He considered that this offered a clue to the future direction of the analysis in terms of her narcissistic pride and inclinations to exhibitionism, but gives no indication as to how he arrived at such a postulate (SE XII, p. 138). Sandor Ferenczi (1955) seems to have looked for nonverbal messages mainly when the patient was stuck for words and regarded these as unconscious communications from the 'inner child'.[1] In discussing the timing of interpretations, Fenichel refers to discrepancies between a patient's words and facial expression (1953). Such authors are not, however, specifically investigating interpersonal perception from the analyst's viewpoint. An interesting exception is psychoanalyst Theodor Reik, who describes his own perceptive processes for the benefit of the reader in his book *Listening With the Third Ear* (1948/1975). This is such an illuminating text, that Reik's accounts will be analysed in some detail in Chapter 10.

Enactment is, however, treated in some detail in certain psychoanalytic writings. This might involve regression to a pre-verbal state, in which the patient expresses an urgent demand for response, often through an action, which might take the form of hitting or throwing. Practitioners are warned to be alert to extreme forms of this kind of behaviour, which can sometimes involve self-harm or danger to the analyst. Bateman and Holmes, for example, describe enactment as follows: 'On the negative side it is destructive, personally dangerous or even life-threatening and may jeopardise the analysis; the unconscious internal drama or phantasy passes directly to the outside, circumventing thought and psychological defence, and so gains expression' (1995, p. 195). Milder forms are simply acts that take the place of recollection or verbal description: 'the patient ... acts it out before us, as it were, instead of reporting it to us' (Freud, SE XXIII, p. 177). Nevertheless, this is treatment of a specific and sometimes dramatic type of nonverbal communication, rather than the everyday sort of body language that sends messages continually.

At the other extreme, Wilhelm Reich (1945) believed that a person's character was held in his or her bodily structure and mode of movement and that physical loosening must occur before change was possible. He coined the phrase 'muscular armouring', referring to the chronic tensions in the body that have been unconsciously formed to protect the individual against painful emotions. This armouring may defend against either threatening internal impulses or from external attacks. Reich's work was carried on by his student, Alexander Lowen, a doctor and analyst and founder of bioenergetics, which aims to use the language of the body to heal the problems of the mind (1975). Bodily expression is therefore central to these theories, but other covert messages are not given prominence.

Only with the introduction of Communication Analytic Psychotherapy by clinical psychologists Ernst Beier and David Young have nonverbal messages been given serious and detailed attention (1984). Yet the authors do not incorporate the process of intuition into their theory, but base it rather on a mixture of analysis and behaviourism, which causes some problems. The Communication Analyst learns to recognize different types of messages, either overt and conscious ones (described as 'simple'), or those that carry covert meanings ('persuasive' or 'evoking') and then to infer the source of the patient's hurt. It is the aim of the therapist to effect change by refraining from giving the expected social responses to the covert communications and thereby avoiding their reinforcement. While recognizing that sensitivity is needed in order to pick up the unspoken messages, the authors emphasize the cognitive mode in the analyst and recommend emotional disengagement in order to understand the patient's hidden motive. This implies a non-empathic attitude, yet the part that feeling plays in the intuitive process is reflected upon elsewhere in this book. It would seem that these analysts run the risk of missing opportunities for helpful spontaneous interventions, with subsequent negative effects on the therapeutic relationship.

If intuition is an innate function and available to everyone, and if communication is at least 65 per cent nonverbal, then it is reasonable to assume that much of the dynamics of any session will concern the transmission of covert messages from the analyst to the patient, which the latter intuitively picks up. R.J. Langs's development of Communicative Psychoanalysis in the 1970s attempted to reconstruct psychoanalytic theory and technique upon the 'adaptive context', or how the unconscious preoccupations of the patient appear to revolve around the behaviour and personality of the analyst. Langs's ideas have been given little credence by mainstream psychoanalysts, and many reasons for this have been put forward by Livingston Smith (1991) among others, such as therapists' defensiveness, but they are relevant here because of their emphasis on unconscious perception. Langs (in Livingston Smith, 1989) considered that the accentuation of phantasy rather than reality for understanding a patient's psyche had developed from the unconscious dread of analysts of themselves being exposed: 'Patients are unconsciously aware of many mad elements in what we do. They understand how our interventions are self-serving, self-gratifying, seductive, narcissistic and so on' (p. 119). After repeated clinical trials, Langs showed that patients offer their therapists hidden commentaries on the helpfulness or otherwise of their interventions, often disguised in analogy, metaphor, dreams or unconscious acts. Livingston Smith (1991) makes the interesting point that clients are in fact more likely to be intuitive and tuned in to the unconscious than their therapists, because they often come to a session in a state of heightened awareness (p. 159). This suggests that patients are attuned to picking up subtle clues concerning the therapist because their perceptive processes are augmented. Indeed, communicative analysts learn to be guided by their patients, but, surprisingly, intuition is not recommended by Langs for the translation of these unconscious messages. Rather, a set of rules is prescribed using directed thought. He appears to be ambivalent about the trustworthiness of intuition.

In searching for descriptions of intuition within the interpersonal process of psychotherapy, Peter Lomas's work is notable (1987). He criticizes analytic technique for its emphasis on cognitive thinking, with the danger that interpretations will be limited to those that are amenable to the theories of unconscious mechanisms. He recommends rather that interpretations should be based 'on a heterogeneous mix that includes immediate intuitions, personal experiences and cultural biases, as well as ideas derived from systems of thought' (p. 41). This indicates that the complexities of humans cannot be well enough understood using analytic thought only. Furthermore he comments that it is ironic that Freud, who gave the unconscious a new respectability, should also have developed a technique that constrains it (p. 46). While giving some examples from his practice of moments of intuition and their effects on the patient, Lomas neglects to throw light on the nature of the intuitive process, other than awareness of his own responses. He links this with the concept of counter-transference (p. 51), not as originally used by Freud to alert the analyst to possible distortions in perception of the patient due to contamination from his personal material, but as more recently applied, notably since Paula Heimann's important paper of 1950. This concerns the analyst's subjective reaction to the patient's unconscious communications, providing valuable clues about the effect of that person's behaviour and hence about the nature of his or her relationships. Some therapists describe this as 'reactive counter-transference' (Clarkson, 1995; see also Chapter 7). Lomas allies this with the intuitive process of everyday life, the main difference being the rigour with which the psychotherapist examines and uses this mode of perception for the patient's benefit (1994, p. 46).

Emotional cues

To understand something of the unconscious aspects of interpersonal perception, it is necessary to return to Darwin's classic work, *The Expression of Emotion in Man and Animals* (1872), which, during the 1960s and '70s was largely ignored, but has more recently regained credibility with the increasing acceptance of biological and evolutionary explanations of human behaviour. His thesis was that all primary human emotional expressions evolved from some functional act. For example, the baring of the teeth in anger could have come from preparation to bite. This then became a warning signal against impending attack. An unexpected onslaught could result in fatalities, but such a disaster could be avoided if aggressive warning displays were involved, resulting in symbolic combat, or the flight of either party. From a biological perspective, people who expressed anger were therefore more likely to survive to pass on their genes.

Psychologists Paul Ekman and Wallace Friesen (1969), having made a number of studies of nonverbal behaviour, concluded that there were three probable origins: inherited neurological programmes, the reflex being the most obvious example; experiences that are common to all humans, such as the use of the hands to put food into the mouth; and experiences that vary with culture, class, family or the individual. Some nonverbal behaviours in this last group can be explicitly learned, for example an adolescent who copies the gestures of an admired film star. Other forms of imitation are often absorbed implicitly, in particular the actions of parents.

Ekman and Friesen distinguished six primary affects, namely happiness, surprise, fear, sadness, anger and disgust, and discovered that these could be easily identified by observers of facial displays not just from Western cultures, but elsewhere in the world, including the South Fore people of New Guinea, some of whom had never previously met a Caucasian. It appears, therefore, that these expressions are pancultural and do not need specialized training for their recognition. Moreover, the fact that they are common to people throughout the world underscores their biological origin. Small infants, while still in the cot and before they can themselves speak, will react to a tone of voice, a facial expression or other body movement, and will quickly learn what they signify. The ability for global processing is inborn, to make sense of much information at once, and rapidly to form an impression of what is happening and respond to it.

We are all aware that in addition to the exposed teeth, anger involves knitted and lowered brows with narrowed eyes, a stare and a tense jaw. The voice will be louder, fists clenched, and there may be stamping of the feet. The noise, the tension in the body and the staring eyes are all likely to create fear in others. The emotion of fear is also characterized by muscular tension, as a preparation either to fight or to flee. There will be changes in breathing, increased heart rate, trembling and perspiration, but with cold extremities. Most noticeable in the face are the raised eyebrows, wide eyes and stretching of the lips. There may also be hiding of the face, protection of the body and cowering.

Although associated with foul tastes and smells, disgust may equally apply to people and situations. The wrinkled nose, half-closed eyes and sometimes protruding tongue typically denote this emotion. Surprise is generally a fleeting expression, in which the jaw drops and the teeth are parted, while the eyes open wide and the brows are raised. This may quickly turn into another response as the surprise stimulus is processed.

Anyone can recognize the pitiful expression of sadness, with the lowered head and brows, down-turned mouth, slumped posture and perhaps tears. Vocal tone will be monotonous and low in volume with prolonged silences. In contrast, happiness is expressed through smiling, character-ized by the widening and upturning of the lips and mouth, the raised cheek muscles and the laugh lines at the outer corners of the eyes. Vocal pitch and intensity will increase, walking style will be lighter and inter-personal distances closer.

Other emotions can be more difficult to identify, because the signals are varied due to idiosyncratic or cultural forms of expression, or because they may be blended with other feelings and are not so obviously distinct. The three 'self-conscious' emotions of shame, embarrassment and guilt may be revealed by a number of nonverbal behaviours. They are referred to as self-conscious, because the strongly negative feelings of inferiority or loss of respect, due to the individual's incompetent, thoughtless or uneth-ical behaviour, engender improved conduct towards others. All three tend to be characterized by avoidance of observation and eye contact, the low-ering of the head or covering of the face and shrinking of the body away in a wish to hide. These may be overlaid by other behaviours in an effort to feel in control, such as the biting or licking of the lips, wrinkling of the forehead and forced or feeble smiles. Blushing is mostly associated with embarrassment, while remorseful or worried facial expressions may sig-nify guilt and a wish to repair the painful situation.

Communication scholars seem to be undecided about whether con-tempt is a separate emotion or a blend of anger and disgust. Ekman and Friesen (1986), however, consider that its distinguishing feature is the curled lip. Nonverbal behaviours associated with pride are more pro-nounced. This emotion is easily recognized from the inflated body position, the broad smile and the celebratory gestures.

Feelings of warmth are demonstrated by a wish to spend more time together, to be physically closer, by smiling and nodding, and by using soft, reassuring vocal tones. Love may include blushing and protracted eye contact, and the very subtle cue of pupil dilation. Nonverbal behav-iours are significantly more pronounced in the communication of love than verbal. As for sexual attraction, this is considered to be displayed almost entirely nonverbally at 93 per cent (Mehrabian and Ferris, 1967).

The dark aspect of love is, of course, jealousy, which may be commu-nicated in a variety of ways, such as cold looks, refusing to respond to the partner, threatening or even violent behaviour, manipulative moves such as flirting with others, or obvious display of symbols that denote posses-sion such as rings.

From a psychotherapeutic point of view, it is important to appreciate that the main way in which emotions are transmitted is nonverbally. Moreover, whenever two or more people are together, it is extremely dif-ficult not to give emotional signals and these will, of course, be imparted in both directions. Social convention governs how these are sent and received, depending on the context. For example loud, aggressive displays will be unwelcome in an art gallery, whereas they may be totally acceptable on the football pitch. Additionally, children, as they develop, learn certain rules regarding the expression of emotion, and these generally fall into five categories (Andersen, 1999, p. 36):

1. *simulation* – showing feelings when you are not experiencing them, e.g. laughing at someone's joke even if it is not funny;
2. *intensification* – pretending you have more feelings than you do, e.g. crying at an aunt's funeral, even though you hardly knew her;
3. *inhibition* – seeming to have no feeling when you really do, e.g. concealing your attraction to someone else when your husband is present;
4. *miniaturization* – showing less feelings than you actually have, e.g. frowning rather than having a temper tantrum;
5. *masking* – covering a real feeling with another that you are not experiencing, e.g. feigned pleasure at an enemy's success.

Unfortunately, difficulty in expressing real emotions can result in psychosomatic disorders, a problem very familiar to therapists. On the other hand these processes can help to keep social interaction harmonious. We all learn to tell white lies so as to protect others' feelings or our own. Nevertheless, this raises the question of deception, which is considered below.

Emotions are contagious, particularly joy, sadness, fear and anxiety (Klinnert et al., 1983). Anyone who has experienced being among the supporters of a winning team can bear witness to the way in which the euphoria rapidly spreads from the players through the crowd, resulting in cheers, clapping, singing and dancing. The same, of course, applies to the losers, but the emotion expressed now is despondency and gloom, which may turn to aggression and even fighting. In relational dyads, it is very difficult to remain cheerful if the other is depressed. Equally, it is far easier to feel joyful if one's partner is happy. There are various hypotheses as to why this occurs. One reason is that people unconsciously copy each others' expressions and body language. Have you noticed yourself smiling when your client does, or the tears beginning to form in your own eyes when the patient cries? The matching of this nonverbal language actually evokes the same mood in oneself, giving helpful data. Are you also aware how gestures such as the crossing of legs, the rubbing of an eye or the scratching of an ear will be reflected by the other person? Indications are that this denotes agreement or liking (Scheflen, 1972).

When working with a client from a different cultural background or ethnic group, it is useful to understand that there may be discrepancies in the manner in which nonverbal messages are sent. Someone from a Mediterranean country, for example, may be overtly self-expressive in terms of gestures and intensity, which a British or American person could find embarrassing. The relationship to time between a Northern European and an individual from a third world country will be quite dissimilar, the first tending towards doing one thing at once according to schedule, and the latter preferring a relaxed flexibility, with several things happening simultaneously. Personal space can also be distinctive. Mexicans and Arabs in particular feel comfortable with closer interpersonal distances than Americans and the British. Moreover, people from country backgrounds will need a far greater personal 'bubble' than city-dwellers. It is important for therapists to familiarize themselves with such cultural divergencies, so as not to misconstrue nonverbal communications.

The clinical setting provides a very particular context, in which the patient may feel very free to express feelings or, conversely, may feel inhibited, according to unspoken messages picked up from the therapist and general environment. How do you imagine that clients feel when they walk into your consulting room? I have mixed memories from my own personal therapy. One room, being small, at the back of the building and having a double door to gain access, gave me a claustrophobic feeling and an overwhelming wish to escape. The impression that the therapist was stressed increased in me the sense of anxiety. Another was an airy and comfortable sitting room with capacious armchairs, in which I felt totally relaxed and at home, and where I was always greeted with a welcoming smile. This I experienced as an invitation to communicate.

Words are very often accompanied by gestures and expressions, which serve to emphasize the verbal content. These are generally referred to as 'illustrators' (Ekman and Friesen, 1972). Someone describing a small child, for example, may indicate the height by holding out a hand, or if talking about a loved pet might enact the pleasure in stroking it, accompanied by smiles. When nonverbal signals are congruent with the verbal material, then communication is enhanced and there is less opportunity for error in interpretation.

More complicated are those hidden messages which are idiosyncratic, particularly those described as 'self-adaptors' by Ekman and Friesen (1969). These were first learned in order to master or manage various problems or needs, such as the facilitation or blocking of speech or sensory input, the performance of ingestive or excretive functions, or the grooming of face or body. They may be repeated in adulthood for their original purpose, or because something in the situation triggers one or other of them. During social conversation, though, only a fragment of the original behaviour is likely to remain. Such adaptors are habitual and mostly emitted without awareness. A typical example is the hand wiping around the corner of an eye, which in its original form would have removed tears. This movement may be unconsciously performed if sadness is present or anticipated. Self-directed adaptors can be rich in meaning, particularly if idiosyncratic. Take, for instance, the eye-cover act, which may have a shared interpretation related to shame, yet the circumstances which trigger it will differ according to the individual. There could be associations with a particular person, or with emotions such as anger, crying or excitement, and these often reach back into childhood. When carefully explored, these connections can provide valuable psychological information. In such cases interpretation of a particular action on the basis of common meaning only would be inappropriate. An example from my own practice springs to mind. One client had the habit of placing two fingers over her lips, which clearly signified 'Don't speak'. She had learned in early childhood not to talk about difficult emotions, and would place her hand over her mouth to help repress the words. When similar feelings were touched on in the session, she would repeat a remnant of the original movement. Another client had a similar hand-to-mouth movement, but, on investigation, we discovered that, although this too arose in childhood, the touching of the lips signified for him a need for sustenance and comfort.

Other types of adaptors are referred to as 'alter-adaptors' as they are derivatives of movements involving others, perhaps relevant to giving or taking, to attack or protection, or to fleeing the situation. They may appear in the session as restless leg movements, related to kicking or running, clenched fists denoting underlying aggression, or an arm that protects the body in some way. Movements that involve items ('object-adaptors'), such as fiddling with a pen or playing with a handkerchief, can sometimes reveal underlying anxiety or even boredom. Here again meanings should not be assumed, but individually explored.

Other cues

Moving on to consider how a therapist knows when to make an intervention, it is useful to ask what the cues are that convey information about tactful timing. Ekman and Friesen (1969) identified a category of nonverbal behaviour on the periphery of awareness, which they termed 'regulators'. These convey information which controls the pacing of conversation, such as a nod of the head, eye or eyebrow movements, small postural shifts and so on. Thus subtle signals are passed from one participant to another, telling the speaker when to continue, hurry up, elaborate, become more interesting, to stop, etc. and to indicate to the listener to pay attention, to wait, and when to talk. People who are insensitive to these regulators are likely to be accused of rudeness. If regulators are withheld, the other interactant becomes disturbed and will cease communicating. Any kind of 'blank screen' attitude maintained by the therapist could therefore seriously inhibit client disclosure, whereas personal involvement in the form of regulators is likely to encourage it.

Patterns of regulators seem to vary with social class, culture and ethnicity and can be a source of misunderstanding between different groups. Scheflen (1963) warns that patients who adhere to social systems other than their therapists may have their behaviour inaccurately interpreted as resistance. He adds that the analyst 'should not ... assume that a behaviour is merely projection or transference, for the reactions of either the patient or himself may be compliance to subtle but compelling signals'. He recommends that the structure of psychotherapy be further studied in its entirety, for the relationship 'may embrace rules – constantly reinforced by mutual nonconscious communication – that are irrelevant, possibly even deleterious to the therapeutic intentions' (p. 136).

Decoding ability

Since the ability to recognize the basic emotions in facial expressions appears to be universal, we can assume that psychotherapists may consider themselves to be as competent as anyone else, but are they equally adept at tuning in to bodily cues? Some unspoken messages are complex. A therapist may notice, for example, that a client's words convey one meaning, but the body denotes something different. The patient may protest, 'But I hate being lonely', yet the avoidance of eye contact, the arms hugging the body, the gloomy facial expression or a superior tone of voice may all serve to keep others away. The therapist may pick up such messages intuitively, recognize the conflict, ask herself what this can be about, and perhaps infer that for this person there is some subtle satisfaction in being lonely. This then becomes an avenue for conscious exploration. (Further evidence of this type of conflict is forthcoming from the study described in Chapter 10.)

A crucial question here is: how skilled are psychotherapists in noticing contradictory body messages? The general expectation is that they will be more expert than the average person. Dittman et al. (1965) set out to discover whether observers' responses to facial cues were influenced by an incongruent message from the body. They used two groups of observers: experienced psychotherapists and professional dancers. When the therapists were shown films of people with their faces masked, they expressed surprise at how much affective information could be read from bodily movements. When shown the whole figure both groups were mostly influenced by the facial cues when interpreting expressions, but there was a difference in ability to respond, in that the dancers were more alert to bodily cues than the therapists. The authors expressed concern at the relative lack of notice taken of bodily cues among experienced psychotherapists, indicating that much important information was missed. However, 13 of the 15 psychotherapists were also qualified as psychiatrists, two were clinical psychologists and only one was a woman, so the study reveals more about male psychiatrists than psychotherapists in general. Nevertheless it demonstrates the tendency to focus on the face and perhaps disregard vital bodily clues.

Some types of training aim to overcome any such deficiency. Gestalt therapists, for example, are specifically encouraged to focus on body language and to draw it to the attention of the client, but without interpretation, allowing the meaning to emerge through exploration. Clarkson states: 'Gestaltists are usually vividly attentive to their own non-verbal behaviour and that of their clients. Crossed ankles, coughing, one shoulder being higher than another, are all important ... especially as Gestalt ... seeks to integrate as many diverse aspects of that person as possible' (1989, p. 81; see also Chapters 11 and 12).

Yet certain of these characteristics are likely to be obscured or overlaid with emotional display rules, because, as we have seen, minimizing or covering up true feelings has become built into the fabric of social life. Adults learnt these procedures so long ago that most no longer realize that this kind of dissimulation is part of everyday interaction. Paradoxically, being a capable communicator necessarily involves the skill of being able to hide one's real feelings and opinions. Since the therapist has also been socialized into learning display rules to the point where it happens out of awareness, how adept can he or she be in detecting where the real truth lies? The importance of becoming conscious of personal socialization processes cannot be overemphasized. This will at least alert the therapist to the ways in which subtle deceptions are employed for the sake of politeness or to cover up one's own shortcomings. It will also expose possible areas of collusion.

Research into deception makes troubling reading. A study into patient–doctor communication discovered that as many as 85 per cent of patients concealed information or else were equivocal, while a full one-third told outright lies; only 3 per cent were openly honest and gave complete information (Burgoon, Callister and Hunsaker, 1994). How much of what we see and hear in the therapy room is therefore real? I am immediately reminded of a major concealment by one client. Having apparently worked productively for almost two years, she became unable to attend sessions due to a mysterious illness. It was only then that I discovered that she had had a malignant tumour on her thigh, which had been gradually worsening for almost a decade. Sadly, she had made the decision not to tell anyone, including myself. By then it was too late to help and she died shortly afterwards. I subsequently spent many painful hours reviewing sessions and wondering if it might have been possible to detect this concealment at an early stage, but found myself unable to reach any conclusion. This experience taught me that, from time to time, especially if the therapy is 'stuck', it can be well worth providing an opportunity to reveal the unspoken. I may perhaps ask if the client has something to relate which is particularly difficult, and suggest that a drawing or a letter might more easily describe the situation.

However sensitive, well-trained or skilled one is, it is not easy to detect different forms of deception, particularly those that are unconscious or at a very low level of awareness. Peter Andersen affirms that there are no nonverbal cues that consistently point to leakage of true feelings (1999, p. 279). So theory does not help in this respect. Even 'shifty eyes', thought to signify duplicity, may in fact simply denote shyness or anxiety. Studies so far seem to suggest that women are generally more accurate than men in detecting deception, particularly in relation to other females, but more research is needed in this area (Andersen 1999, p. 300).

What if the nonverbal cues are of a nature that they are not available to conscious attention, but can only be picked up subliminally? The communication researchers Ernest Haggard and Kenneth Isaacs (1966) filmed psychotherapy sessions, then ran them in slow motion. These exposed fleeting signals, which were not visible at normal speed. They termed them 'micromomentary' expressions, noticing that they often occurred when the patient was in conflict. For example the words might be 'I am not angry', but a brief angry expression could be ascertained from the slow-motion film. These 'micros' appeared to reveal leakage of true feelings.

Using a tachistoscope that could flash pictures on to a screen at high speed, Paul Ekman (1975) discovered that many expressions are completed in one-half to three-quarters of a second. Moreover, they are surrounded by other bodily movements and words, some of which may be conflicting. When he showed a film incorporating micromomentary expressions to students and then to experienced nurses, the students were able to detect them only when viewed in slow motion. The nurses, however, spotted them at normal speed. This suggested that experience of working with people enhances one's ability to capture fleeting expressions.

Ekman thought that children are discouraged from paying attention to such leakage of feelings, because too much is revealed concerning the adults. He also discovered that various subjects had a subconscious block to a particular emotion, and might miss, for example, anger or disgust, but could identify all the others. Ability to reconnect with their childhood propensity for intuition, and knowledge of their own blind spots would therefore appear to be crucial for counsellors and psychotherapists.

It is worth noting that some nonverbal forms of behaviour, according to Ekman and Friesen (1969), do not convey any particular meaning but are derivatives of infantile movements which have become habitual. Vestiges of them may be carried into adulthood and could arouse inappropriate curiosity from some therapists. Unfortunately, however, Ekman and Friesen do not give any clear examples and admit that further research is necessary.

Clinical assessment

Whenever two or more people meet, each invariably sums the others up, making rapid, unspoken judgements concerning their characters. This of course also happens in counselling, but, from the therapist's perspective, the emphasis needs to be on how the prospective client can best be helped. Chapter 4 considered personal differences in ability to make these sorts of assessments. Not only must the clinician judge whether or not the person is suitable for the type of treatment that is being offered, but the severity of the problems presented must be gauged, hypotheses about the nature of the difficulties have to be formed, and a prognosis made. This is a complex task, particularly as there is no framework for differential diagnosis that is generally accepted by contemporary psychotherapists as reliable, although a variety of schemata exists.

The psychoanalytic literature on this subject is summarized by Bateman and Holmes (1995, pp. 148–50), who make the point that such theories are useful in alerting the analyst to possible pitfalls and may suggest the most helpful technical approaches, but ultimately the decisions have to be contextual and dependent upon the relationship between analyst and patient. How does the clinician make such judgements and on what type of information are they based? Not only must factual data be gathered during the interview, but an ambience needs to be established whereby unconscious material also becomes accessible. A balance has to be struck between direct questioning and attentive listening, to reveal both the content of a patient's story and the subtext of the narrative. As has been seen, nonverbal aspects, such as the tone of voice, gestures, facial expressions, emphases or important omissions can provide significant psychodynamic clues, forming the basis for interpretation.

Because of the amount of information available at any one time, the interviewer will have collected much of it subliminally. Indeed, the clinician may have difficulty in explaining exactly how he or she arrived at any particular conclusion and claim that it was a 'hunch' or 'gut feeling' or other term denoting intuition. Assagioli attached high value to the employment of this faculty by counsellors and psychotherapists: 'We cannot conceive a true and successful therapist who has not developed and uses the intuition' (1965/1975, p. 221).

How much of clinical perception is actually intuition and how much is simply inference? Some definitions of clinical intuition can be found in the literature, but there is no clear agreement as to its nature. S.R. Hathaway (1955) describes it as inferential 'in which the inferences have their source in cues or cognitive processes that the percipient is unable to identify or specify with satisfactory completeness'. Having declared that intuition is inferential, he subsequently states that it is not possible to specify the nature of the process – if it exists at all (p. 229). The establishment of its presence would be based on the demonstration that inferences are made in the absence of recognizable forms of communication. However, the experimental studies designed around this assumption and described in the paper are inconclusive.

American psychoanalyst Alexander Guiora (1965) seeks to identify three specific modes whereby diagnostic and predictive clinical judgements are made, namely inference, empathy and intuition. Inference, he states, is characterized by conclusions derived 'from a given set of data or premises in compliance with the rules of Aristotelian logic' (p. 780). Intuition, on the other hand, depends upon 'allological principles', a form of comprehending in which the external cues are inadequate for logical judgement, yet immediate and accurate prediction is made through 'the mediation of idiosyncratic associations' (p. 782). In such a case retracing of the sequential steps whereby the conclusion is reached cannot be made. Guiora thus makes a clear distinction between inference and intuition and claims that intuition is non-inferential. As for empathy, this subject is investigated further in the next chapter.

Eric Berne, founder of Transactional Analysis, wrote a series of papers on intuition (1977) which make a significant contribution to the subject. He states that the intuiter does not know how the conclusions are arrived at, and agrees that the process is subliminal, but he defines it, within a clinical context, as being based on experience and input from the senses: 'it is knowledge based on experience and acquired by means of preverbal unconscious or preconscious functions through sensory contact with the subject' (p. 4). The question of the sensory basis of intuition has been explored in detail in relation to Jung's typology (see Chapter 4).

Theodore Sarbin of the University of Chicago, in attempting to discover whether clinical psychology is an art or a science, refers to intuition as a 'crude empirical method' (1941, p. 394). He notes that a clinician may make a diagnosis on the basis of the 'general feel of things', but if pushed can usually determine the empirical basis. This is very much in contradiction to the other definitions discussed above, which state that the process whereby intuitive judgements are made cannot be described. However, his position on the question of the experiential basis concurs with Berne's. Like Hathaway, he takes the inferential standpoint, referring to clinical intuition as consisting of 'informal inferences', but he is not in favour of the use of such a method within the context of clinical psychology, which, he concludes, should be considered a science depending on logical inference only. As such, he seems to be dismissing unconscious processing as invalid.

Rosalind Dymond, also of the University of Chicago, takes up the argument between the scientists and *Verstehenists*[2] and asks whether clinicians can predict individual behaviour (1953). Moreover, is this best done using the classical objective approach, that leads to laws of behaviour in terms of central tendencies, or by taking a phenomenological point of view which observes behaviour of the individual from this person's own perspective? What should the frame of reference be? Sarbin's argument is that to predict for any individual it is necessary to refer to other similar cases, and to sort particular characteristics into classes, and then a probability statement can be made. In this framework, therefore, past frequencies of the subject's behaviour, or of the behaviour of others with whom he has been classified, are the principal bases for prediction.

The phenomenological point of view, however, emphasizes the uniqueness of the individual which should not be lost by focusing only on characteristics shared with others. Dymond studied ten psychotherapists and their predictions of what clients would be like when therapy was completed, as compared with the clients' own descriptions of themselves at the finish, using Q-sort.[3] While this was a small study, the conclusions were challenging to those who were taking the inference-only position. She showed that the clinician can shift any prediction away from the stereotype should this be necessary, that is if the client is highly idiosyncratic. Otherwise general knowledge and experience of clients is used when appropriate for the particular case. Moreover, the most accurate predictions concerned both the person very like and the one very unlike the general class. She was able to claim that 'some clinicians can make predictions of individual behavior over and above what can be accounted for by chance, a knowledge of the group norm, or their stereotype of the group' (p. 160). This seems to indicate that both inference and intuition are involved in clinical judgement, and that 'intuition' is not necessarily just informal inference by another name.

Ronald Taft (1955) recognizes two ways in which judgements concerning others can be made, either with the analytic or the non-analytic method. The first mainly involves inference, using for example the rating and ranking of traits, but in the second the judge responds 'in a global fashion' (p. 1). Material in Chapter 3 has demonstrated how central this feature is to intuition: the perception of the whole rather than the parts.

As far as psychotherapy is concerned, the evidence suggests that both inference and intuition are involved in diagnosis and assessment. The clinician will be listening to the verbal content, using logic to analyse the information received, and at the same time the intuitive process will be at work, taking in many nonverbal messages. As an overall impression of the case emerges, the practitioner will be drawing on past experience from which comparisons will be formulated and inferences made, until some kind of conclusion can be reached. The clinician will again connect with rational processes in order to verbalize the diagnosis.

How accurate is clinical intuition?

Tony Bastick, in his list of properties of intuition (1982, p. 25), specifies the two following features: 'intuition need not be correct' (property no. 9) and 'subjective certainty of correctness' (property no. 10), a quality already considered in Chapter 3. Just because an individual believes an intuition to be accurate does not, of course, make it so.

A feeling of confidence is often quoted as being a feature of intuition. This clearly has implications for the clinical situation, since confidence gives no guarantee at all of accuracy. Stuart Oskamp of Stanford University, in a well-designed study of 1963 which was relevant to everyday clinical practice, found that confidence is significantly decreased by general experience.[4] In other words, the experienced clinician is more cautious when making predictions and more aware of appropriateness. This supports an early study by C.W. Valentine (1929), which set out to assess the relative reliability of men and women in making judgements of children. This warned that confidence might be an indication of poor reliability. Indeed, Oskamp recommends caution, since he discovered a 25 per cent inaccuracy in distinguishing between psychotic and non-psychiatric patients, based on their MMPI profiles, whether either actuarial or clinical methods were used. This study therefore indicates that phenomenological approaches are as accurate as statistical methods, at 75 per cent, on that particular task.

Women are popularly thought to be more intuitive than men, but Valentine's research showed no difference in accuracy of judgement of children's characters. However, there have been some studies subsequently that demonstrate that women universally are more accurate and more sensitive receivers of nonverbal communication, an advantage which seems to be both biological as well as learned. This is particularly so in the presence of an expressive sender, a point which is of direct relevance to the practice of counselling and psychotherapy (Hall, 1984). There does, therefore, appear to be some truth in the old saying.

A characteristic of intuition which is often remarked upon is its suddenness. Bastick lists this as property no. 1: 'quick, immediate, sudden appearance' (1982, p. 25). Drever, in his dictionary definition (1952) describes this feature as 'immediate perception or judgement'. The questions that then arise within a clinical setting are whether speed is a useful attribute (for example because of shortage of time or money) and whether it is related to accuracy of perception. Eric Berne's series of studies are of especial interest here. In late 1945 he had the job of giving a psychiatric examination to around 25,000 soldiers in less than four months. He therefore had between 40 and 90 seconds to make each assessment and, due to the pressure of time, Berne's judgements were of necessity intuitive. The task was made more difficult because all the soldiers wore the same garments. He became curious as to how he made his judgements, especially after noticing that he could predict the men's replies to his questions with 'surprising accuracy' (1977, p. 7). He therefore formalized the process and, over a period of 17 days, attempted to guess the civilian occupation within a few seconds of meeting the man, and also to set out the data on which these suppositions were made. There was a 55 per cent accuracy overall, but Berne noticed a drop in this percentage if there were distractions, or with fatigue (after 50 guesses). He also noticed that the success rate improved if the process was allowed to remain unconscious, rather than incorporating the deliberate use of criteria.

The disadvantages of Berne's study are its subjectivity and lack of a control group, but it nevertheless has the advantage of being based on a real-life situation, rather than being dependent on an experiment artificially set up in a laboratory. Bastick asserts that, in intuition, speed is possible on account of the 'parallel processing of a global field of knowledge' (1982, p. 51), whereas analytic thought 'only compares two elements at a time'. Logical deduction is a conscious, linear, step-by-step process and therefore often slow. The speed of intuition is clearly of value in certain situations, particularly when time is short, but because it is not necessarily accurate needs to be carefully checked.

Clearly, judgements involving people are somewhat haphazard affairs, with no guarantee of certainty. While both inference and intuition appear to be involved in clinical assessment, is the one approach any more accurate overall than the other? After careful weighing of the available evidence, G. W. Allport (1965) considers that people who take a reflective, analytic approach to perception are generally less accurate than those who adopt a more global, intuitive approach. This conclusion is challenging to practitioners of therapies that emphasize logical analysis.

* * * *

My researches into intuition had thus led me to study the work of psychologists in the field of interpersonal perception. This was new territory to me, but the relevance to my own practice quickly became clear. Communication analysts had developed a precise framework for understanding what goes on between people on a nonverbal level. Applying this to my own situation within sessions proved extraordinarily helpful. Paradoxically, being able to give names to the different types of unspoken signs, such as 'kinesics', 'adaptors' and 'regulators', helped me to recognize when intuition was needed and to be more aware of my own preconscious processes. Moreover, having intuition affirmed as being at least as good as, if not better than, logical analysis in forming judgements, gave me greater trust in this faculty. At the same time I was careful to note any possible inaccuracies.

Additionally, I began to examine my own socialization processes, the display rules which I had absorbed, and to question how much this might be influencing the progress of the therapy. There was pleasure, too, especially when with supervisees, to notice how much we reflected each others' body positions, affirming our underlying agreement and liking. Emotional contagion, on the other hand, was sometimes painful, but being alert to this phenomenon helped me to retain objectivity.

Touching in to others' feelings motivated me to consider empathy in greater depth and the part that this plays in intuition. I therefore retraced my steps to Senate House Library at London University to see what more I could discover.

Notes

1. The 'inner child' constitutes the part of the psyche carrying those childhood experiences which continue to influence adult behaviour. Ferenczi's opinion is not wholly supported by my own researches (see Chapter 10).
2. The term 'Verstehenist' is derived from the German *verstehen*, to understand. It usually refers to someone working in the human sciences who takes the agent's point of view, making primary how the individual under investigation understands him- or herself.
3. Q-sort was developed by W. Stephenson in 1953. It refers to a method employed in either qualitative or quantitative research, in which the respondent sorts through cards containing self-referent statements. There are successive sorts using different criteria. The final position of the cards indicates how the individual perceives their self-concept. Any change in self-perception over time can be recorded through repeated sorts at later dates.

4. Oskamp increased reliability by re-running the judging task one month later. This involved two groups, one composed of 44 experienced clinicians and the other of 28 inexperienced undergraduates. They had to distinguish, from MMPI profiles, patients hospitalized psychiatrically and those for medical reasons alone. Training was introduced to the undergraduates on the re-run, involving intermittent pauses during early phases of the judging session to discuss how well they were performing and why. There was a notable improvement in judging the last group of profiles.

CHAPTER 7

Empathic attunement

In searching for a definition of empathy, I was very surprised to discover that the word entered the English language only comparatively recently, at the beginning of the twentieth century. Freud had recognized the importance of a good rapport between analyst and patient before attempting an interpretation (SE XII, p. 139) and he used the German term *Einfühlung*, which means literally 'a feeling in' or 'feeling within' (SE XVIII, p. 108). The English translation is derived from the Greek *empatheia*, indicating 'affection' or 'passion' from within, which conjures up in my mind the idea of a strong feeling for someone else with a loving and caring intent, based on imaginatively transposing oneself into the other person's place. Freud also used the term in the context of humour, in the sense that we have to take the joker's 'psychical state' into consideration, 'put ourselves into it and try to understand it by comparing it with our own' (SE VIII, p. 186). In other words, in order to see the humour, we have to be able to empathize with the joker. As such, it is a route to understanding. Freud expressed this more directly when discussing group psychology, calling empathy that 'which plays the largest part in our understanding of what is inherently foreign to our ego in other people' (SE XVIII, p. 108). Thus, by connecting with another person through feeling, we are better able to comprehend whatever is different from ourselves.

The subject was taken up a little later by Sandor Ferenczi when discussing psychoanalytic technique (1928/1955). He featured tactful timing as being of crucial importance if the analyst were to avoid causing unnecessary pain to the patient, and he considered this to be based on the 'processes of empathy and assessment' (p. 100). Here we can begin to see a connection with intuition. After all, how does a therapist know when to intervene and say something or when to stay silent and wait for further associations? The therapy may take an unexpected twist, or the patient may react in an uncharacteristic way, so how then should the therapist respond? When should conclusions be drawn and in what manner should these be presented and at what point in the proceedings? One might say that a good therapist knows such things intuitively. Poor timing and lack of tactful consideration of the patient's feelings can result in the person withdrawing and thereby jeopardizing the therapeutic alliance. Ferenczi considered that professional experience combined with personal analysis were helpful in assessing the timing of empathic responses. Moreover, empathy was necessary for estimating the strength of the patient's resistances. In this the analyst should not be guided by feelings alone, but should 'weigh the situation coolly', conjecture upon any withheld thoughts and unconscious trends. Not having the resistances oneself allowed this to be possible. This process, which was largely pre-conscious, guided the analyst when to form judgements and present material.

Such observations apart, empathy in the context of psychotherapy had been little studied up until the middle of the twentieth century, which is remarkable bearing in mind that it is a quality highly valued in a therapist. Writing on the vicissitudes of empathy in 1960, psychoanalyst Ralph Greenson comments 'it is striking how little psycho-analytic literature exists on the subject of empathy', and that 'particularly for therapy, the capacity for empathy is an essential prerequisite' (p. 418). He places intuition on an equal footing with empathy in this regard: 'Both intuition and empathy give one a talent for psychotherapy; the best therapists seem to have both.'

Since any such studies would of necessity reveal the inner processes of the therapist, psychoanalysts Beres and Arlow (1974) admit that few of their colleagues would be willing to subject themselves to this kind of 'public scrutiny'. Is there a fear here that aspects of the supposedly rational process of psychoanalysis might be exposed as simple everyday emotional intelligence? Yet these authors consider empathy to be 'of focal significance' in their employment as psychotherapists (p. 26) and later in their paper regard it as an 'essential tool in psychoanalytic work' (p. 47).

The strongest assertion of the central significance of empathy within the psychoanalytic context came from Heinz Kohut, who declared that psychological fact could only be arrived at through this process, which he described as 'vicarious introspection' (1959, p. 462). By adopting the patient's experience second-hand, as it were, and reflecting upon it, we are able to appreciate the person's psychological reality. Moreover, if we fail to use our own feelings in this way, we fall into the error 'of a mechanistic and inert conception' of the patient's interior world. Here we find another parallel with intuition: theory, other people's explanations and ideas, can get in the way of deep understanding of the unique individual concerned. Indeed, Kohut saw empathy as a process of observation via feelings, a way in which data could be assembled, but taking into account the patient's own point of view. At the same time it was important to be able to step beyond empathy and to use analysis and reason in order to find explanations (1971, p. 303). Language has to be accessed to describe those feelings in all their complexity and subtlety, and then other associations made so that a full understanding can be achieved.

Empathy used in this way implies an acceptance of the patient's perception of his or her own experience. Kohut offers a straightforward example, one that will be familiar to many practitioners: a patient was very annoyed with him because he had arrived just one minute late for the consultation. Kohut was able to understand this apparently extreme response by empathizing with that insecure child who had grown up with erratic and unpredictable parents.

It is notable that Kohut came under critical attack by other psychoanalysts, who feared that, by giving empathy such a central role, the scientific status of their profession would be put in jeopardy. Kohut responded by saying that empathy should not be confused with sympathy or compassion, nor with intuition. He did think, however, that it was occasionally used in an intuitive fashion, that is, 'with great speed and without the awareness of intermediate steps'. Such a process should not, in any scientific context, stand by itself; rather, the intermediate steps need to be brought into awareness and scrutinized. (1980, p. 483.)

The speed with which both intuition and empathy can offer insight and comprehension, was also noted by Ralph Greenson, who saw a similarity between the two processes: both were 'special methods of gaining quick and deep understanding'. Suddenly, the therapist's perception of that particular point of the case becomes clear. Yet Greenson makes a definite distinction between the two modes: 'One empathizes to reach feelings; one uses intuition to get ideas' (1960, p. 423). So he associates intuition with thinking rather than feeling. Either way, the practitioner is better able to grasp the psychological constellations in the patient.

Unlike Greenson, Kohut seems keen not to compromise the scientific status of psychoanalysis, by aligning empathy with intuition. He issues a warning against the over-hasty use of intuitive knowledge and advises analysts to resist being swept away 'by the comfortable certainty of the "Aha-experience"'. Rather, the practitioner should continue to keep an open mind and test the newly acquired insight with 'trial empathy' in order to collect as many alternatives as possible before drawing any firm conclusions (1977, p. 168). The analyst must therefore not offer interventions or interpretations too quickly, but keep the intuition in mind while further connecting with the analysand's feelings. This is no doubt a wise recommendation, but it is interesting that he suggests testing the intuition via feeling. Tony Bastick concurs with this point, with some qualification, noting that the accuracy of the intuitive evaluation will depend upon the appropriateness of the feelings empathically aroused (1982, p. 81). This in turn may rely to a large extent on the therapist's past experiences which are likely to be used as a referent for understanding the present.

In his eagerness to uphold his scientific standing as a psychoanalyst, Kohut applauds empathy at the expense of intuition: 'Whereas empathy is the scientific analyst's greatest friend, intuition may at times be one of his greatest enemies.' He quickly qualifies this statement by suggesting that the analyst should not relinquish his spontaneity, but rather be aware of explanations that suddenly arise with a sense of conviction (1977, p. 169). It is not intuition itself which is the 'enemy', but rather the feeling of certainty that tends to go with it. Indeed, as we have seen, intuition is not always an accurate form of perception, but then neither is empathy. Other people's feelings can be misassessed. Indeed, the client may indicate that the therapist is on the wrong track by saying so, becoming angry, going silent or changing the subject. An experienced practitioner will always be alert to such messages.

Developmental roots

How, then, do humans come to be able to empathize with one another, to be capable of dipping in to each other's feelings, so that the one understands the other from the inside? Some writers consider that the roots of empathy lie in the infant's ability to apprehend the mood of its mother, well before verbal concepts become available, or indeed before the child experiences itself as a separate individual. Equally, the attentive mother knows instinctively what her baby needs and when and how to attend to those needs. This kind of empathic relating is a direct emotional knowing, which needs no words. Guiora describes it thus: 'There is in the empathic act a temporary suspension of ego functions in favor of an immediate, pre-cognitive experience of another's emotional state as one's own' (1965, p. 781). Here he is drawing on object-relations theory by referring to the temporary fusion of self-object boundaries.

This primary ability extends beyond the baby-mother relationship, as psychological studies have demonstrated. Even tiny infants will respond to the hurt feelings of another child and will themselves become upset. At this stage there is no sense of themselves as separate beings, of who it is who hurts. So that if a child injures its fingers, another might put its own fingers into its mouth to check if they hurt too. This is generally referred to as 'motor mimicry'. Only after the age of about two and a half can children clearly distinguish between others' feelings and their own. Moreover, after this age, children differ markedly in their sensitivity towards others' moods. This appears to depend on the responses of parents and whether or not children are encouraged to appreciate the effect that their own actions can have on others (Goleman, 1996, pp. 98–9).

The psychiatrist Daniel Stern made intensive studies of the subtle exchanges that occur between mother and infant, examining thousands of hours of videotaped material. He saw how caring mothers would tune in to their baby's moods, so that if the child shakes its rattle and squeals with pleasure, the parent will laugh and smile, take up the infant's tone of voice and perhaps shake the rattle too, or give a little tickle to increase the fun. In this way the baby's mood is affirmed. Through this kind of 'attunement' the infant feels emotionally understood and connected (Stern, 1987). This then becomes the basis of the person's emotional life. Knowing that other people can share his or her feelings offers the possibility of future intimate relationships.

What happens if attunement is lacking, or if mismatching of emotions occurs in those early years? Stern noticed that if mothers failed to tune in to the child's feelings, it immediately showed distress. If empathy from the parent was lacking for long periods, the child would stop expressing the feelings and become withdrawn.

It seems, therefore, that empathy is partly inbuilt and partly learned. Its development can be blocked if the adults are not well attuned to the child, if they fail to facilitate it, and if they themselves are poor models of how to respond empathically to others. Indeed, studies of adults show a wide variety in ability to empathize, and this of course includes therapists (Raskin, 1974). Carl Rogers, father of person-centred therapy, came to the disturbing conclusion that therapists who were confident in their personal relationships and not afraid of intimacy were more able to respond empathically to clients than those who were less sure of themselves (1980, p. 148). Those early lessons in emotional attunement provide a sure foundation for a rewarding relationship, therefore, whether personal or professional. Nevertheless, there are indications that empathy can be learned, or at any rate improved upon, even at a late stage, and this will be examined in Chapter 12.

Psychologists have also studied another phenomenon, usually referred to as 'interactional synchrony' (Andersen, 1999, p. 157). As was mentioned in chapter 6, people unconsciously match the facial expressions and actions of each other, so that if one person smiles, so will the other, or equally if the expression is sad, the partner may well wipe away an imagined tear. Apparently it is the 'mirror neurons' in our brains that account for this unconscious imitation. I have often noticed how a client will copy my posture, for example leaning one way or the other, head in hand or ankles crossed the same way. Equally, I may become aware of how I automatically do the same. After reading up on some of this research, I had a sudden revelation of why I often felt uncomfortable with a particular client. This individual is naturally extravert and extravagant in her gestures and expressions. By nature I am considerably more introverted, so it was difficult for me to match her actions and I therefore felt awkward. Quite literally, I was 'out of sync' with her.

When discussing contagion of emotion in the previous chapter, we saw how feelings may change along with facial expression, so that frowning will tend to induce irritation or anger, smiling pleasure and so on. As the second person unconsciously mimics the first person's expression, the mood is also matched (Andersen, 1999, p. 158). This is one way in which we unconsciously pick up other people's emotions. Psychotherapists are well aware of the contagion of feelings, although how and why the phenomenon occurs is generally not examined. Curiously, there appears to be a gulf between therapy theory and the discoveries of psychologists – but I will take up this theme in Chapter 11 when considering training.

In the clinical situation it is important to be aware of the possible danger of merging too closely with the client, and the therapist needs to be able to have access to cognitive control. Moreover, while the internal representation of the client is forming in the therapist's imagination, it is essential to retain a notion of the self as a separate individual. Yet the feeling of being in tune with a client can be so powerful that it seems to be almost telepathic. Some authors describe this as 'resonance' or 'vibration' between the two persons, while others place the experience in the realm of the transpersonal. We will consider this further towards the end of the chapter.

The links between empathy and intuition

Certain similarities between these two phenomena have already been noted. Both have a 'primitive' component in that everyone is born with the potential to empathize and to intuit. Each involves a non-logical, irrational way of knowing. They operate out of awareness at a pre-conscious level, so that the intermediate steps are not apprehended, except possibly in retrospect. Both can therefore offer understanding at great speed.

The question now is, does the one depend on the other in any way? There is some agreement that empathy can act as a forerunner to intuition, leading to an immediate cognitive understanding of the client that is feeling-based. This is the position taken by Ralph Greenson: 'Empathy often leads to intuition. The "aha" reaction is intuited .... intuition picks up the clues that empathy gathers' (1960, p. 423). By tuning in to the client through the sharing of feelings, there is an experience of some new understanding beginning to form, perhaps via some bodily sensations or fleeting images, until suddenly it all makes sense and the intuition crystallizes. In this context the idea within the intuition is created from the feelings. Beres and Arlow take a similar view, seeing empathy as facilitating the emergence of intuition. Here, it is empathy that offers the clues needed by intuition. Interpretation then follows the analyst's intuitive understanding, which in turn may lead to insight in the patient (1974, p. 47). Indeed these authors make clear that the therapeutic relationship demands that empathy and intuition go on to interpretation and insight, otherwise all that exists is a mutual experience consisting of transference on the part of the patient and counter-transference for the analyst.

A session with a former dancer, who was presenting with depression, comes to mind. She had a very quiet and somewhat inexpressive voice and felt very 'stuck' in her life. I was finding it difficult to concentrate and follow her narration, when I had a distinct impression of her as a child standing on her toes in point shoes, very gingerly treading around a stressed and angry woman. In that instant I recalled myself as a ten-year-old, practising ballet steps in the school hall. The headmistress walked in unexpectedly with some visitors. Although I had obtained permission to use the hall, I was nevertheless quaking with fear in case I should be reprimanded. As I connected with my own fear of this authority figure, I could well understand how frightened my client must be of any situation in which she might be judged. Indeed, she had transferred this into the counselling situation, imagining that I would in some way condemn and scold her, just like her enraged mother. The therapeutic task was now to build more trust in the working alliance, so that she would feel able to reveal more of herself with confidence. If empathy and intuition had not guided me, then I might have stayed as stuck as my client, as she continued to transfer the unspoken fear into the sessions.

At this juncture I am reminded again of the whole notion of feminine intuition. Even today, with greater sexual equality, women remain the chief carers of small infants. They are therefore the prime teachers of empathic attunement, of nonverbal rapport leading to intuitive understanding. Women therefore have a most important role in the development of empathy among humans in general and therefore of intuition also.

Tony Bastick based his theory of intuition on extensive examination of the psychological and allied literature, rather than personal experience of what happens in a psychotherapy session. His searches led him to conclude that empathy can play a prominent role in the intuitive process, which is accessed 'through appropriate feelings'. These are evoked 'mainly subconsciously through empathy' (1982, p. 279), which gives substance to the theory expressed above that empathy can lead to intuition. He founds his definition of empathy on the one expressed by Rosalind Dymond (1949) as 'the imaginative transposing of oneself into the thinking, feeling and acting of another', extending this process to objects as well as people (p. 279). So a therapist may subjectively ask, 'What is it like to stand in that person's world?' or a poet may enquire 'What would my experience be if I were that object?' We can see from this how important it is for therapists and counsellors to be emotionally variable, sensitive and imaginative. Indeed Bastick goes so far as to state that 'emotional involvement is central to all aspects of intuition' (1982, p. 84). It has to be remembered, however, that when using the term 'emotion', he also includes body sensations, kinaesthetic responses, as well as feelings. His theory sets out to demonstrate that intuition is very much a complete mind-body-feeling process.

How often have we said, 'It's just on the tip of my tongue', as we search for a word, phrase or explanation with that strong feeling of knowing that we know? Here feelings, or maybe images, such as that of a letter, or recall of sounds, are used as retrieval cues. At the same time there are body responses, a state of tension and real physiological arousal. At last that forgotten name or event comes to mind, and the feelings now are of relief, satisfaction and a warm sensation of being right. At the same time the tension of not-yet-knowing subsides. In addition to the picking up of someone else's feelings, it is clear that the actual process of intuition is often an emotional one.

While empathy may indeed lead to intuition, Greenson warns that there can be antitheses between the two processes, having observed that empathic people are not necessarily intuitive and that intuitive people can be unreliable empathizers. This author does not offer reasons for these observations. To look again at Jung's typology, however, we can see that people who have the feeling function predominant, with the thinking mode in the inferior position, might run the risk of sharing deeply in the client's mood without any useful understanding arising. In this case the feeling may well be that of sympathy rather than empathy. Moreover, intuitive people who have the feeling function in the tertiary position, may decide to avoid empathy, not wishing to become emotionally involved. It seems, therefore, that intuition does not always depend on empathy.

In examining my own practice again, I can see that intuition can sometimes be thought-based rather than evoked through feeling. While doing my best to understand the extreme disgust of spiders experienced by my arachnaphobic client, I can honestly say that I felt little true empathy for her. I myself find spiders fascinating little creatures and am not in the least afraid of them. It was therefore difficult to appreciate her description of them as 'horrible' and 'evil'. This client came across as a humorous and very agreeable person, who spoke of her upbringing as being secure and happy, and of herself as a good and obliging child. It struck me as odd, therefore, that she had such a deep frown, and I quietly held a question in my mind about this. During one session the word 'projection' popped into my head, apparently from nowhere. Perhaps I had made a connection, out of awareness, between the word 'evil' and the frown. Then the thought followed that, in trying to be the perfect little girl, she had disowned her own shadow. What place could there be for it in this happy household? The safest place would be into the bodies of spiders. When I offered this interpretation, she agreed that it made good sense. In this case, therefore, the intuition arose from a series of thoughts rather than empathic feeling.

A therapist may experience different degrees of empathy according to how much his or her own responses resonate with the client's situation. If there is some difficulty in empathizing, it may be that the verbal mode is inadequate for the client to convey the extremity of feeling. I recall a client who had a terrible fear of travelling. Since I myself love to explore unknown terrain, it was hard fully to appreciate the extent of her apprehensions. Partly to assist myself and partly as a therapeutic tool for her, I suggested she evoke an image for her fear and then draw it. A howling mouth with jagged teeth, wide-open crazed eyes and spiky hair on end quickly appeared on the page. As soon as she showed it to me, I felt horror-struck. Through the medium of drawing rather than words, she had been able to reveal her terror. Now I could grasp the extent of her fear and our work together could begin.

Tony Bastick warns that negative emotions, such as anxiety, can block empathy and therefore intuition also. Clearly, if a therapist is overwhelmed with personal worries, then he or she cannot be empathically open to the experiences of the client and therefore not receptive to intuitive information.

Identification and projection

In asking that subjective question of what someone else's experience must be like, we have to transpose ourselves into that other world. How then do we do this? The intuitive type of person, according to Tony Bastick, empathizes with the elements of the situation described, in order to evoke appropriate feelings. He or she then projects these feelings to the situation in a process of temporary identification, experiencing in fantasy as the object does. Other connections and cognitive associations are made, which in turn produce the intuition. Empathy therefore helps with the retrieval of stored information. Bastick offers the concept of 'empathic projection', in which these two processes are concurrent and interacting, leading to a brief at-oneness with the other. The therapist thus uses his or her body as a kind of intuitive processor, a sensitive instrument through which this two-way operation of empathy and projection can take place.[1] Bastick considers that this is fundamental to intuition (1982, p. 280).

To test this theory, I recalled working with a bereaved client. The emotional impact was very considerable, as I, too, had lost a close family member at a young age. As she described her pain, I was quickly in touch with mine, but I knew it was imperative to be very clear about what belonged to the client and what to me. If I stayed too closely connected to my own suffering, then my response might be sympathetic rather than empathic, which would be unlikely to help the client. It would be equally unlikely to prompt an intuition or any true understanding of that person. However, by projecting my own feelings into her situation, and empathizing through our shared experience of loss, at the same time recognizing how different her circumstances were from mine, we could begin to find a way forward. The understanding I was able to offer helped her to complete the process of mourning.

In that moment of feeling at one with my client, it was clear to me that I was identifying with her grief. Yet there has been some argument in the literature about the part that identification plays. In examining the future of psychotherapy, Vanaerschot is emphatic that empathy is not the same as emotional identification, the difference being that 'the therapist is continuously aware of the fact that these feelings belong to the client and are not originating from himself' (1993, p. 49). Nevertheless, even if the feelings are evoked by the client, they are still experienced in oneself. The therapist must always enquire, 'To whom do these belong?'

To turn again to psychoanalysis, Fenichel (1945) considered that empathy does indeed involve identification with the object, together with a subsequent conscious awareness of one's own feelings, so that it is then possible to comprehend the feelings of the one identified with. Although pre-dating Bastick's psychological approach by several decades, the two descriptions bear a resemblance. Fenichel even equates empathy with intuition, describing it as 'the intuitive grasp of the real psychic states of another person'.

The oscillation between identification and separation is given prominence by Beres and Arlow (1974), because it is important for the therapist to maintain a sense of self with access to the cognitive function at will. For example, it is not necessary for the therapist to feel depressed when the client is depressed, but rather simply to connect very briefly with the emotional state presented. From experience, the therapist will be able to remember what it is like to be that way. This brief identification is referred to as a 'signal affect', alerting the therapist to the unconscious motivation and fantasy. Thus memory, comprehension and conceptualization are all involved in the empathic response. This suggests that the phenomenon requires ego development, and increases with maturity. The more that a therapist has been exposed to life in a great variety of situations, thus accumulating a store of knowledge and experiences, the more he or she is able to identify with material presented. The therapist feels with the patient, but also separates and thinks about him or her.

Carl Rogers places the emphasis slightly differently. It is well worth taking note of his reflections on this subject, as they are based on original research involving many hours of taped sessions. The result was that empathy became pivotal to his person-centred approach. His earlier writings imply that the separation between therapist and client remains constant throughout, so that empathy now becomes the ability to perceive the internal frame of reference of the other person as if you were that person, 'without ever losing the "as if" condition' (1959a, p. 210). Barrett-Lennard warns that if this separateness is not maintained, then the counsellor's thoughts or feelings may become merged with those of the client (1965, p. 2). Indeed, this hazard has already been commented upon.

Although Rogers makes passing reference only to intuition, a non-judgemental attitude and a real desire to understand were considered by him to be essential to the empathic process (1961/67, p. 44). We have already seen how intuitive types are naturally non-dogmatic and open to novel experiences, wanting to weigh up the evidence in their own way. The therapist needs to step into a client's private world with sensitivity and without any wish to judge, or with any pre-conceived ideas, but with the desire only to perceive the person's experience from the inside, from his or her own point of view (p. 53).

Rather than reaching out towards the client and metaphorically stepping into those other shoes, the opposite is sometimes reported of intuitive experiences, that is, the person is received, or introjected, into oneself. In opening oneself to the other, an area is freed up for the client to enter and be welcomed. A participant in Claire Petitmengin-Peugeot's study describes this clearly: 'I have the impression that it is the other who comes into my space. Open yourself up and leave the space to the other' (1999, p. 65). Reik specifically refers to the 'introjection' of the patient by the analyst in order to achieve understanding: 'We can attain to psychological comprehension of another's unconscious only if it is seized upon by our own, at least for a moment, just as if it were a part of ourselves – it is a part of ourselves' (1948/1975, p. 464).

A deeply empathic therapist may even be able to formulate in words experiences that are only dimly grasped by the client, helping the person to comprehend why he or she behaves in this or that way. Gerard Egan in his book *The Skilled Helper* (1975/1994) refers to this as 'advanced empathy' (see below). Moreover, such acceptance of the client's thoughts and feelings helps to consolidate the therapeutic alliance, offering the person the freedom to explore all aspects of the self, however difficult, in an atmosphere of safety. It is in such an environment that intuition also flourishes.

Advanced empathy

When discussing intuition with colleagues, I have noticed that the phenomenon is sometimes associated with advanced empathy, or even equated with this process. It seems important, therefore, to examine just exactly what the relationship is, so that the connection can be clarified.

Although the term 'advanced empathy' is generally associated with Gerard Egan and his problem-management approach to counselling (1975/1994), Carl Rogers points to it precisely in the following quotation:

> it means sensing meanings of which he or she is scarcely aware, but not trying to uncover totally unconscious feelings, since this would be too threatening. It includes communicating your sensings of the person's world as you look with fresh and unfrightened eyes at elements of which he or she is fearful. (1980/1995, p. 142)

This, then, is a deep kind of empathy, prompted by the sensitive picking up of clues perhaps half-consciously or unconsciously provided by the client. It means formulating into coherent language something that the client may merely be hinting at or struggling to understand. It may be about bringing into the open something only implied, perhaps through body language or some other form of nonverbal communication. This does not deal just with problems, but perhaps also with the client's potential.

My work with a stressed accountant offers a useful example. When talking about his life at the office, I noticed how his voice became flat and monotonous, and the feeling conveyed to me was of joylessness and emptiness. Moreover, from restless movements of his hands and feet, I had an intuitive sense of long-repressed energy as my client described his day-to-day world. It was these sensings that prompted me to ask what, if anything, had ever made his heart sing. As he recalled a horse-riding holiday in his teens and the thrill of trekking across the Welsh mountains, his voice changed noticeably. Now it had varied pitch and vitality. On further probing, it transpired that all he had ever really longed for was a stud farm, where he could breed and work with the horses that he so loved. Yet he had been coerced into a position at his father's firm, where he had spent the past twenty-five years. By simply reflecting back to him the change in vocal pitch and energy, his secret longing was given new force. This became a first step towards bringing horses and riding back into his life.

In describing advanced empathy, Gerard Egan stresses that, while digging deeper, it deals with what the client is actually expressing or trying to say, not with the helper's interpretation of it (1975/1994, p. 180). So counsellors need to ask themselves, 'What is this person really hinting at, or only half saying?' or 'What message is implied behind the explicit narration?' The client may be defending against this semi-hidden material and have difficulty in accepting it, so the therapist must tread carefully in voicing the covert communication. In making more explicit whatever is implied by the client, opportunity for fuller and more conscious expression is offered. In this way, misunderstood aspects of the person can be brought into focus and explained, or perhaps real, underlying feelings disclosed.

One of my clients was mystified as to why she always put herself at the bottom of the pile when it came to the work arena, even though she used to be extremely bright at school and always passed examinations effortlessly. She had now reached the age of fifty and despaired of having apparently done nothing with her life. Friends and relatives had often tried to encourage her to apply for this or that job, clearly aware of her considerable gifts, but none of these suggestions was ever followed through. She herself was lively and energetic, got along well with people and was not obviously suffering from low self-esteem, so what was the problem? I began to pick up some clues from her clothes and mannerisms. It was noticeable that she had the habit of tossing her head and swinging her long grey hair, generally made into a plait. She wore either dungarees or little mini-skirts and flat bar-shoes or trainers. She smiled and laughed a great deal and I often felt charmed and amused by the stories she brought to sessions. While many of her thoughts were well considered and mature, she was unconsciously presenting herself as someone less than a third of her real age. I had a growing sense of a poor fit between this persona and the demands and responsibilities of a full-time job. How could I best help her to see what was going on? I suggested that she draw a picture of herself. We were then able to discuss the needs of the childlike figure depicted in the drawing in an objective and non-judgemental way, and she began to realize that as long as she was identified with this part of herself, then she would feel disinclined to apply for a challenging position. My experience of this process was partly intuitive and partly inferential.

The making of connections between different elements in a client's narrative can be completely conscious, or else performed at speed and out of awareness. This type of advanced empathy may or may not be intuitive therefore. Either way, the aim is to help individuals to identify themes, especially those that reveal self-defeating patterns, or else to make the links that offer better understanding and therefore a guide as to future action. Once again, an example from my practice can best illustrate this.

A social worker came to see me suffering from depression. The relationship with her boyfriend had recently come to an end, which had left her grief-stricken, and a complaint had been lodged against her at work. While this was being investigated, she was suspended and in fear of losing her job. The complaint concerned a perceived bullying and arrogance, which my client considered to be unjustified. I also initially found this surprising, until various elements of her story began to come together. She herself had been bullied as a child at school for being overweight and incompetent at games. In her relationship with her boyfriend, she admitted that she had been furiously jealous if he even looked at a slim girl. She would goad him into going out with someone more attractive, in her desperate need to hear that she was the only one for him. In the end she had pushed him too far. At work she had become the champion of the underdog to such an extent that she had started to exert undue pressure on junior staff. When she realized that she was in fact overcompensating for her own unhappy childhood, she was able to begin to learn how to be more relaxed in her dealings with others. These connections were formed jointly over a number of sessions, until we both arrived at the insight of why the complaint had been brought. In this case, the process was more inferential than intuitive.

Advanced empathy may well follow on after the therapist has empathized in a basic way with the client. David Berger in examining this process in the clinical situation gives a clear example to illustrate his point (1987, p. 90). The analyst appreciates his patient's emotional state during a reported quarrel with her daughter, and this of course is empathic. He then experiences the sudden recognition that this particular quarrel resembles arguments with her mother that the patient had previously reported. This is an intuition based on the parallel structure of two sets of relationships – or the making of connections, as in advanced empathy. Berger emphasizes the elation of discovery that the analyst experiences, which is typical of the intuitive process.

As with many intuitive responses, advanced empathy may lead to a challenge because it makes explicit something of which the client is only dimly, or even not at all, aware. The chances are that repression or other defence mechanisms have been put in place, because it may be something which the person would rather not know. The therapist needs to be very sensitive about the timing of responses, therefore, and the manner in which any insights are presented.

Counter-transference

Just like advanced empathy, strong associations are frequently made between intuition and counter-transference, particularly by therapists trained in psychoanalytic or psychodynamic approaches. In these methods transference plays a central role in the therapy. The subject is complex and has been given considerable space and scrutiny within psychoanalytic literature. It is therefore only necessary here to reflect on its associations with intuition.

Originally Freud used the term 'counter-transference' to describe the effect on the analyst's feelings of the patient's transference, whatever he or she unconsciously brought into the analytic situation from childhood (SE VII, 1905). He thought of it as an intrusive element, inasmuch as it interfered with the analyst's neutrality and evenly hovering attention. In this type of counter-transference the analyst remains fixed in the identification and caught up in conflicts similar to those of the patient. As a result he or she may act out or respond defensively, unable to 'see' what the material consists of. In so far as this disturbs the evenly hovering attention, it also interferes with the empathic and intuitive processes. As we have seen, the identification in empathy needs to be transient while the therapist remains clear about what belongs to the patient's psyche and what to his or her own.

Another form of counter-transference response, however, is clearly described by Paula Heimann in her paper of 1950, which acknowledges that analysts have a wide range of feelings towards their patients, which are by no means all inhibiting. They must, however, be subordinated to the analytic task and used for research into the patient's unconscious. In following the patient's free associations, the evenly hovering attention is employed to listen on many levels, to hear the allusions and implications, the latent as well as the manifest meanings. Heimann writes from the basic assumption that the analyst's unconscious intuitively understands that of the patient, enabling a rapport on a deep level. This very deep kind of empathy rises to the surface in the form of feelings, or counter-transference response, giving the analyst information about what the patient is really trying to communicate. Moreover, in comparing his or her own feelings with the patient's associations and behaviour, the analyst can confirm whether or not this intuitive understanding is on target. In addition to the thinking mode, therefore, it is evident that feelings can be used to check intuitions. (See also Chapter 10.) Heimann continues by asserting that the analyst does need to have a 'freely roused emotional sensibility' (p. 82) in order to be able to track the patient's feelings and phantasies. Here again, there is a striking similarity with Tony Bastick's 'emotionally sensitive and variable' intuitive type. Paula Heimann issues a warning against extreme emotions, however, which are likely to incite the analyst to action rather than reflection. The emotional sensitivity needs, therefore, to be broadly differentiating and flexible rather than narrow and intense.

Sometimes the intuitive, unconscious perception will be ahead of the therapist's comprehension and this may leave a feeling of puzzlement. The following case offers an example. A male client of mine wanted to look at the anger he was experiencing. He described a number of situations which had led to an accumulation of excessive emotion, most specifically having had his part-time teaching hours reduced without proper consultation. Yet when I suggested that he look at his anger as a vital source of energy which could be used for self-assertion or other creative purposes, he was immediately resistant and quoted a spiritual leader whom he admired. This guru advocated acceptance and tranquillity as a response to adversity. However, the edge in his voice indicated to me that he was far from tranquil. Though he insisted that this belief system was profoundly meaningful and the right path for him, I remained quietly unconvinced. I had a sense of unease and felt that something else was going on, perhaps to do with authority figures, but this eluded me. There was little point in challenging the teachings of a spiritual leader, so I suggested a piece of Gestalt with the headmaster at his school and that he evoke this person in imagination. When, during the dialogue, I encouraged my client to express his discontent, his voice dropped and his body slumped. I reflected back to him how I saw his energy draining away and asked what was going on. He said that if he raised his voice or asked for what he wanted, the head would turn his back and walk away. He felt hopeless. All immediately became clear to me. He had learnt in childhood that to express anger or make demands meant being ignored and was non-productive. I had unconsciously perceived that this man was not following the guru's path out of a sense of religious conviction, but that it was an excuse for his inability to be assertive and stand up for himself. Here, from a psychological perspective, was the real motivation. My unease had emanated from his difficulties in following the guru's advice. In this case my unconscious perception had been in advance of my conscious conception.

Clearly, counter-transference feelings are by no means always a disturbing factor, as Freud postulated. Indeed, if an analyst remains unfeeling and detached, then an important route to intuitive perception is likely to be blocked.

Over the years, counter-transference responses have been categorized into different types. Jung anticipated Paula Heimann's stance as early as 1929, referring to the phenomenon as a 'highly important organ of information', pointing out that the patient influences the analyst unconsciously (CW 16). To continue within the context of analytical psychology, Fordham in 1957 introduced the term 'syntonic counter-transference'. He had adopted the word 'syntonic'[2] from radio communications to describe the adjustment of circuit settings in a receiver so as to produce maximum response to a particular signal. Thus, in the clinical situation, the analyst's unconscious is tuned in to whatever signals may be emitted by the patient. Through introspection, the analyst notices feelings or behaviours that are in response to the patient's unspoken messages. The neurotic or interfering kind of counter-transference, on the other hand, Fordham refers to as 'illusory'.

In 1985 Andrew Samuels proposed two further terms to convey different aspects of the helpful type of counter-transference. The first is 'reflective counter-transference', in which the analyst unconsciously takes on the mood of the patient. For example, he or she may not normally experience depression, yet nevertheless be overcome by low spirits after being with a particular individual. In this case the analyst's feelings reflect those of the patient.

The other sort he refers to as 'embodied', because the analyst's low mood, to continue with this hypothetical example, may be caused by the imago of a depressed significant person held within the patient's psyche. Here, the feeling absorbed by the analyst is the embodiment of that figure or entity. Samuels emphasizes the fact that many of the counter-transference states are nonverbal or pre-verbal, which are, as we have seen, characteristics of the intuitive mode.

To move forward into the integrative frame of reference, in which the therapeutic relationship is the focus, Petruska Clarkson also describes two main types of counter-transference (1995), one being 'reactive' and the other 'proactive'. It is the first variety that provides intuitively acquired information. This type was previously referred to by Winnicott as 'objective counter-transference' (1975, p. 195), because the analyst is reacting objectively to the patient's projections, personality and behaviour. Reactive counter-transference may be subdivided into on the one hand 'complementary', in which the therapist experiences accurately the emotional, cognitive and behavioural responses which would complete or be complementary to the client's projections. If the patient projects aspects of his or her young self on to the therapist, this is the part that the therapist feels induced to play, while the client takes on the role of the significant parent. The reverse may also happen if the client projects the parent on to the therapist, so that the therapist feels invited to become the child. On the other hand the reactive counter-transference may also be 'concordant' (Racker, 1968/1982). Clarkson describes this as an 'emotional attunement to an affective or feeling state which is problematical or painful to the client' (p. 91). This is comparable to Samuels' reflective counter-transference.

Clarkson's proactive counter-transference has to do with the psychotherapist's own material, and is most similar to that originally recognized by Freud. It is crucial for the therapist to be able to identify the source of his or her affective responses and their significance within the therapeutic relationship, so that the work with the client can move forward. Do the feelings experienced stem from unresolved issues concerning the therapist's own past, or do they clearly emanate from the client, offering valuable information about patterns of behaviour and ways of responding that may or may not be useful within the context of the person's present life? Such questions need to be carefully and honestly assessed by the therapist and, if in doubt, taken to supervision.

Sometimes the differences between these two main types of counter-transference are not clear-cut, because the historical experiences of the therapist and client may overlap. I debated just such a case recently with a supervisee, who described feelings of anxiety when her male client talked about setting up a business with a particular female partner. These prompted her to enquire whether he trusted his partner, but she remained unsure why she had asked such a question. We came to the conclusion that not only had she been unconsciously invited to adopt the position of the client's father, who came from a poor north-east of England background and who seemed fearful of financial matters, but she had also connected with her own thrifty Yorkshire upbringing. The counter-transference was therefore partly reactive and partly proactive. By sorting out what belonged to whom, my supervisee was in a position to accept the genuinely useful intuitively acquired information and put aside the rest.

Meeting at depth

Later in his career, the writings of Carl Rogers became more personal and philosophical, in part covering a terrain that, by his own admission, could not be scientifically proven. While the basic characteristics of empathy had been clarified by objective research, he became increasingly aware of experiences that could not be studied empirically. He was expressing a very deep empathy, in which there seemed to be a touching of souls. It involved 'the transcendent, the indescribable, the spiritual' and mostly occurred when he was connected with his 'inner, intuitive self' (1980/1995, p. 129). Moreover, there was a sense of something larger at work, a feeling of oneness and unity which had to do with the whole of nature. This happened most especially in groups. He quotes the eloquent words of a participant: 'I felt the oneness of spirit in the community. We breathed together, felt together, even spoke for one another. I felt the power of the "life force" that infuses each of us – whatever that is. I felt its presence without the usual barricades of "me-ness" or "you-ness" – it was like a meditative experience' (1980/1995, pp. 196–7). The empathy was so complete that all the barriers between individuals had dissolved. At this level, the interconnectedness of persons and the created order was beheld. When a meeting takes place at such a relational depth, then no longer do clients feel abandoned and alone. This in itself can be healing.

Brian Thorne highlights the personal work necessary in order to achieve this degree of empathy. In writing about the mystical elements inherent in person-centred therapy, he suggests that 'the loving connectedness with the self is the prerequisite for the adventure of connecting with the other' (2002a, p. 41). First, then, the therapist must learn to accept and appreciate him- or herself fully, before unconditional love can be offered to another. Thorne continues: 'Essentially it is a discipline which focuses on the nature of the other and draws from this the intuitive inspiration which makes for interpersonal connectedness at the deepest level.' Along with this, there can be a state of heightened consciousness, and a sense of 'mystical communion through relationship' (p. 50). This in itself can offer the client a new perspective in which life's sufferings and difficulties can be rendered 'of little or no account'. This involves the surrendering of the psychological and emotional disturbances to the empathic therapist, which frees the client to move forwards. Rogers also emphasizes that it is who the therapist is that counts, and how fully he or she can invest his or her own being in each moment of the relationship. Then, as spirit meets spirit, within the context of something larger, immense energy can be released, 'which transcends what we thought was involved' (Baldwin, 2000, p. 36).

Rogers throws a challenge to those who uphold transference as central to the therapy. He sees it as a sophisticated device for forestalling relational depth, for defending the therapist against involvement and a means by which access to the spiritual is prevented (in Thorne, 2002a, p. 56). Clearly, there are different degrees of empathic understanding, all of which can be helpful, but the type that Rogers later promotes is of the very deepest kind. He moves beyond the 'as if' condition into becoming a direct participant in the client's world.

Tobin Hart writes about deep empathy in the context of transpersonal knowing (2000). Here the other's feelings are experienced 'directly in my own body' (p. 253). The emotions seem to reverberate physically within the therapist. Alvin Mahrer refers to the client's words 'as if they are coming in and through the therapist' (1993, p. 33), which is followed by a further stage, in which he or she 'literally enters completely into being the person'. The sensitive body of the therapist now contains the client's experiences so utterly, that he or she is transformed into this way of being. Because of the intimacy and unity that occurs, the client also becomes transformed and walks away from the session a new person. Stanislav Grof (1993) refers to this type of transpersonal connection as 'dual unity' (p. 91). Physical boundaries appear to have been dissolved and there may be a strong sense of merging with the creative source from which we have all come. Tobin Hart reminds us that deep empathy is not a particular technique, but 'more direct knowing that involves a shift in being, consciousness, or awareness' (2000, p. 260). Again, there is an emphasis on who we intrinsically are in such moments, rather than what we do. What remains unclear, however, is how far the therapist, through such a fusion, can still remain in contact with him- or herself. In such very deep transpersonal empathy the 'as if' condition can no longer apply.

This type of experience is redolent of the *participation mystique*, first studied by the anthropologist Lévy-Bruhl (1910/1966). His writings on what was then referred to, in somewhat derogatory terms, as 'primitive mentality' were widely discussed during the earlier part of the twentieth century. *Participation mystique*, as described by Lévy-Bruhl, is marked by the difficulty of the subject in distinguishing him- or herself from the object. Yet it is in this mystical oneness with the other that absolute illumination about the person or object is provided in a direct intuition. Jung, who had a deep interest in Lévy-Bruhl's work, was very clear that the identification occurring in this process was one that was given, an *a priori* oneness of subject and object, not one resulting from pathology (CW 6, para. 781). Van der Post, writer and explorer and a friend of Jung, gives a detailed account of the behaviour of a Kalahari Bushman residing in America: 'He had a gift ... that enabled him ... to enter into the spirit of whatever they happened to be doing and even partake of the character of the people who came and went ... as if it were food for his own. It was not just that he appeared to know what the people were like within their own hidden selves but could actually become them' (1975/1989, pp. 68–9). It is possible therefore to use *participation mystique* at will and for more complete understanding of the other. There is, of course, a difference between unconsciously merging with someone else and losing one's identity in the process, and choosing to allow dissolution of personal boundaries for the benefit of the other. Therapists working in this way need to be scrupulously honest about their own intentions and motivations.

There seems to be a subtle distinction between empathic fusion and empathic resonance. If two violins are in the same room and a string on one is plucked, the string tuned to the same frequency on the other will also resonate. Therapists may vary in their responsiveness to the sensations and feelings of clients, depending on how well tuned in to the other they are. David Elkins equates empathic resonance with soul:

> To know the soul, we must lay aside our rational ways of knowing and open ourselves to the world of reverence, feeling, and imagination – the world of I–Thou encounter, imagery, poetry, art, ritual, ceremony, and symbol ... Soul is the empathic resonance that vibrates within us at such moments. She is the catch of the breath, the awe in the heart, the lump in the throat, the tear in the eye. (1995, p. 83)

Such responses are markers as to the presence of soul. It is in the imaginal world that souls may meet, touch and resonate with each other.

Hart suggests that empathy, refined even further, does not involve simple observation, nor stepping into the other's shoes, nor reacting to, fusing with, resonating with, nor attuning to; rather perception seems to occupy manifold perspectives all at the same time. One seems to become the very field of intersubjectivity itself (2000 p. 261). Multiple layers and patterns of experience are intuited directly and at once.

Hart declares that all empathy is 'potentially transcendent in the sense that it takes us beyond ourselves' (p. 267). Whatever the level of empathy that individual therapists may achieve, courage is often needed to reach towards another person at relational depth.

* * * *

After re-reading this chapter I was particularly struck by the different varieties of empathy that might be applied in therapy, ranging from the everyday sense of a good rapport, to transposing oneself imaginatively into another's world, and onwards to the very highest, or deepest, form where there is a true touching of souls. At any level, the connection might prompt an intuition, which in turn may enhance the understanding of the case. Yet I was left with the distinct impression that so much depends on the development of the therapist, on the degree of responsiveness and emotional sensitivity, and willingness to meet, accept and relate to the client in a profound way. Too heavy a reliance on theoretical considerations, anxiety over intimacy, or lack of love for the self, were just some of the problems that might intervene and jeopardize the process. So I was left with the question: What can the therapist draw on, from within, to assist and support this closeness to the other, so that it might feel a little less difficult or risky? Material that I was putting together concerning that secondary sub-waking self might provide at least some of the answer.

Notes

1. 'Projection' in this context should not be confused with the classic defence mechanism, in which one unconsciously projects on to someone else the disowned elements in oneself. It is noticeable, particularly in couples, how the one blames the other for his or her own shortcomings. In this way, one does not have to admit to one's own failings.
2. The term 'syntonic' is derived from the Greek *suntunos*, meaning in harmony with.

CHAPTER 8

The secondary self

During my investigations into intuition, it was noticeable that a theme kept reappearing from time to time that had to do with some kind of other self. This other self, often only dimly perceived, seemed to represent in symbolic form a source of inner wisdom, an intuitive knowing, that might offer guidance as to the way forward, the actions that might best be pursued or avoided. Sometimes the advice seemed to take the form of monitions or warnings. Most striking was the image that consistently appeared to the individual concerned, clearly apprehended as a particular figure, to whom a name may be given. As trust was built in this source of wisdom, a relationship was formed with the figure, to the point that it could be evoked at will, whenever the person needed consolation or help. As I pondered this phenomenon, I began to wonder how much we, as therapists, might benefit from such a process. In personifying this source of understanding, could we have more direct access to our intuition, and thereby be of greater assistance to our clients?

The daemons of Classical times

As my researches continued, it became apparent that the concept of a source of intuitive understanding as some kind of inner voice or presence other than the usual rational self has an ancient history. Many examples can be found in the classical texts of Ancient Greece, including Homer's *The Odyssey*. Here, certain psychological states that characterize some kind of intuitive insight or understanding are attributed to the intervention of supernatural beings, generally described as daemons or gods, that are very often nameless. Any sudden memory, insight, inspired idea, or warning, or the meaning of an omen, particularly when there has been no prior deliberation, is experienced as having been put into the person's mind by some external being. For example, Helen intuitively comprehends the meaning of an omen and thereby prophesies Odysseus's homecoming saying 'I shall be your prophet, the way the immortals put it into my heart, and I think it will be accomplished' (XV, 172. Lattimore,

1965). Interesting here is the idea that the prophecy itself comes from the gods, but that its interpretation, the manner in which it will be carried out, it hers. So reflection may follow intuitive knowledge.

Perhaps we need to remember that self and not-self were less clear to Ancient Greeks than to the modern person. As E.R. Dodds points out, Homeric man had no concept of the 'soul' or 'personality' as different entities. The poems recognize a person's *psyche* only after death or if threatened with death, or in the act of fainting or dying. Dodds's discussion of the *thumos* is of especial interest here, described as an 'independent inner voice' that advises on a course of action, such as when to eat, drink or kill the enemy. For example, Odysseus 'plans in his thumos' to kill the Cyclops forthwith, but a second voice restrains him (IX, 299ff.). Lattimore translates this as: 'Then I took counsel with myself in my great-hearted spirit', rather losing the sense of separateness of the thumos (1965, p. 145). Usually the protagonist takes the advice offered, but may also reject it, as here. Dodds suggests that in Homer the thumos may be roughly defined as 'the organ of feeling' (1951, p. 16). At any rate, it can be consulted and conversed with and its admonishments are to be taken seriously. Here, of course, the source of counsel is located within the person, usually in the chest or midriff, yet some kind of divine intervention may operate on the thumos, as in *The Iliad*, when Diomedes remarks that Achilles will fight 'when thumos in his chest tells him to and a god rouses him' (IX, 702). From a psychological perspective, emotional drives are thus objectified and treated as not-self.

The influence of Homer on the culture of Ancient Greece must have been profound, for, as Bertrand Russell asserts in his *History of Western Philosophy*, from the reign of Peisistratus onwards (560–527 BC) Athenian youth learnt Homeric poems by heart and these were 'a most important part of their education' (1946/1961, p. 31). It would surely seem quite natural, therefore, for the intelligentsia to consult with some divine being whenever good counsel was needed.

In the case of Socrates, he relied on a personal daemon for guidance in times of stress. He gives a very precise account of his experiences of this daemon or 'prophetic voice' that acts as his 'constant companion, opposing me in even quite trivial things if I was going to take the wrong course'. Even under sentence of death, he puts trust in his daemon: 'I suspect that this thing that has happened to me is a blessing, and we are quite mistaken in supposing death to be an evil. I have good grounds for thinking this, because my accustomed sign could not have failed to oppose me if what I was doing had not been sure to bring some good result' (Plato, 4th c. BC/1954).

In discussing intuition, Carl Jung refers to Socrates' daemon, taking it as an example of how this aptitude occurs: 'To describe such a function is naturally very difficult on account of its irrational and quasi-unconscious character. In a sense one might compare it to the daemon of Socrates ...' However, Jung considers that, being 'strongly rationalistic', Socrates repressed his intuitive side 'so that it had to make itself felt in the form of concrete hallucinations since it had no direct access to consciousness' (1923/1971, pp. 145–6). This is a speculative remark, perhaps made because Jung had trouble in reconciling Socrates' intuitive nature with the high degree of rational thought clearly demonstrated in Plato's descriptions of him. Indeed Jung implies that Socrates was not, in his view, an intuitive type. Apparently he fails to take into account the cultural background of Ancient Greece, in which unconscious processes were commonly ascribed to deities or daemons and were not considered to emanate from the person.

A concept similar to the thumos appears in Japanese culture, that of *kufu*, which is not about sorting out difficulties just in the head, but rather a state that is evoked whereby the physical self is involved in the solving of a problem. The intellect may raise the question, but it is the body that provides the answer. In writing about this phenomenon, Suzuki explains:

> The Japanese often talk about 'asking the abdomen' ... The abdomen, which includes the whole system of viscera, symbolises the totality of one's personality ... Psychologically speaking, [kufu] is to bring out what is stored in the unconscious, and let it work itself out quite independently of any kind of interfering consciousness. (1959, pp. 104–5, 109)

In this case, it is supposed that unconscious material is stored in the body, along with the overall impression of who one is as a person. By turning the awareness towards the sensitive area around the abdomen, with a question well formulated, elements of knowledge held here recombine to present the person with a sense of the best way forward.

Psychoanalyst George Frankl describes the developmental origins of this process in terms of what a baby may ingest from its mother, both physiologically and emotionally. He refers to the solar plexus as a 'primitive brain', because it is this area that evaluates whether the object that the mouth wants to devour is either acceptable or disagreeable. If unacceptable, it will constrict, giving a feeling of unease. It is these primary responses that are so influential in the formation of character (1994, p. 70).

Gendlin's 'felt sense'

In reading about the ancient customs of taking counsel from the thumos and through the process of kufu, I was reminded immediately of Eugene Gendlin's concept of the 'felt sense', which has been mentioned in

Chapter 3. He describes it as 'an internal source' that can be 'consulted many times every day' through the technique of 'focusing' (Gendlin 1978/1981, p. 4). The person learns how to get in touch with a particular kind of inner bodily awareness, which forms after first attending to the feelings. It is information which we acquire from the body about any presenting difficulty. At first it seems hazy and vague, but by continuing to focus upon it, meaning will emerge. Gendlin emphasizes that the felt sense is not mental, but rather physical, a bodily store of knowledge about a person, an event or situation, perceived as a whole. Its location is generally in the stomach or chest.

This experience has significant implications for the practitioner as far as the therapeutic relationship is concerned. Not only do we hold information in our bodies which is all about ourselves, but we also store there knowledge of others, including, of course, our clients. Our bodies know the effect that a particular person has on us as soon as that individual enters the room. With some people our physical selves are experienced as comfortable and free; with others we may feel tense and tight and have difficulty in breathing. We can then use the focusing technique and consult with our bodies to give us understanding about this counter-transference response. For instance, whenever a particular male client arrived in my consulting room, I was aware of a tightness across my chest and around my shoulders. By turning my attention to my body, I realized that it was in fact unconsciously mimicking his. I could then go into the experience of what it was like to have a body held in this way and images arising from my felt sense helped me to understand the kind of stresses that he was carrying.

Gendlin makes the point that, in order to be alert to the felt sense, a space must first be cleared (1996, p. 286). This means putting aside all personal concerns as well as theories and techniques, so that the client can enter a clear area, where nothing lies between the person-to-person meeting. He sees the relationship to be of prime importance for future change, and describes how we are alive to each other in a bodily sense. So if, for example, a client believes that no one could ever care about him or her, and may state this in words, nevertheless the message will be picked up via the body that the therapist does in fact care. The thoughts will reach consciousness later.

The felt sense helps the therapist not only to be genuine, from a person-centred point of view, but also to make the genuineness manifest. Sometimes a client may pick up a cue from the therapist, perhaps from a fleeting expression, and ask what is happening. The therapist needs firstly to validate the client's perceptiveness, and then to consult quickly with the felt sense and decide whether or not it would be helpful to reveal what was going on, or whether it was a purely private matter unrelated to the client material.

Sometimes there appears to be a hiatus in the working alliance and it is then important to verbalize what is happening on a covert level, so that the work can continue. The helper's felt sense message may be that the client is holding on to some kind of resentment. The difficulty can then be alluded to, rather than pretending that everything is fine. When this kind of interactional material is brought into the open, there can be a feeling of relief on both sides, and levels of trust are enhanced.

These are just a few examples of how effective this consultation with the felt sense can be in revealing intuitive knowledge concerning the therapeutic relationship and client material. Gendlin's work is therefore warmly recommended.

Jung's Philemon

It can now be appreciated that the intuitive source can be connected with in different ways. This can either take the form of some sort of consultation with a sensitive area of one's own body, or else it can be an imaginative dialogue with an all-knowing person or creature.

If we turn to Jung's autobiography (1963), we can discover how the notion of a secondary self had been a reality for him since childhood. His mother, Emilie Preiswerk, came from a family of theologians. While her Protestant attitudes and values were conventional, she had another side to her, an 'unconscious personality', that made unexpected appearances. This secondary personality Jung found unnerving as a boy, for, when in this mode, he records that she had the ability to be absolutely forthright and truthful in what she said to the point of ruthlessness. He ascribes both godlike vision and animal instinct to her pronouncements: 'like one of those seers who is at the same time a strange animal, like a priestess in a bear's cage' (1963/1995, p. 67). It seems that she was able to lay aside her customary self and allow her intuitive nature to provide her with startlingly direct perception of a person or situation.

Although Jung's young cousin was ultimately exposed as a fraud as far as her séances were concerned, nevertheless his dissertation of 1902, based on his observations of her, provides a useful exposition on how a secondary personality might be formed. In this case, it manifested itself as a 'spirit', who apparently spoke through the medium in High German, whereas the girl normally spoke only the Swiss dialect (CW 1). It is clear from this endeavour that scientific enquiry about the natural world was not enough for Jung; experiences of the supernatural were a reality to him and equally deserving of study. The part of the psyche that was in touch with such phenomena was the intuitive. It must have seemed obvious to him that this function had to be included in a comprehensive typology. Indeed, in the popular literature concerning the paranormal the words 'psychic' and 'intuitive' are frequently found to be interchangeable.

It has to be said that Jung, according to his own admission (1963), was brought up not only in a religious atmosphere, but also within the prevailing Swiss peasant culture, of which superstition was a necessary part. It therefore never seemed surprising to Jung that clocks should stop or glasses shatter at the moment of death, or that dreams should foretell such events. While he found some accounts of occult phenomena dubious, he nevertheless had a deep interest in the supernatural and was disappointed that his student comrades, who had been brought up in urban environments, treated such subjects with anxious defensiveness or even derision. Unlike them, he kept an open mind. Since experiences of occult phenomena had been consistently reported through the ages, this was sufficient reason, so Jung believed, to investigate them. Moreover, he wanted to have an explanation for his own encounters with the paranormal, such as the walnut table in the family's dining room that inexplicably split with a loud report, or the knife that shattered equally audibly in the sideboard. At least he found sympathetic understanding in his mother's 'No. 2' personality.

Critics of Jung might simply dismiss him as superstitious and thereby discredit the inclusion of intuition in his typological structure. There could well be a naturalistic reason why an old table might unexpectedly split, due, for example, to a sudden change in atmospheric humidity, and perhaps someone had deliberately broken the knife in the sideboard; Jung was not even present when this happened. Whatever the truth may be about such events, their impact on Jung was profound and his belief in the reality of the supernatural motivated him to enquire into such phenomena from a psychological perspective. The fact that they were experienced as both real and significant by himself and others made them worthy of serious study.

This leads to a consideration of Jung's psychological make-up. Like his mother, he also contained a secondary self which he first recognized at age twelve, as an old man of great authority who belonged to the eighteenth century. When seeing an antique carriage driving by one day, he had a powerful feeling of recognition and nostalgia; moreover, an eighteenth-century statuette at his aunt's home had buckled shoes of the type he believed he must have worn himself. People who maintain that there are successive states of existence would say that these were 'past-life' experiences, while rationalists would dismiss them as the fantasies of an imaginative boy. Jung would by now have been aware of the notion of *karma* from his readings of stories about Oriental religions and no doubt the idea that he had once been an influential man would have strongly appealed to his twelve-year-old mind.

Jung describes such impressions with verve and their impact on him is obvious. A few lines further on in his autobiography, however, he counters them with the rational part of his mind, which tries to find a reasonable explanation, and even repudiates the idea of being two different persons. He acknowledges his own confusion (1963/1995, p. 207). Here we can observe the dialectic between intuition and reason. His intuition confirms the reality of his experiences, while his intellect demands rational elucidation.

Ultimately intuition triumphs, for his secondary personality eventually develops into an image of the prophet Elijah, and subsequently 'Philemon', a winged being, who brings with him an 'Egypto-Hellenic atmosphere with Gnostic colouration' (1963/1995, p. 207). This figure first appeared in a dream and later in visionary form, representing a source of wisdom from Jung's unconscious. Most importantly, this being seemed to have a life of its own, producing notions that were not a part of Jung's conscious mind:

> For I observed clearly that it was he who spoke, not I. He said I treated thoughts as if I generated them myself, but in his view thoughts were like animals in the forest, or people in a room, or birds in the air ... It was he who taught me psychic objectivity, the reality of the psyche. (1963/1995, pp. 207–8)

Philemon represented 'superior insight' and conveyed to him 'many an illuminating idea' (p. 208). By summoning up this figure, therefore, through a process that Jung was to refer to as the 'active imagination', he was able to tap into the wisdom contained within his own unconscious, a deliberate way of having access to intuitive knowledge. He could put himself into such a state by letting himself 'drop', or fall into a trance, as Anthony Stevens sees it (1990, p. 168), and use imagery and dialogue to evoke special insights. Jung describes Philemon as 'quite real, as if he were a living personality. I went walking up and down the garden with him, and to me he was what the Indians call a guru.'

There is an interesting parallel between the two personalities of Jung and his young cousin, Hélène Preiswerk. In each case the secondary personality offered superior wisdom and insight. Jung had concluded in his dissertation concerning the girl that the more dignified, mature 'control', which she called Ivène, was a manifestation of the adult personality contained within Hélène's psyche, but not yet expressed in daily life, due to environmental and psychological factors. The same might well be said of Jung's 'Wise Old Man', the part of him constrained by the conventional attitudes prevailing in the Protestant vicarage in which he was raised. These independent parts of the psyche, apparently autonomous, were later referred to by Jung as complexes and became a fundamental aspect of analytical psychology. The aim was to bring such unconscious material into full awareness so that complete maturity and wholeness, or 'individuation' as Jung termed it, could be attained. The intuitive process whereby such unconscious elements could be accessed, involving the suspension of reason and the use of receptive meditation, was thus crucial to Jung's psychology. Imaginative personification of the complexes assisted with this practice. Individuation also incorporates the realization of potential. The figure of Philemon was Jung's future self, that of the wise old man and spiritual leader.

In principle there appears to be little difference between Jung's Philemon and Socrates' daemon. Each had been experienced since childhood and each was used for a similar purpose, to have access to superior knowledge. However, it seems that the daemon indicated to Socrates what he should not do rather than pointing to a positive course of action: 'it always signifies to me the abandonment of what I am about to do, it never incites me' (Plato, 4th c. BC/1954). He took its warnings very seriously. During a banquet, when a member of the party, Timarchus, rose to leave, Socrates knew intuitively that he must try to stop him, being totally unaware that he was plotting a murder:

> 'By no means', said I, 'rise up; for there has been to me the usual daemon signal.' Upon this he stayed. And after a slight interval, he was again going away, and said – 'Socrates, I am going.' And there was again the voice. Again therefore I compelled him to stay.

The third time, however, Timarchus slipped away unobserved to commit his crime. It seems, from this and other quotations, that the daemon generally came to Socrates spontaneously and was believed to be an external entity, whereas Jung learnt to evoke Philemon deliberately and understood that the figure emanated from his own unconscious.

The active imagination

Like Jung, we as therapists can learn to evoke some kind of symbolic figure that represents our own inner source of wisdom. Equally, we can evoke such a creature at will and, through imaginary dialogue, find answers to problems that we are encountering either in our work or else in our personal lives. First of all, however, the appropriate attitude is necessary. Jung makes a distinction between active and passive fantasies. The former are consciously evoked and the attention is specifically directed towards elements that so far remain out of awareness. The expectation is held that, by associating the images that arise with parallel elements, meaning and understanding will result. In this, there is a positive participation of consciousness. Passive fantasies, on the other hand, appear uninvited, if at all, and, according to Jung, may often be morbid in character or due to a dissociated state (CW 6, paras. 712–14). He considers that active fantasy is one of the most superior forms of psychic functioning, because the conscious merges with the unconscious to create something beneficial.

One difficulty in fully understanding Jung is the loss of certain subtleties through the process of translation. The German word *betrachten* is relevant here, generally translated as 'to look at', 'consider', 'contemplate' or 'reflect upon'. However, Jung himself makes reference to the allied meaning of *trächtig*, an adjective referring to pregnancy. Held within this is the idea of offering the image received such undivided attention that it becomes alive and is able to produce something: 'one concentrates upon it, and then finds that one has great difficulty in keeping the thing quiet, it gets restless, it shifts, something is added, or it multiplies itself; one fills it with living power' (1930–34, quoted in Chodorow, 1997, p. 7). More is involved than simply looking; total absorption is needed, while at the same time allowing the fantasy free play, until the image becomes pregnant with meaning.

While personal work may involve focusing attention on a feeling or bodily state until an image arises, and then working with that, for professional purposes a more directed route needs to be followed. Firstly, as we have seen, intuition responds best to a relaxed state, so this must be induced. It is therefore worthwhile to ensure that there will be no interruptions, and then to go through a process of deep physical relaxation either lying flat on the floor, or sitting in an upright chair. One useful method is to work through the body, clenching and then releasing each major muscle group individually (see Charles, 2000, pp. 13–14 for more detailed instructions). It is also important to close the eyes and empty the mind of intrusive thoughts by, perhaps, focusing on the breathing and allowing busy mental activity to quieten and drift away. Then it is necessary to bring to mind the problem with which one needs help, or question to be answered, along with the expectation that a way forward will be found through the meeting with an archetypal figure that represents loving wisdom. After that, a visualization is followed, during which the imagination is allowed to supply all the details, in terms of all the senses. This generally begins in a tranquil location, such as a meadow. A path is seen, which leads through a forest and then upwards towards the top of a mountain, symbolic of a timeless realm beyond everyday concerns. Here, some kind of temple is found, where the meeting takes place with the wise being. This figure or presence wants only the very best for both you and your client. The difficulty or question is posed and then the answer is awaited. This may be heard as a verbal message, or a sign may be received. Trust is needed that the communication will be helpful even if the meaning is not immediately obvious. The path down the mountain is retraced and the reply is brought back into the world within the context of the client work. If a symbol was given, it may be helpful to create the form through some kind of artistic expression until the message emerges. It is always important to make an ethical check at this stage to ensure that the advice offered conforms to best practice. The archetypal being can also be drawn or painted to make it more real and bring it more fully into consciousness. Images for this that have been reported vary greatly, from the spirit of a tree, a Chinese sage, to some kind of animal, or a bird figure such as an eagle. Thereafter, the being can be called upon to provide intuitive knowledge when needed.

Piero Ferrucci (1982/1995) suggests that the wise presence represents the transpersonal Self, and through this technique direct communication can be set up between the personality and the superconscious. Thus, inner truth and guidance can be accessed at will. Within the context of psychosynthesis, this is the region which is the source of spiritual energy, containing our higher intuitions and inspirations (Assagioli 1965/1975, pp. 17–18).[1] John Rowan likes to refer to this conscious use of symbols and images as 'opening the third eye' (1993b, p. 54). It is as if one had suffered from myopia, or some other form of eye disease, whereby only limited perceptions and insights could get through. This third eye, however, has vision which is bright and clear, a centre of pure awareness, which transcends the personality.

Another technique which Ferrucci advocates is writing a letter to the Self, setting out the difficulty (1982/1995, p. 149) and then waiting patiently for the response. Answers may not be straightforward, but rather the personal qualities needed to assist with the problem may be demonstrated in symbolic form. Moreover, these may take some time to reach consciousness and could arrive via a dream, through an element in the environment in the form of synchronicity, or perhaps as an impulse to take some course of action. He emphasizes the importance of silencing the mind from busy intrusions. It is helpful to include the quality of silence during any visualizations offering access to the superconscious, as it is into this quiet space that messages can be received.

These techniques can, of course, also be suggested to clients, whereby they can learn to become their own therapists through having access to their own inner guidance. In this way they can gradually discover how to become independent of the external helper as trust in their own 'still small voice' is gained.

When taking a professional problem to the secondary self, it needs to be remembered that intuitions often appear as whole forms, rather than the parts produced by the analytic mind. It is therefore likely that you will see the client's difficulties in a different light altogether, with perhaps an overview of the person's life, and whatever it is that the soul persistently struggles with. Moreover, the emphasis may well be on the future, a strong sense of what the client may become, of that person's potential and what he or she needs now to move forward.

Joan Chodorow, in writing on Jung and the active imagination, comments that this dialogue with the Self represents the religious attitude, the meeting with the god within, for the purpose of recreating the personality towards individuation. She writes: 'In the deepest sense, active imagination is the essential, inner-directed symbolic attitude that is at the core of psychological development.' (1997, p. 17). This is the attitude that practitioners and clients alike need to cultivate if they wish to release intuitions to consciousness.

The internal supervisor

By now it can be seen that different models of therapy may supply a variety of techniques whereby the helper can have better access to some kind of inner guidance. From within psychoanalysis, Patrick Casement (1985/1990) suggests an 'internal supervisor', whose purpose is to monitor the progress of therapy and review the interaction between patient and analyst, anticipating possible interventions and their consequences. He recommends that therapists cling less tenaciously to theory in order to be more receptively open to whatever their patients are communicating to them at diverse levels (p. 27). This means listening not just to the words and the story, but also being responsive to those nonverbal signals and covert messages that the patient may be transmitting. Clearly, this implies going more by intuition than by the book (p. 21). He considers that he has learnt most from those patients with whom he has been responsively different according to the needs of the case. Yet in allowing oneself to do this, some kind of adequate orientation is needed, so that the therapist does not stray too far from course.

As we have seen, intuitive types tend to have their own locus of inner authority, relying on their own personal judgement, rather than on external authorities or theories. It is precisely this ability that Casement utilizes, but in a more formal way. He sees the internal supervisor as offering some kind of paternal support from within, the part of oneself that is both concerned for the analyst and patient and yet sufficiently watchful and detached to be on hand to offer sound advice when needed. Casement compares this process with the 'nursing triad'. He, as analyst, can care best for the client when supported by this internal supervisor, just as the good-enough mother will best look after her child when she herself is 'held' by the other parent. The qualities of the internal supervisor, therefore, include maturity, loving concern and the ability to reflect, a trustworthy figure who can be relied upon for sound advice and support when needed.

It is within this context that the therapist can find 'an inner play-space where clinical options can be explored (either silently or with the patient) rather than remain blinkered by past thinking' (p. 27). By placing one's trust in this inner supervisor, therefore, and allowing oneself to let go of the rule-books, the therapist can respond creatively to each unique individual. When a 'play space' is thus opened up, thoughts, images, feelings can jostle together, allowing those vital connections to take place that in turn can offer fresh insights about the patient. Indeed, we have already noted how play can enhance the intuitive process. In this way the analyst can share the patient's creativity in a spirit of exploration.

W.R. Bion encouraged analysts to allow themselves space for 'reverie' during which a patient's images could be played with (1967). In this state the patient's material may combine and re-combine with the therapist's own thoughts, feelings, past experiences and further associations, until out of the mélange meaning and understanding may emerge. At the same time, a monitoring process takes place to check how well (or otherwise) the therapy is progressing and by sensing how the client may be experiencing the work. If the impression is that the therapy is not moving forward, the decision may be made to take an alternative approach.

While Casement recommends discarding strong adherence to a particular school of thought, or position on technique, he nevertheless resorts to other practitioners' theories to guide the internal supervisor. For example he relies on Matte Blanco's theory of 'unconscious symmetry' (1975) to assist with the abstraction of themes from the patient's material (1985/1990, p. 5). This has to do with primary-process thinking, whereby we unconsciously assume all relationships to be symmetrical, so that if John is angry with Mary, the assumption is that Mary is also angry with John (p. 6). In psychoanalytic listening, therefore, it is useful to be aware of this process, so that 'self' and 'other' may be heard as interchangeable, as may 'inside' and 'outside', and so on. Casement provides an example from his own practice whereby, by hypothesizing unconscious symmetry, he links the patient's wish to know the future through a meeting with a clairvoyant, to her past. As he plays with this material, therefore, he surmises that the theme communicated out of awareness could be to do with making contact with someone difficult to reach, either in the future or the past. While Casement highlights 'unfocused listening' and the need to take into account the form of the communication (as far as its weight or volume is concerned) as opposed to its content, nevertheless the distinct impression gained from the examples given is that the work of the internal supervisor is essentially intellectually based.

Casement also ascribes aspects of his mode of listening to the influence of R.J. Langs (1978), a theorist referred to in Chapter 6, who underlines the interactional nature of the therapeutic relationship (p. 57). In this model, the analyst needs to be aware of the patient's perception of the analyst's reality and responses to that reality. Casement describes how this attitude helps him to be in touch with the effects that he has on a patient as distinct from that which arises more autonomously from within the patient. Equally, he tries to monitor the patient's effect on himself (1985, p. 59). Here again, his internal supervisor relies on a theoretical position, which aids his listening technique. Could it be that once this way of listening has become customary, one's intuitive capability is enhanced? The therapist then automatically tracks what is occurring in the relationship and is more alert to the cues and prompts that have a bearing on it.

My impression on reading Casement's work is that he has an underlying wish for a more intuitive mode of operating, whereby conscious thought processes are relaxed, to allow in other signals. However, the very word 'psychoanalysis' implies a cognitively based approach, in which logic and language predominate. Indeed, the many examples he provides of his internal supervisor in action feature the analyst's intellect. He specifically describes the internal supervisory process as 'what I was thinking, in the session, and how I arrived at each intervention' (p. 102). There seems to be a tension between his wish to play and be more intuitively open, and psychoanalytic pressure to give logical explanations for the most minute details of each case. On p. 127 he admits that the examples given around his work with a particular Mrs B. do not provide a suitable illustration of 'how a more autonomous and relaxed process of internal supervision should be'. Because he had agreed to presenting this case to a seminar, he had internalized a severe critical supervisor, which discouraged the more subliminal way of working which he wished to advocate. How important it is, therefore, to visualize this internal guide as a caring helper!

A more intuitive approach is evident from the case quoted on p. 142, concerning a woman who had been sent away from home by her mother on her refusal to eat. During the session, after expressing rage at her husband and throwing a cushion at her analyst, she then picks it up, holds it close and starts to cradle and rock it. At this, Casement describes how he begins to sense an element of hope along with the despair, and that he might perhaps be able to hold the hurt child within the patient so that there was no need to send her away. Although the process is later discussed in terms of projective identification, the needs of the patient are intuitively obvious from her actions.

* * * *

While it was clear to me that the procedures collected together to form this chapter were all different ways of contacting intuition, it was striking how rarely the word itself was mentioned, the main exception being Jung's writing, and, to a lesser extent, Assagioli's. Although the strategies within the psychotherapeutic context were at variance with each other, there were also some similarities, whether the internal consultant was from the transpersonal, humanistic or psychodynamic models. All agree that a relaxed approach is necessary at the outset, together with a sense of exploration, to promote therapist insight. The main difference is where the attention is focused, either on the imagination, the body and or on verbal play. Yet all encourage the practitioner to let go of theory, with the aim of learning to rely on the inner intuitive authority rather than on any external specialists. At the same time it is not suggested that these techniques should replace professional supervision, which remains an important requirement of clinical practice.

Some of this material has taken us into the imaginal realm. This is the area we will now explore in greater depth.

Note

1. Assagioli's map of the unconscious contains three main parts: the lower unconscious which includes such elements as the body's control mechanisms and the fundamental drives and urges; the middle unconscious, formed from our waking state and elements close to awareness; and the higher unconscious or superconscious, where intuitions, inspirations and ethical imperatives are located. The personal self is placed in the middle region, and this may have access to the Higher Self, which is experienced at the superconscious level. The collective unconscious surrounds this model, which is normally portrayed in the shape of an egg. Assagioli asserts that there are no strict dividing lines between these areas, but that all are permeable (1965/1975, pp. 17–18).

CHAPTER 9
The spiritual connection

Within the realms of spiritual, religious and philosophical writings, intuition makes some deeply significant appearances. In this terrain, however, we have to take a step away from scientific psychology, leave logic and reason in a side alley and explore the highest and deepest of human experiences. Intuition is here regarded not as a haphazard occurrence that may or may not bring with it a flash of inspiration that could lead to some productive invention, rather it is seen as the prime, the ultimate, the very highest form of knowledge. The intellect is now not only secondary; it may even be viewed as an obstruction to the route towards attainment of enlightenment.

To begin with, let us have a look at three Western philosophers who present theories of ultimates. It is intriguing to see how some of their ideas reappear in contemporary transpersonal psychologies, underlying some of the central precepts.

The 'Classical Intuitionists'

This phrase was coined by the psychologist Malcolm R. Westcott (1968) to describe the philosophers who laid emphasis on the concept of intuition as the way to acquire special knowledge. He selects just three philosophers, the first of whom is Benedict (Baruch) Spinoza (1632–77), Dutch by birth, whose Jewish father and grandfather had fled to Holland at the end of the sixteenth century to escape religious persecution. The form that Spinoza was pursuing was that of absolute truth. The second philosopher selected by Westcott is Henri Louis Bergson (1859–1941), influential French thinker, who offered the concept of prime reality. The third is Benedetto Croce (1866–1952), Italian philosopher renowned for his aesthetics and his investigation of ultimate beauty, central to which is his view of intuition.

It strikes me as strange that Spinoza should currently be regarded as one of the outstanding rationalists of the seventeenth century, and yet he himself considered that intuition, not logic, was the highest form of knowledge, and, moreover, the most satisfying method of attaining truth. Is this just another example of how intuition has been marginalized by certain commentators, especially during the predominantly scientific and technological age of the twentieth century? By contrast, Romantic writers, beginning with Goethe and later Shelley and Coleridge, saw Spinoza as a mystical pantheist, whose great work, the *Ethics*, was based on a metaphysical system in which there is only a single substance, God or Nature, which is the cause of itself and exists of necessity. Knowledge of this substance is perceived intuitively, with absolute certainty and complete satisfaction.

In his *Treatise on God and Man and his Well-being* Spinoza illustrates various mental processes mathematically with the calculation of a sum in proportion. One person would simply reproduce what he had been taught; another would test his calculations, but could not be sure that these would serve as a rule for all; the third would use pure reason; but the fourth 'having the clearest knowledge of all, has no need of hearsay or experience or the art of reasoning, because, by his penetration, he sees the proportion in his calculations immediately' (in Wild, 1938, pp. 19–20). This, then, is instant insight as to the solution. A later example emphasizes that it is not the finding of the number that is intuitive, but the sense of proportion within the group, of how the numbers relate to each other. Moreover, this is accompanied by a feeling of 'adequacy'. 'Clear knowledge' he asserts, comes 'not from our being convinced by reasons, but from our feeling and enjoying the thing itself, and it surpasses the other by far.' Intuition, then, has a satisfactory feeling of rightness about it, which is based on the perception of harmonious relationships.

A later work, *On the Improvement of Understanding*, delves deeper into the process, which 'alone comprehends the adequate essence of the thing, and, that without danger of error'. Intuition, then, can perceive the very core, the very nature or soul of a thing, which gives direct understanding. This does not stand in isolation, though, but is recognized as the meaning of the particular in relation to the whole, which he describes as 'God' or 'Nature'. He explains in his *Ethics*: 'The more we understand individual things, the more we understand God.' He perceives one element as being common to the nature of all things: 'Now this kind of knowledge proceeds from an adequate idea of the primal essence of certain attributes of God to the adequate knowledge of the essence of things' (Spinoza in Wild, 1938, p. 25).

Although his ideas are set out with the utmost objectivity, nevertheless there is a sense that Spinoza was writing from direct experience of the use of his own intuition, which involved a complete identification with the thing observed. Thereby the nature of the object is spontaneously revealed. Through the unification with the very essence of the object concerned, one is also unified with God. This experience of intuitional illumination is described in the fifth book of the *Ethics*: 'this kind of knowledge does not result from something else, but from a direct revelation of the object itself to the understanding. And if that object is glorious or good, then the soul becomes necessarily united with it ... Hence it follows incontrovertibly that it is this knowledge which evokes love. So that when we get to know God after this manner, then ... we must necessarily become united with him. And only in this union ... does our blessedness consist.' (ibid., pp. 29–30.) Here can be sensed the ecstasy of the mystical union with the whole of nature.

Spinoza was by no means the first writer to link intuition with mysticism. During the previous century, Jakob Boehme, a shoemaker and German Protestant, wrote of the 'divine intuition'. Having himself received little formal education, he seems to have arrived at his own wisdom quite intuitively. In this he acknowledges the intercession of the Holy Spirit: 'By my own powers I am as blind as the next man and can do nothing, but through the Spirit of God, my own inborn spirit pierces all things ... When the Spirit of Divine Love passes through my spirit then the animal creature and the divinity form but one single being, one single conception, and one single light' (Boehme/Berdyaev, 1958, p. vii.) Here also we have the idea of unification with God and of penetrating insight seeing to the very essence of things.

I find it fascinating that there is an intuitive sense of an element that is common to all things, an impression that finds resonance in modern quantum physics. Einstein spent many years trying to discover this miniscule subatomic unit, and since then physicists have come up with a number of ideas, including string theory, whereby the essence of absolutely everything in the universe can be conceived of as oscillating curled strings of energy. While this theory remains speculative, current physics has banished our traditional concepts of solid objects and of space and time. Rather than three spatial dimensions, there may in fact be as many as eleven, with humans living in one 'membrane' and parallel ones nearby. As long ago as 1975, the physicist Fritjof Capra stated that 'the universe is ... experienced as a dynamic, inseparable whole which always includes the observer in an essential way'. Within this framework the idea of cause and effect has lost all meaning. He makes a direct comparison between contemporary physics and the experiences of Eastern mystics and concludes that each is taking a separate but complementary route to the same knowledge concerning the nature of the universe (1975, p. 81).

Spinoza's psychology is remarkable, with direct parallels in contemporary humanistic and transpersonal approaches. He considered that most everyday moral condemnation was based on ignorance of human passions and actions. By gaining understanding of these, a person could become free. If knowledge of a high order could be arrived at, then the emotions and desires from which a person suffers become transformed into an enduring interest in eternal truths. Most of Spinoza's writing could not be published during his lifetime, as it was considered to be so heretical.

Let us now turn to Henri Bergson and his notion of prime reality. Bergson considered that it was due to the neglect of intuition that so many contradictory theories had been put forward. He perceived prime reality as movement, as change. During the course of change, life has appeared, and eventually intellect, which developed out of survival needs. Intellect has provided choice, and to assist this, humans have classified everything, thus giving all objects permanence. In doing this, however, reality has become altered from a perpetual happening, or 'duration', to a 'patterned immobility'. Life and movement, in which all elements are interconnected, are in reality so complex that the intellect is incapable of comprehending them. Only through intuition can their meaning be grasped, which in turn releases one from the contradictions provided by the intellect.

How does one go about this? By freeing oneself from reasoning powers and sinking back, one can engage totally with the flow of current happenings within the personality. It is then that pure duration can be intuitively experienced. Bergson describes how the summoning of images can assist with this process. Each must be given equal attention, which in turn produces a tension, and then consciousness adopts a particular disposition, revealing itself to itself as it really is, without any veil. It is through this attitude that the intuition spontaneously arrives. He explains later in *Creative Evolution* that 'in order that our consciousness shall coincide with something of its principle, it must detach itself from the *already-made* and attach itself to the *being-made*' (1913/1954, p. 250). Thus, one has an intuition of the perpetual happening which is prime reality.

Sadly, however, intuition never lasts more than a few moments, so that one must then depend again on reason to push the ideas forward, until the next revelation. 'It is a lamp almost extinguished ... but it glimmers wherever a vital interest is at stake. On our personality, on our liberty, on the place we occupy in the whole of nature, on our origin and perhaps also on our destiny, it throws a light feeble and vacillating, but which none the less pierces the darkness of the night in which the intellect leaves us.' (1913/1954 p. 282.) Intuition thus casts light on the nature of our selves and how we relate to the entire world. We can only move from intuition to the intellect, never the other way round.

To the philosopher, says Bergson, intuition is indispensable, because it is in this manner that the phenomenon can be perceived as 'mind itself, and, in a certain sense, life itself' (1913/1954, p. 282). He then offers the image of the intellect being 'cut out of it by a process resembling that which has generated matter'. It is thus that the unity of the spiritual life is revealed. The mystical divinity of intuition is here implied. He then criticizes religious doctrines for suspending spirituality high above the earth, apparently beyond attack. In doing this, the connection with the body, of spirit within, is lost. Consciousness he likens to a great wave, which arises replete with innumerable potentialities. It flows onwards as the river of life, through the body of humanity, each tiny rill a new soul being created. This image brings home to us Bergson's fundamental principle of life as movement and change.

Bergson also has much to say on intuition and artistic creation. Once again we have the concept of the artist melding into the object 'by a kind of *sympathy*, in breaking down, by an effort of intuition, the barrier that space puts between him and his model' (1913/1954, p. 186). He or she momentarily enters into the object observed, becoming one with it, in order to gain a deep understanding as to its nature. Only then can its essence be expressed.

Benedetto Croce in his *Aesthetic* (1901/1953) is in agreement with Bergson, in that intuition is the prime route to knowledge, with logic dependent upon it. As Wild explains (1938), intuition in this context presupposes mental activity, a spontaneous process whereby a selection is made among impressions to form a whole or unity, which becomes clear to the mind and can then be expressed in terms of sound, colour, shape and so on. In order to produce a creation, however, the will has to be engaged. The synthesis that draws together the elements to produce a unity Croce regards as 'spiritual' and this is also synonymous with beauty. It is not that beauty is the characteristic of any one intuition, but rather of all. Beauty is form and it is the form that is intuited. Croce also writes of the deep satisfaction that intuition can bring in the 'divine joy of creation'.

Each of these philosophers regards intuition as the highest form of knowledge, with logic a second best. Intuition is spiritual, divine, of the soul, whereas logic is the down-to-earth product of human thought processes.

Parallels with humanistic psychology

The encountering of ultimates, as described by these three philosophers, is not within the realm of everyday human experience, and its onward communication may present considerable difficulties. At the same time, such an experience is declared to be sufficient unto itself, and, as Spinoza suggests, can lead to a spiritual orientation.

Psychologist Abraham Maslow, in studying fully functioning individuals, has shown that 'peak experiences' as he terms them are indeed intrinsically meaningful to the people concerned: 'experiences which are so precious in themselves as to prove that not everything is a means to some end other than itself' (1970/1976, p. 75). Moreover they are phenomena associated with psychological health and do appear to be available to anyone open to them. Since these experiences are subjective, it is impossible to assess to what extent those that Maslow describes match the 'ultimates' discussed by the philosophers. However, some of them clearly do lead to the attainment of knowledge which is deeply significant to the individual and may be life-enhancing or even transformative: 'if it were never to happen again, the power of the experience could permanently affect the attitude toward life' (1970/1976, p. 75).

In assessing the nature of such revelations, Maslow concludes that they involve a 'shift in attention' and in the 'organization of perception' (p. 77). There is therefore a move away from the level of consciousness normally employed by the person into a different state, and it is this that results in the intuitive knowledge. For example, intense fascination with someone or something involves a concentration and focusing of the awareness, to the exclusion of disturbances, tiredness or boredom. Alternatively, the attention may be widened and all-embracing to the point that everything is seen as a meaningful whole. In Gestalt terminology this might involve a change in the figure-ground relationship, of perceiving patterns within apparent chaos or of creating an entirely new Gestalt (Köhler, 1929). Maslow terms this state 'Being-cognition',[1] shortened to 'B-cognition', in which the world is seen as purely good, beautiful and worthwhile. He asserts that it is possible to describe perception during peak-experiences in terms of Being-values, which are recognized as ultimates, as ideals and far goals. It is notable that beauty and truth, along with a number of other characteristics, feature in his list of the attributes of reality as perceived during peak-experiences.

The concept of 'Being-values' can also be helpful to a psychotherapist in terms of perceiving not just the pathology, but the highest and best in the client. In other words there may be a perception of potential, leading to a facilitation of the reappearance of submerged attributes and hence to a more rewarding life. Moreover, clients often report being in a state of confusion. The counsellor may therefore have to help the individual make sense of the inner chaos. This may involve the perception of patterns as the life story unfolds and the offering of such observations to the person. Maslow's ideas were the inspiration behind 'Third Force' or humanistic psychotherapy,[2] which emphasizes the realization of potential.

There is further agreement between Maslow and the Classical Intuitionists in their observation that communication of these special experiences can indeed be problematic. In his attempt to elicit information of the ineffable during interviews, Maslow had to adjust his procedures to incorporate what he describes as 'rhapsodic, isomorphic communications' (1970/1976, pp. 84–90). Analytic, rational and linear approaches had to be abandoned in favour of poetic, metaphorical, primary-process language and the incorporation of nonverbal messages deduced from gestures, facial expressions, tone of voice, body posture and so on. If he adopted a brotherly I–thou attitude, rather than that of a cool, detached investigator, subjects were far more likely to reveal the detail of their experiences. It is interesting that he recommends this particular approach by psychotherapists during sessions, rather than the dispassionate observation of classical psychoanalysis, which he considers to be unsuitable for exploring the peak terrain. It is well worth asking ourselves, as therapists, how much our general approach invites or inhibits communication of unusual experiences.

All three philosophers discussed by Westcott place intuition as independent of, indeed opposed to, intellect, maintaining that truth reached by intuition can never be reached by reason. Equally, reason cannot refute or even fully describe or explain the truth acquired by intuition. Maslow, however, emphasizes the need for independent, external validation of intuitive knowledge. He quotes the example of falling in love which leads to greater attention and care, but may also prompt exaggerated statements such as 'my husband is a genius' (p. 77). Psychiatrist Roberto Assagioli agrees with this, underlining the importance of employing 'careful scrutiny' to verify intuitive information (1974/1984, p. 156). Indeed where the building of hypotheses or the making of clinical judgements are concerned it would be irresponsible not to check out the usefulness and relevance of any such notions. Ways in which psychotherapists go about this form a topic in the next chapter.

Transpersonal psychotherapy

There can be no doubting the impact that out-of-the-ordinary experiences can have on people, whether they be intuitive apprehensions of the connectedness of the whole of life, a revelatory feeling of contacting the divine, seeing to the very essence of a thing, or simply of having a sudden insight as to the solution to a problem. Yet the model on which psychotherapy has traditionally been based is the medical one, in which there is no place for the mystical, spiritual or intuitive. The 'patient' is seen as 'sick', as having something wrong with him or her that needs to be fixed, and the analyst or therapist is thought to be the expert who knows how to do this. Thus a whole area of vitally important human experience, that might in itself be both transformative and healing, tends to be left out of the equation. Worse, sublime experiences may be pathologized, unwittingly defended against, and not allowed into consciousness.

The growth of transpersonal psychotherapy, however, sometimes labelled the 'fourth force', has helped to redress the balance. As the word 'transpersonal' implies, the sense of identity is seen as extending beyond the personal self into the realm of spiritual experiences. This in no way disallows the personal; rather the transcendent may be expressed through the personal. Individual concerns may, however, be seen within a wider context, that of the whole of the cosmos as interconnected, in which each person plays a part. From this follows an intuitive sense of life as sacred, and that the world needs to be cared for, rather than defiled or despoiled. Higher states of consciousness may be encouraged, in particular through the use of meditation and contemplation, and qualities such as beauty, truth and love are sought.

Despite advances in quantum physics, which challenge many long-held scientific assumptions about the nature of the cosmos, the main paradigm under which we live in the Western world is that the universe happened by chance and that there is no particular point to its existence. A person who holds such a belief will respond very differently to the self and the environment than someone who sees the universe as purposeful, alive and evolving. Equally, the prevailing assumptions about the nature of humans are that they are separate bodies and that consciousness resides solely in individual brains. Moreover, consciousness is purely a human faculty, which gives people the right to exert dominance and control over the rest of the natural world, to fulfil materialistic desires. Death of the body brings individual consciousness to an end. Spiritual psychologies, however, maintain that a person is more than the body, and include the concept of soul or essence, or higher Self, which is vitally connected to the source of all life. It therefore has continuity beyond the body. As for the brain, this is not the seat of consciousness, but rather an instrument of it, acting like a kind of transmitter. The medical model considers the emotions to be dependent upon electrical and chemical shifts, which can be altered with drugs, whereas the transpersonal therapies view them as energy sources which can be used for spiritual growth. Additionally, they are considered to be not exclusively confined to the body, but able to have a direct effect on others. Despite the fact that scientific advances become quickly out of date and are superseded by yet newer technologies, there is a general belief in the West that one day we will know everything. Transpersonal approaches, in contrast, recommend humility. While not denying the usefulness of the intellect, the task here is to help those on the spiritual path to cultivate their intuition so that absolute, eternal truths can be known directly. Therapists can only assist with this process insofar as they themselves have progressed along that way.

It can be appreciated, from this brief résumé, that there are fundamental differences in attitude between those who adhere to the prevailing scientific viewpoint and those who incorporate spiritual values into their practice. The important thing, however, as Charles Tart (1975/2000) emphasizes, is to be aware of our own perspective by challenging assumptions, so that they do not remain implicit. Clearly, our outlook as therapists will radically affect our work with clients. To be blunt, a soulless approach is likely to produce a soulless result. At the same time it is appropriate to be respectful of any particular client's world view.

I became especially conscious of this recently, when a stressed executive came to see me, a highly intelligent and thoughtful person, indeed the ultimate rational man. Nevertheless, he had suffered a serious breakdown and had been off work for several months. His quiet reserve, difficulty in meeting my gaze and flat tone of voice told me that his emotions had been packed away for a very long time. What he wanted was to be able to function again and return to work as soon as possible. Would I help him to create strategies so that he could better cope with the demands? While this was how we could safely make a start, I had at the same time a strong image of his true self, his soul, struggling to be expressed. When the time was right, we were able to explore his longing to be close to nature, and he began to experience himself as much more than an intellectual machine, capable of producing high-level reports.

If we are to take intuition seriously within the therapeutic context, then we need to have more than just a kitbag full of useful techniques. While everyday intuitions to do with the comprehension of nonverbal communications are crucial, there is also the higher, or deeper, realm of transpersonal experiences. To understand the different varieties of intuition better, John Rowan has provided a useful hierarchy consisting of six different levels (1993b, pp. 14–17), each of which involves another notion of the self. The first is the 'child self', when intuitions of occurrences in the environment may be very rich, but expressed not in words (since this is a pre-logical time) rather in play or drawings. Creative people may deliberately return to this stage. The second is termed the 'magical self', which denotes a trance-like state emanating from a close identification with a group. It is the *participation mystique*, which has been discussed earlier in the book. The next stage is the 'role-playing self', in which intuition is mainly adopted at the service of society. It is seen as a technique that can be learned, a skill that may produce practical and original things, useful inventions and discoveries. After that comes the 'autonomous self' in which the person is beginning to tune in to the spiritual aspects of intuition in a fresh and original way. Here there is much greater dependence upon imagery and symbols rather than words. The fifth level is the 'surrendered self', in which it is realized that intuitions arrive from a source other than the personality. There is therefore an opening up and receptivity to this wellspring, which may be conceptualized as a Muse or Archetype, or Wise Being offering guidance. At the highest level there is a complete identification with the intuitive source, a state of illumination and transcendence, which is accompanied by bliss and ecstasy, as described by the mystics. Now there are no longer any difficulties.

Therapists who wish to work transpersonally need to understand, and hopefully experience, the different types of intuition, even though many, especially the highest degree, can never be deliberately induced. This is asking a great deal of individuals, since it is has to do with the very essence of oneself. It also involves the willingness to submit to the discipline of spiritual practice and to be open to whatever it has to offer. Trust and fearlessness may be needed along the way, and much encouragement from other guides. At the same time, personal rewards can be substantial and great opportunities present themselves for rich work with clients.

Such an approach is encountered not only in transpersonal therapies, but also in, for example, person-centred therapy. Brian Thorne (2002a) writes, from a Christian perspective, about the commitment to living out of the three core conditions as 'practical mysticism' (p. 84). This involves ongoing self-exploration and self-awareness (congruence), the acceptance of other people without judgement (unconditional positive regard), and the ability to understand others' experiences from their point of view (empathy). Dedication of this kind can lead to the release of 'divine energies', an aliveness in the presence of the other and a perception of intrinsic truth and beauty, which he describes as more profound than being in love, but full of the same 'delight and vibrancy'. Such a description points to heightened awareness and perhaps even a super-normal state of consciousness.

This reflects mystical aspects of person-centred work described by Carl Rogers. He writes with great sensitivity about how his inner spirit may sometimes reach out and touch the inner spirit of the other. Then the therapeutic relationship 'transcends itself and becomes a part of something larger' (1980/1995, p. 129). This occurs when he is closest to his 'inner, intuitive self' and perhaps in a slightly altered state of consciousness. It is in such moments that whatever he does 'seems to be full of healing' and that simply his presence is 'releasing and helpful to the other'. Such a state can never be forced, but may spontaneously arise when feeling relaxed and close to his transcendental core.

The benefits of meditation

With science providing so many solutions to our problems, it has become customary in the West to rely on external observation and experimentation.

It is almost as if we have forgotten about the wisdom within. Our usual waking state is accepted as the norm, and there is considerable suspicion of any heightened or altered state of consciousness. Yet the ancient psychologies of the East accept that it is through the transformation of ordinary consciousness to a state of enlightenment, whereby human suffering, in the form of fear, neediness, greed, pride and so on, spontaneously drops away. Such a state is arrived at through meditation. Moreover, aspects of the higher state begin to enter the normal realm of consciousness, so that the adherent begins to perceive life from a different perspective.

My first experience of meditation happened not as the result of any attempt to achieve enlightenment, but rather to offer my body the best chance of healing itself. I was at the Cancer Help Centre in Bristol, fearful for my life and willing to try anything that might assist in overcoming such a menacing illness. Group meditation was part of the programme and we were invited to allow our thoughts to float away and focus simply on our breathing. Not only was I able to achieve deep relaxation, but when I opened my eyes after just half an hour, I was stunned by how dazzlingly beautiful the room appeared. The large houseplant opposite was no longer a static object; I could 'see' the energy with which it climbed and twisted itself around its supporting pole. The carpet, which I had assumed to be beige, was now filled with innumerable tiny blobs of colour. Paintings seemed filled with movement and meaning, while shafts of sunlight shining through the window gave an extra intensity to the shapes of furniture. Clearly, I was in a heightened state of awareness. Indeed, the physiological changes that accompany meditation are well documented. The brainwaves lengthen from beta rhythms (mental activity at 13–26 Hz) to alpha (relaxed state, 8–13 Hz) and then theta (hypnogogic reverie, 4–8 Hz). Meanwhile, serotonin is released into the bloodstream, giving a feeling of well-being (Green and Green, 1977).

Meditating on a client, or praying for him or her, either between sessions or just prior to one, can similarly enhance perception and deepen intuitive understanding of the case. One becomes more sensitive to moods, atmospheres and nonverbal communications of all kinds. At a superconscious level, apprehension of the person's destiny, his or her potential and life's purpose may be revealed.

Psychosynthesis recommends two forms of meditation: reflective and receptive. The first involves focusing the mind on a particular quality, such as love, beauty or courage, especially something that you wish to bring into your own life, for fifteen minutes or so. All the associations, the people who exude the quality, personal experiences of it and so on are reflected upon. If the mind wanders, it is gently brought back to the subject. Piero Ferrucci proposes that just at the point when you become bored, feel that the subject is exhausted and want to give up, you must continue, because it is then that lucidity is experienced and insight is most likely to occur (1982/1995, p. 96). The more that one concentrates on a subject, the more one can rely on unconscious processing to bring that quality into everyday life in a meaningful way. The technique can of course be offered to clients, especially when they feel that their life is lacking in something important. Inspirational phrases can be used in the same way. Not only can personal attributes be enhanced, but this form of meditation may also allow the opening to superconscious energies and direct intuitions.

The second type of meditation proposed by psychosynthesis, being receptive in nature, may follow on from reflection. The person lets go of the focus of attention and allows the mind to be free. In a state of quiet attention, one waits for whatever will enter. Ferrucci describes how this silencing of the mind is crucial for the awakening of intuition (1982/1995, p. 233), which may appear in the form of an image to which significant meaning is attached. The intuition may be of an everyday kind, providing information about someone from one's private life, or about a client, or the solution to some problem, or it may be from the superconscious, concerning some universal law, the interconnectedness of all things, feeling at one with everything. This latter kind is often accompanied by a sense of awe or wonder.

I had just such an experience only a few weeks ago. The evening had been an exciting one, and I felt too revved up to fall asleep easily, so I imagined myself in a quiet, green meadow and reflected on the word 'consciousness'. I then emptied my mind and drifted off into a semi-slumber. Unexpectedly I had a kind of vision of the flowers and leaves in the meadow turning to face the sun, and afterwards of petals closing as the light faded. It was then that I had the sudden realization that all of life is 'conscious', in the sense that everything is responsive to whatever the environment provides. I could then 'see' how this connects every living thing on earth and that we, as humans, are just one element in the chain of being. There was a deep satisfaction in feeling so intimately a part of nature.

There are, of course, many varieties of meditation from different spiritual traditions. Another form of potential benefit to the therapist is 'mindfulness', during which the practitioner becomes totally aware of everything that happens, moment by moment, both within the body, feelings and the mind, and also outside the self. This is raw perception, without interpretation and with the letting-go of pre-conceptions or any habitual ways of responding and thinking. This can lead to meaningful insights. There are some similarities with the Gestalt approach, in that the focus is on the immediate present, with the aim of comprehending the client experientially. Indeed, Zen Buddhism was a fruitful influence when

Gestalt theory was being compiled. Fritz Perls (1973/1976) writes about the 'relational awareness' of everything that occurs within the entire field of the clinical situation. The therapist needs to be attentive to his or her own reactions, needs, thoughts and feelings, as well as responsive to the patient's communications, plus sensitive to the whole environment and all that happens in the space in between (see also Chapter 12).

According to Richard Schuster, who studied Buddhist meditation in India, the regular practice of mindfulness not only improves ability to empathize, but also the depth of concentration is positively related to openness to experience (1979, p. 74). Through the daily practice of mindfulness, one becomes accustomed to giving bare attention to each successive moment, without the intrusion of the analytic mind and conditioned thought. It is pure recognition of what is. This process, in the words of Schuster, aids 'therapists to grasp intuitively their clients' communications and experiences with greater ease, clarity and fluidity' (p. 76).

Jung had been deeply influenced by Eastern mysticism. Through the practice of Yoga, energy (libido) is withdrawn from all affective ties to the object. This results in the process of *tapas* (introversion), or meditation without content, until the self is fused with the essence of the object and *atman* is attained. Of particular interest is the psychological description that Jung gives to the process of Yoga:

> Yoga introverts the relations to the object. Deprived of energic value, they sink into the unconscious, where, as we have shown, they enter into new relations with other unconscious contents, and then reassociate themselves with the object in new form after the completion of the tapas exercise. (CW 6, para. 191)

This procedure is none other than that of intuition, whereby thoughts and images reassemble themselves in the unconscious making new connections, with the possibility of offering insight, understanding and novel ideas to the conscious mind.

Psychiatrist Roberto Assagioli gives explicit instructions for the technique of the use of intuition within psychotherapy (1965/1975, p. 219), which, particularly as regards the introspection and withdrawal of emotional attachments, show a marked resemblance to Jung's description of the practice of Yoga quoted above:

> Constantly sensations from the outer world or from the body intrude into the field of consciousness, and makes either the entrance or recognition of intuitions impossible or difficult. Therefore, it is necessary to carry out what we might call a psychological cleansing of the field of consciousness ...

The second stage is that of 'relaxation and quiet waiting', which is 'not purely passive', until the subject contacts and even identifies with the sought-after experience of reality or truth, equivalent to the state of atman. During this process the will stands on guard until the intuitions enter the field of consciousness.

Within the context of transactional analysis, Eric Berne recommends that the therapist should approach the session 'like an innocent new-born babe' and with an 'unencumbered mind', which is clear of any prior preparation and of all he knows about the patient, free of all his personal problems, and of everything he has learned about psychotherapy. It is upon this *tabula rasa* that the impressions are made and noted. (1966, p. 62.) Here again, the value of an open mind, cleansed of extraneous distractions, is emphasized.

There are many parallels in these descriptions and the evidence suggests that therapists can considerably enhance perception and moment-by-moment interactions with clients through the regular practice of meditation. A quotation from the writings of the sixteenth-century mystic, Jakob Boehme, seems apt at this point: 'When thou standest still from the thinking of self, and the willing of self; ... and when thy soul is winged up and above that which is temporal, ... then the Eternal Hearing, Seeing and Speaking will be revealed in thee, ... and so God appeareth in thee, and whispereth to thy spirit' (Boehme in Wild, 1938, p. 98).

Divine homesickness

Most psychotherapies direct attention to the content of personality, feelings of poor self-worth, to strong negative emotions, neuroses, and the damaging experiences of childhood, much of which can help the person to live a more fulfilling life. However, an existential crisis may be encountered in which the great questions are asked about what life is for, and what meaning there can be to it. Despite progress on the personality level, there is still a longing for something more. This is sometimes referred to as 'divine homesickness'. The transpersonal therapies see the existential crisis as a call to spiritual awakening. Just when the world appears to be at its most grey or empty, a peak experience may suddenly occur, a moment of inspiration or illumination when all is transformed and the way forward suddenly becomes clear.

A colleague described just such a moment. Her life had completely fallen apart after the recent death of both parents, the break-up of her marriage and a crisis in relation to her new baby's father. She felt totally trapped, was fearful of the future and could see no way out of her situation. Friends in a remote part of Wales were caring for her. One day she was driving along a nearby country lane, the gloomy, overcast sky reflecting her mood, when suddenly a shaft of sunlight emerged from behind a cloud. It illuminated a rusty old tin shed at the side of the road, trans-forming it into a shimmering, golden refuge. She gasped in wonder, was completely transfixed and had to stop the car. At that same instant the thought crossed her mind, 'I don't have to go back', and she experienced an intense sense of relief, of a burden being lifted. The illumination that had occurred within the depths of her psyche was the realization that she was free to choose, that she could build a new life for herself here in Wales and heal her relationships with significant people at a distance. She subsequently rented a cottage in the village and embarked on a whole new way of living and being. Each time she passed the tin shed, she was reminded of that crucial transformational moment, when her soul was touched.

James Hillman, a Jungian analyst and founder of archetypal psycholo-gy, has made it his mission to 're-vision' psychotherapy from the perspective of soul (1975). After all, the very word 'psychology' comes from two Greek words, *psyche* and *logos*, translated as study of the soul, while 'psychotherapy' denotes servant or attendant of the soul, and 'psy-chopathology' suffering of the soul. As academic psychologist David Elkins points out, Western psychology cut itself off from these ancient roots and allied itself to the physical sciences (1995, pp. 78–9). He believes that psychology is both art and science and that reintroducing soul in its original humanistic meaning, will bring back the depth and pas-sion for life that has been sadly missing in our mechanistic age. Elkins continues: 'The soul reminds us that there is ... a world far deeper and more primordial than our logical processes. Soul is the door to this ancient imaginal world; she ... is mythic and poetic in the deepest sense of these terms. To know the soul, we must lay aside our rational ways of knowing and open ourselves to the world of reverence, feeling, and imag-ination ... ' (p. 83). He recommends that each of us seek to know the soul personally and experientially, because it is only from this depth that we can find some common understanding. The true knowing of oneself Hillman likens to a painting, a lyric poem; it is 'revelatory, nonlinear, dis-continuous' (1990, p. 59). Moreover, to see into the soul of another human, we need to work imaginatively, 'searching for images with images'. In order to perceive a person's essence, 'we must look into his imagination and see what fantasy is creating his reality'. Loss of meaning Hillman equates with loss of image in which archetypal significance resides. So the therapeutic task is to rediscover those images, not to inter-pret them, but allow them to give us whatever they bear (1990, p. 60).

Clients may sometimes spontaneously bring images in the form of pic-ture postcards or reproduction paintings, which carry some deep significance for them. It is almost as if words are inadequate to express whatever needs to be communicated. Striking images brought to me in this way have included a pale young man who is painting a portrait of himself, a bedraggled whore full of self-loathing, and a dovecote amid a peaceful rural scene. Rich and productive work has invariably followed such an offering. The young man was struggling with a crisis of identity, the whore turned out to be representative of the woman's 'victim' sub-personality, while the dovecote depicted a longing for peace and tranquillity and freedom from the daily grind of the office routine.

Similarly, a well-chosen poem or story can speak directly to a distressed client, and point towards a solution. From personal experience, I vividly recall an occasion during group process when the facilitator read out a poem by Rumi about a donkey cruelly laden down and whipped by its owner. I instantly recognized that I had been mistreating myself in just the same way, by working ludicrously long hours and whipping myself into action early each morning. Drawing the donkey, identifying its deep needs, allowing it to rest and play, and supplying it with a bell to call for help, proved to be deeply therapeutic. Through poetry and imagery, change was possible.

* * * *

As I finish this chapter, I am aware that I feel excited and energized by the subject. The reading and researching has been deeply involving and moving, and any fears or cynicism I may have had concerning the transpersonal domain have significantly diminished. Altered states of consciousness now become full of creative possibilities for intuitive apprehension, and negative associations have been placed in proportion. In addition to feelings of connectedness, I was left with a strong empathy with other writers who attempt to define the indefinable. It is as if my own spirit has been touched and it wants to reach out and explore further.

A quotation from David Elkins's paper perhaps offers a fitting conclusion to this chapter: 'The soul is ontologically thirsty; if this thirst is not met, life becomes barren and dry, and the soul begins to die.' What it needs is to be 'nurtured by love, goodness, truth, beauty, and passion' (1995, p. 91).

Notes

1. Maslow uses the term 'Being-cognition' to denote a transcendent state in which one experiences life at the level of pure being.
2. The first and second forces are psychoanalysis and behaviourism respectively, while the fourth refers to transpersonal psychology. Humanism moved away from the earlier tendency to emphasize pathology and studied, rather, psychological health.

CHAPTER 10

The therapists' diaries

For some time now I had been tracking my own professional work in terms of intuitive moments, noting in a diary format each time such an event occurred, what exactly it consisted of, and what had happened before and afterwards. While my researches into theoretical writings were by now very considerable, I needed to supply more empirical evidence collected from actual practice in order further to substantiate the claims made. The focus group had proved useful in forming a picture of the nature of intuition, as experienced by therapists, but many other questions had been left unanswered, in particular how exactly an intuition is employed in therapy. I also wanted to know, from others, what prompts an intuition, the form in which it appears, whether or not it is acted upon, what happens as a result, how it is validated and whether or not it has an effect on the progress of the therapy. As a result of this information, I was hopeful that other recommendations could be made for the profession in addition to those collated from the theoretical literature.

The diary format was selected as the basis of the design to give access to information concerning therapists' subjective experiences of intuition and also because independent monitoring of sessions was impossible due to issues of confidentiality. This type of design is recommended by Robson (1993) as suitable for situations where direct observation is impracticable. As with the focus group, participants were tested with the Myers-Briggs Type Indicator, to see if there was any connection between their personality type and their responses, and as a check for possible bias in terms of their favoured functions.

Data collection

Data were assembled from three main sources with the purpose of increasing internal validity. These were as follows:

(a) diary notes made by four psychotherapists over a period of one month during 1999, concerning moments of intuition within their clinical practice;

(b) diary notes assembled from the only suitable textual source: the clinical work of psychoanalyst Theodor Reik, whose cases are described in detail in *Listening with the Third Ear* (1948/1975);

(c) diary notes assembled from detailed case notes of my own clinical practice over a period of one year, September 1998–99.

In each case the notes were systematically made on a form (see Appendix C), either by the therapists concerned from group (a), or by myself as researcher to cover data from sources (b) and (c). The therapists contributed 10 forms as follows: C. 3, M. 5, N. 2 (see codes for names listed below). Reik's material constituted 24 forms and mine 19. A total of 53 diary forms was therefore collected, each representing one therapist intuition. The significance of the emphasis on sources (b) and (c), and the possibility of bias, will be discussed under 'The question of validity' (see below).

The participants

The selection of respondents was purposive, not random. This was in keeping with the aims of the study, to provide rich and detailed material (Strauss and Corbin, 1998). In the first instance seven experienced psychotherapists known to myself were invited, verbally in person or by telephone, to keep intuition diaries over a period of one month. Of these, three responded positively, but only two actually kept diaries (P. and N.). Two further therapists who had attended the focus group were also invited to participate, and both of these kept the diaries (C. and M.). In all, therefore, four of the nine took part in the research. This uptake was lower than expected, and it was difficult to establish reasons why therapists did not wish to participate. There was some resistance to recording information on a form, a process thought to be too demanding. However, those who used the form encountered no problems. With permission, one of the four therapists (P.) spoke onto a tape in preference to writing down his records and this tape was subsequently transcribed, but it was not possible to complete any forms from this material due to insufficient detail.

All four therapists nominated themselves as intuitive, although one (C.) was shown to favour sensing when tested with the MBTI. Each had practised for a minimum of five years and all belonged to recognized professional associations. Two were men and two were women. All worked in a private setting one-to-one and with couples. I coded myself as R. and Reik as K. Reik's type was deduced by examination of his writing style and content, as an introverted thinker supported by extraverted intuition.[1] His cases covered 35 years of psychoanalytic practice. Table 10.1 gives a summary of the participants, with initials used as a code for all names.

Table 10.1 Summary of participants: groups a, b and c

Therapist	Gender	Orientation	Years practised	MBTI type
C.	Male	Psychosynthesis/psychodynamic	8	ISTJ
M.	Female	Psychodynamic/humanistic	13	ENFJ
P.	Male	Gestalt	13	ENFP
N.	Female	Psychodynamic	6	INFP
R.	Female	Integrative	11	INTJ
K.	Male	Psychoanalytic	35	INTP

The four participants were sent a letter at the outset of the study, which gave instructions for keeping the diary (see Appendix D). No operational definition was provided; rather the emphasis was on each individual's own experience of intuition within the context of their professional practice. A request was made that intuitions should be recorded as soon as possible after their occurrence.

Design of the diary format

Initially, as researcher I ran a small pilot study to test out various types of format, by recording my own intuitions on to these, and the one chosen was shown to be the simplest and most inclusive design (see Appendix C). The aim was to assist respondents to incorporate information about all phases of their intuitions, with extra space for further comments and descriptions. It was also important to know approximately how often intuitions occurred, and whether they happened during, between or after sessions. In asking for the session number, indications might be forthcoming as to whether intuitions tend to occur early or late in therapy. Brief details of clients were requested in case any relationship could be found between the client and type and frequency of intuition experienced by the therapist.

Confidentiality

This presented a difficult problem and had to be carefully considered. Initials only were used for clients, plus indications of age, gender and ethnic origin, but no other information was obtained whereby they could be identified. M., in particular, was extremely concerned about confidentiality, as part of her practice involves a referring agency which specifically forbids use of client material for research purposes. Some of her diary forms therefore had to be excluded from the study. Other therapists considered that insufficient details were given about clients to enable identification and they were therefore less concerned. Moreover, they understood that the emphasis of the research was on the process within the therapist rather than the particular case of the client.

The advantage of including material from a published source (Reik's work), was that it was in the public domain and issues of confidentiality were therefore already cleared. Considerable detail of these cases is revealed as well as descriptions of the intuitive processes occurring within the analyst. They could therefore be transcribed onto the diary forms with ease.

Data analysis

As with the focus group study, it was important to allow the findings to emerge from the data, so the process of grounded theory was instigated, following the method originally proposed by Glaser and Strauss (1967) and subsequently Strauss and Corbin (1998).

After collecting together the 53 diary entries, each was coded with the initial of the participant (see above) and the page number, starting with '1' for each therapist, for example C.2, R.16 or K.23. If two intuitions occurred in the same session these were numbered M.1a, M.1b and so on. Thus, any entry could be quickly identified.

The material was then placed into seven categories, following the general format of the diary page, as follows:

1. The prompt.
2. The form of the intuition.
3. Therapist's response.
4. Application in the session.
5. Client's response.
6. Perceived outcome.
7. Validation.

Definitions were created for each category giving guidelines for the inclusion of units of meaning taken from the diary entries. It could then be seen that these units could be further grouped into sub-categories, and again definitions were drawn up. In each case units were assigned using the constant comparative method for inclusion or exclusion (Glaser and Strauss, 1967). Each sub-category was given a title which captured the essence of the rule for inclusion. The content of all categories was then reviewed and some alterations made until internal consistency was achieved. Initially some overlap was noted between the first two categories, but a distinction was made between cues noted by the therapist in the external environment (category 1), and the form the intuition took subjectively (category 2). In some cases it was found that units of meaning could be assigned to more than one category, so a decision was taken as to best fit.

The construction of models and diagrams was based on recommendations made by Ian Dey (1993).

During the process of analysis theoretical memos were made, which formed the foundation for the discussions below.

The findings

Whereas there is some debate in the literature of topics covering categories 1, 2 and 7 (the prompt, the form of the intuition and validation), there is no research to my knowledge which specifically explores what happens in a session as a result of a therapist's intuition. This therefore is original material. (For more complete information concerning the findings, see Fulcher, 2002.)

Category 1: The prompt

This category attempts to answer the question: What, in the external environment, prompts an intuition in the psychotherapist? In the focus group study, the picking up of clues or cues was listed as an essential feature of the intuitive process. A question remained, though, as to whether this was in effect sensory rather than intuitive in terms of Jung's psychological functions. It was thought that the intuition might include keen observation, but that that did not invalidate the intuition. There is support for this view from the diary data.

Of the five kinds of prompts that appear in the present study (see Figure 10.1) two of them, 'mismatch' and 'actions of client', are clearly the result of observation involving the sensation function. In the first, the therapist sees that the body language or degree of emotion displayed does not fit with the words spoken:

> An amiable grin – like a mask he couldn't take off – appeared at inappropriate times, when other people would have been sad or furious. (K.13)

In the second, what the client does appears to the therapist to speak louder than the words:

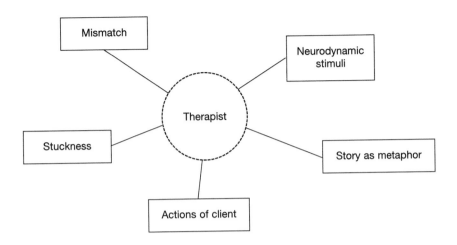

Figure 10.1 The prompt.

> She kept showing me all her files, plans, schedules, lists. Why? I'm aware that the content of these isn't the issue, but the process of showing me. (R.18)

Such observations help to initiate the intuitive process.

'Neurodynamic stimuli' are similar in character to the 'micros' researched by Haggard and Isaacs (1966) and reviewed in Chapter 6. These do not involve conscious observation, but are small signs taken in at a subliminal level. If they are not at variance with words spoken, then they are even more difficult to detect:

> I suddenly recognized that ... a profound fear must be at work ... certain expressive movements that we understand, without our conscious perception really being at work. (K.5)

Another type of cue noted is 'story as metaphor', in which the client's narration about other people appears to carry a message about the therapy or therapeutic relationship.

> The realization that she's using her son as a metaphor for herself, and subtly asking for encouragement (R.16)

The fifth type of prompt is 'stuckness' in which the client is unable to proceed with the therapy. Yet a new opportunity for creativity arises, because a different approach has to be taken:

> Going round and round something very familiar, then one time you come at it at a slightly different angle. (C.1)

Later discussion with the therapist suggested that the intuitive mode could be deliberately invoked by working with the stuckness itself. For example, the therapist may use meditation to conjure up a symbol for it. Equally, the client may be encouraged to produce an image and perhaps draw it and joint work will follow from that, giving information about what is obstructing the flow of the session.

None of the last three types of prompt necessarily involves conscious observation. It appears, therefore, that cues used for the intuitive process may or may not utilize the sensation function. Jung had allowed for some degree of sensory involvement in his definition of intuition, by distinguishing between the 'concrete' and 'abstract' forms, the first being linked with the actuality of things, and the second with ideas (CW 6, para. 771). Since he does not give any examples, it is difficult to detect his exact meaning. Nevertheless, the material in this present study would seem to fit with his theory. It indicates that subtle clues may give information about how things really are for the client, for instance if the individual's true feelings are 'leaked' through body language or actions, despite best efforts not to show them. Such examples could be called 'concrete' intuitions, or rather intuitions based on concrete observations. 'Story as metaphor' however, offers the therapist the idea that a covert meaning is being transmitted. In the example given above (R.16), the client describes how her son is nervous of learning to swim, but that his teacher encourages him and thereby boosts his confidence. The therapist has a 'sudden realization' that the client is really asking for encouragement for herself within the session. This could therefore be described as 'abstract intuition' in that there is a connection of ideas.

A feeling rather than an idea may be the therapist's reaction to the story. For example a client criticizes her family for not appreciating her and the therapist wrote, 'I felt she was angry with *me*.' Jung in his definition of intuition declares that this function may appear in the form of a feeling, but not that feeling may prompt an intuition. This seems to be an omission in his theory.

As mentioned in Chapter 6, Ferenczi (1955) looked for nonverbal messages when the client was unable to express him- or herself verbally, and considered that these mainly came from the 'inner child'. Of the two examples from the diary data under the sub-category of 'stuckness' neither concerned such messages, R.1 stating that information was forthcoming about the client's state of health, and C.1 that the couple concerned were no longer lovers. However, nonverbal messages from other subcategories are interpreted as coming from the inner child. To take as an example diary page R.2 (categorized under 'mismatch'), the reply to 'what prompted the intuition?' is:

He smiled while describing the manipulative and destructive behaviour of his ex-wife. His eyes also grew larger with an expression of innocence.

This produced 'a hunch that it had to do with a childhood experience'. There is a note under 'further comments' that several weeks later the client had a sudden memory of having been bullied by an older sister from age three years, whereupon the client agreed that the hunch was correct.

The picking up of clues has been allied to the process of detection in some of the psychological and psychoanalytic literature. In an essay of 1914 Freud wrote of the influence upon psychoanalysis of the work of art-connoisseur Giovanni Morelli in distinguishing fakes from originals through observation of minute details: 'It seems to me that his method of inquiry is closely related to the technique of psychoanalysis. It, too, is accustomed to divine secret and concealed things from unconsidered or unnoticed details, from the rubbish heap, as it were, of our observations.' Psychologist Guy Claxton (1997, p. 169) makes the point that this kind of detection comes into its own when the answer to a problem is not obvious. He continues: 'It requires "clues": pieces of information whose significance, or even presence, is not immediately apparent.' Moreover, 'the successful detective trains her awareness on the outside world, in order to find meaning in the minutiae of experience'. As is obvious from the diary pages, the clues that lead to intuitive knowledge are often extremely subtle and it is important to pay close attention to such details.

Category 2: The form of the intuition

Within this category are examples from the diary pages of another way in which the therapist may pay attention, and that is to the activities within him- or herself, the subjective process as the intuition takes shape and enters awareness. These are of 13 types and some may be combined (see Figure 10.2).

The sub-category with the most numerous entries (14) concerns the making of connections, also considered by the focus group members to be an essential aspect of the intuitive process. As was noted in the discussion of the group debate, support for this notion is found in Bastick's work. Further corroboration is gained from Claxton, who writes, 'this kind of detection requires a particular mental mode in which details can be dwelt upon, at first without knowing what their meaning may be, so that slow ripples of activation in the brain may uncover any significant connections there may be'. He emphasizes the importance of a rich background of knowledge and experience with which new associations can be made. He continues: 'Without this patient rumination, the clue, the problem and the

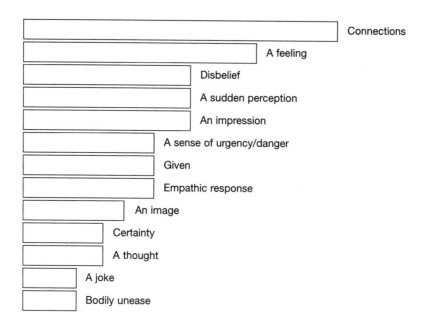

Figure 10.2 The form of the intuition.

database will not come into the fruitful conjunction that reveals the ways in which they are related' (1997, p. 169). Reik gives an example in which he made a connection between the bizarre behaviour of a patient and prior experience of other cases, which led him to understand that the strange rituals demonstrated a reversal of particular childhood experiences:

> Where, for instance, did I get the idea that the real text or content of his behavior could only be recognized by a reversal? Certainly not from remembering the reading of analytic books or attending lectures or seminars ... when I tried to find whence it came, I could only answer: from experience, that is, from memory-traces of phenomena I had observed before. (1948/1975, pp. 218–19)

The 'rumination' that Claxton refers to is called 'conjecture' by Reik. This author also makes the comparison with detective work: 'In this preliminary stage [of conjecturing] the analyst behaves like the detective, who ensures the preservation of every clue, follows it up, and makes use of it.' Logic is not employed, but rather 'the principle of poised attention', during which the analyst may pursue 'contradictory trains of thought', which in turn increase the opportunities for the making of new associations between the clues and knowledge already held within the memory (pp. 222–3). As the work with the patient progresses, so one can conjecture with increasing assurance.

An interest in the arts was discussed in Chapter 4 in relation to the ability to judge people. The diary pages produce four examples in which the process of the therapy was assisted by the making of connections between the case under consideration and characters from plays, operas or books. These are typical of the process of 'bisociation' described by Koestler (1964/1989). Light was thrown on one of Reik's cases through the recollection of a melody from the opera *Don Giovanni* (K. 12), in which he became aware of its hidden melancholy. The case in question concerned a man who felt impelled to seduce women who were tied to another man, after which he had no further desire to see them. Yet he was not quite the classic Don Juan character and there seemed to be no sense of triumph over another male. The melancholy tune prompted Reik to ask himself the question why his patient never thought of himself as a beloved man, which ultimately led to his understanding of the case. Examples such as these indicate that Taft was indeed correct in making the observation that an interest in the arts can assist in accurate judgement of people (1955).

Connections may also be made between the client's outside relationships and the one that is formed in the clinical setting or vice versa, as is evident from R.10, listed under sub-category 'disbelief'. Here the therapist 'knows' that her client cares very much about his wife's opinion of him, despite his protestations, because she makes connections with her own experience of this man during sessions:

> He said of his wife, 'I don't care what she thinks of me', but I immediately thought to myself, 'Yes, you do'. How did I know he did care what she thought? It might have been because I had noticed how sensitive he was to *my* opinion of him. (R.10)

Associations may involve picture-fragments, or the form of the intuition may appear as a clear single image without awareness of other connections. The symbol itself may lead to the next step in the session, as described on diary page R.17 regarding an image of impotent men:

> We looked at her relationships at work and considered that perhaps the men around her actually resented her competence and wanted to pull her down. She found this 'insightful and helpful'.

More examples of the use of imagery had been expected other than the four described on the diary pages. When discussing the lack of them with participants, it was suggested that when an image occurs, the experience is so striking that it is remembered by the person and perhaps takes on greater importance than it deserves.

Less clear are those fleeting 'impressions', which seem to be made up of a number of elements taken in at a subliminal level. At the time, the therapist cannot work out how he or she arrived at such an impression, although on later reflection it may be possible to recall some of the ingredients. Reik emphasizes the importance of trusting one's impressions as soon as they enter awareness (1948/1975, p. 151). One case, diary page K.7, involves a professional woman, who appears on the surface to be sincere and friendly, yet Reik is left with the distinct impression that her former analyst had lost patience with her. Later meetings with her confirmed that this first impression was made up of a number of small provocations. This insight became central to the work, which revolved around the subtle ways in which she made herself disliked. (See under category 4.)

The making of connections can also involve a sudden perception or, equally, the experience of immediacy may itself mark an intuition, and seems to be a well-recognized feature in the literature. Bastick (1982) lists it as property no. 1: 'quick, immediate, sudden appearance' and, as already mentioned, ascribes it to parallel processing, rather than to the slower method of linear, logical thinking. There are 22 references to the speed of intuitive processing on card 5 of the focus group and the eight that appear in the present study together increase the evidence in support of this theory.

The topic of humour occurs from time to time in the literature on intuition, and a sense of fun and ability to play were considered in Chapter 4 to be characteristics of the intuitive type. With just two entries in this study, it does seem that humour sometimes plays a role in clinical practice, in these cases to provide relief and to help the client to gain a new perspective or some objectivity over the problem. Koestler (1964/1989) writes at considerable length on the topic of laughter and varieties of humour in relation to creativity. His view is that the process depends primarily on its surprise effect, a 'bisociative shock', the result of the 'collision of incompatible matrices' (pp. 91–2). Here again can be seen the making of unusual or unexpected associations. Bastick describes this as 'recentring', or a change in the relationships between the elements of an 'emotional set'. The 'surprise' element Reik regards as an indicator to an analyst that he has touched on the most vital piece of knowledge for the understanding of a case: 'the most valuable of our art and craft have learned to appreciate the heuristic value of surprising ideas emerging from the unconscious, and gladly welcome them' (1948/1975, p. 247). This sense of surprise or shock, which the patient experiences when presented with something he has hidden away for a long time, can have a cathartic effect, often released in laughter. Reik devotes an entire chapter to psychoanalysis and wit, to which the reader is referred.

Jung does not mention the speed of processing in his definition, but he does include the impression that the contents of an intuition are 'given' rather than being derived from or produced by conscious thought. This aspect appears five times on the diary pages, indicating that therapists sometimes experience this quality in their work:

> I never made any conscious attempt to interpret the dream; it interpreted itself, so to speak. (K.1)

Here, the intuitive process appears not to be under personal control.

The monitoring of feelings in response to the client is well documented in the psychoanalytic literature. If the therapist is sure that the feeling does not concern his or her own material, but is an unconscious communication from the patient, then this can point to intuitive knowledge which may be useful in the session. Within integrative psychotherapy, this is generally referred to as 'reactive counter-transference' (Clarkson, 1995, p. 89), as described in Chapter 7. The 11 diary entries provide clear examples of this process, involving feelings within the therapist such as anxiety, irritation and embarrassment; two further entries illustrate how the reaction may be perceived in the body. Page R.3 describes how the therapist notes her feelings of self-consciousness when with this particular client, and of being 'unable to find a way in amid the volume of words'. She reflected them back in the form of a question. This led to useful work with the client's inner 'perfectionist' and hence to an understanding of why his relationship with his sons was always so strained: they had formed the habit of comparing themselves unfavourably with him. Subsequent interviews with participants revealed that all had received some training in this aspect of the intuitive process, although it was not referred to by that name but was usually categorized under 'counter-transference'.

There were only five entries under 'empathic response', which seems remarkable, bearing in mind the emphasis that a number of authors place on its central role in the intuitive process. Type may be causing selectivity, since C., R. and K. all prefer the thinking to the feeling function, being ISTJ, INTJ and INTP respectively. The participants may therefore not be representative of the profession as a whole, in which the preferred functions seem to be NF, at least among American counselling students (76%) (Myers and Myers, 1980/1993, p. 151). Members of the focus group placed the emphasis on 'being in tune' with the client and the examples from the diary pages are in agreement with that view. Sometimes this took the form of guidance as to timing of interventions and pacing of sessions. Hints concerning these aspects took the form of subtle movements of the eyes and head and other body-language signals. These are called 'regulators' by Ekman and Friesen (1969) and discussed in Chapter 6. Diary page R.8 asks, 'How do I know when to say something?' and refers to the client's 'narrowed eyes – she appeared to be thinking hard, so I stayed silent'. The page includes the comment that this kind of sensitivity helps to build a good working relationship.

The members of the focus group failed to produce instances from clinical practice of a sense of urgency or danger, but it is evident from the five accounts in this study that the impression can be a powerful one. As a result, the therapist is impelled to act upon it, in terms of making the client feel more secure, of extending usual boundaries by changing appointment times at short notice, or in taking care with personal safety. It is not always evident what causes this sense of urgency or danger, but it may be subtle stimuli such as 'something in her voice?' (M.1a) or a 'gut feeling' taking the form of bodily unease as in N.2:

> I had a physical sensation in my lower abdomen, which said 'Be terribly careful'. (N.2)

Category 3: Therapist's response

Participants were requested to state on the diary forms whether the intuition occurred during a session while with the client, or afterwards between sessions. Generally (43 times) it came into awareness in the presence of the client, but sometimes also appeared between sessions spontaneously or while reflecting upon the individual (10 times). This suggests that some intuitions require an incubation period for the making of connections, which concurs with Bastick's theory. However, intuitions may also occur on first meeting a client. The data also indicate what happens after the therapist is aware of an intuition, whether or not it is acted upon and in what manner. Responses are of three kinds (see Figure 10.3): a verbal communication, an action, or the withholding of the intuition.

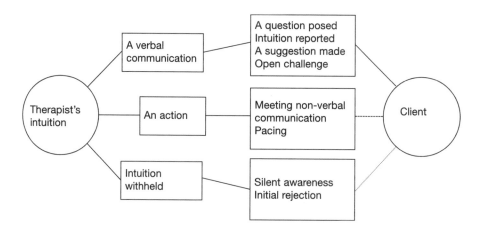

Figure 10.3 Therapist's response.

It is clear from the material assembled on the forms that an intuition is not necessarily acted upon immediately. It may be silently noted and held within the memory until there is an opportunity to use it, or it is maintained as another piece of information. Using the forms, an assessment was made concerning the timing of the therapist's response. On 20 occasions the intuition was not employed at the time it happened, but at a future date ranging from the next session to several months later. It was marginally more likely to be used immediately (25 times) or some time later in the same session (8 times).

No correlation could be found between the session number and the occurrence of an intuition. In other words, it might be experienced on first meeting a client or at any time during the work together.

In the judgement of the therapist, it may not be appropriate to express the intuition directly to the client, but it is used as additional information. M. responds in one instance by reflecting privately on what she might be missing of the client's needs. When more is known about the client, the intuition may be seen as just one piece of the puzzle to be used at a later time; it may also turn out to be an important link between other elements giving a new understanding:

> My initial feeling that the absence of grief at the father's death and the excessive mourning for the dog must have been connected subterraneously was correct. I had not spoken of my ideas to the patient and I had waited until her memories began to speak and my waiting was rewarded by sudden insight. (K.22)

If the therapist decides to employ the intuition, a judgement may be made to do this in an indirect way. Despite the impression given by the focus group members, this would seem to suggest that therapists exercise caution when acting upon an intuition in their work. Eleven entries indicate that a question is formed from the intuition. This has the dual purpose of eliciting further information from the client as a result of the intuition, and also of checking that the therapist is on the right lines. Quotations from R.5 illustrate this:

> He was talking about an ex-girlfriend ... Her need for security had been the problem ... It suddenly struck me that he was talking about himself – his own need for security. I asked him if this was so and he admitted he felt 'comfortable' at home (despite his unhappiness with his wife).

Rather than asking a question, a suggestion may be made which points towards a future direction of the work. This may be forthcoming at the time of the intuition or in a later session, when the client is judged to be more open to the suggestion and in a better position to respond to it positively. R.14 demonstrates this:

She declared that she wanted to be 'out there' doing it all – but I am not convinced. I'm not sure how I knew that she didn't really want to be out in the world 'doing it all'. It could have been the tone of voice which was high and whining ... I later suggested that we look at what gets in the way of her making progress with her working life.

Psychotherapists may also respond directly to what they perceive to be a nonverbal communication by acting upon it, although not reiterating it. The five cases reported in the diaries all have to do with meeting an unspoken need of the patient, either by creating a feeling of safety when self-destructive urges are sensed, by offering comfort of some kind, or by saying what the individual apparently wants to hear in an affirmative way.

Although client looked robust ... I used much of the session to work on creating a safe and stable setting. (C.3)

However, the intuition is quite often reported directly (10 entries), and occasionally may even result in an open challenge from the therapist (1 entry):

The second I saw her, I thought 'Too much responsibility'. It was a most extraordinary first session. I challenged her openly, not aggressively, but forthrightly. (N.2)

The giving of personal response may involve revealing counter-transference feelings, when the therapist is reasonably sure that this feedback will be useful to the client. Even so, apprehension may accompany this kind of reporting: 'I took the risk of saying that I felt deskilled' (R.17). Body language may be pointed out to the client, if the therapist judges this to be significant. P., as a Gestalt therapist, does this without offering any interpretation, eliciting meaning rather from the individual (tape transcription). Within a psychoanalytic context, there is more likely to be an interpretation which is discussed with the patient:

I ... received the impression that below her unemotional and detached surface there existed superstitious survivals of her religious upbringing ... The course of the analysis proved the accuracy of my at first vague impression that the abortion experience she mentioned so casually had been of paramount importance for the development of her neurosis. We learned that she was preoccupied by the unconscious idea that the abortion had been an act of murder for which she would be punished by God. (K.20)

If there is a 'mismatch' between body language, or tone of voice and content, then the words spoken will be perceived to be of secondary importance and the emphasis placed on the intuitive information, as in R.2:

> [I had a] sense that he was also telling me something else, on a deeper level, which was important ... I pointed the smile out to him. He had been unaware of it.

Such behaviour on the therapist's part contravenes the social conditioning of Western culture, since we learn not to make personal remarks based on intuitive information for fear of embarrassing the person. Therapists therefore have to endeavour to override such conditioning.

Category 4: Application in the session

The data under this category provide evidence of the impact that a therapist's intuition can have on the immediate session and also on the future course of the work. There may be a joint activity, the client may experience insight through the work that follows, or the next stage in therapy is instigated (see Figure 10.4). When the diary examples are looked at more closely, it can be seen that the intuition may be helpful to either the client or the therapist or both.

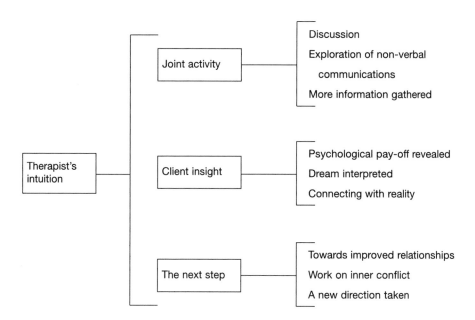

Figure 10.4 Application in the session.

If the work follows a new direction as a result of the intuition, this is generally instigated by the therapist and used as a guide concerning the next step to take. In R.10 the intuition resulted in an exploration of the individual's identity as a man.

> I didn't tell him this thought, but asked him for more descriptions of his wife. Only then did it emerge that she used to hit him and that she had violent parents. This initiated work with his identity: who is he as a man? (R.10)

An intuition may also point to some kind of inner tension or conflict, perhaps perceived as a result of a 'mismatch' as in R.15. The client had mentioned that she felt passionately about the environment, but the therapist 'knew' that she would do nothing about it because the voice was so lacking in energy. The work was therefore diverted into looking at what prevented her involvement in environmental issues:

> The following week she told me she'd felt quite angry with me [after I had reported my feelings of frustration] – but admitted that she also feels frustrated with herself. This led to some work looking at the inner conflict which prevents her from acting upon her convictions. (R.15)

The gathering of further information is of particular assistance to the therapist in deepening understanding of the case. In the quotation given below (K.6), the analyst realized that the student's deliberate and controlled manner of speaking was more important than his words. Exploration of this feature revealed much illuminating background information concerning the behaviour of his parents:

> We soon arrived at the insight that his low voice and dignified manner had developed as an expression of his opposition to the shrieking, high, excited voices of his parents, especially of his mother. (K.6)

Often the intuition provokes a discussion or psychological exploration that leads to an increase in the client's self-understanding, particularly in terms of what is happening on an unconscious level. This may involve making links to the causes of symptoms, which give new insight about the presenting problem. R.7 describes work with an arachnophobic. The intuition, which resulted from use of the word 'evil', prompts the discovery that the client projects the 'bad' part of herself on to the spiders which she so fears.

Nonverbal communications can reveal significant aspects of the client's process, which can throw light on unrewarding behaviour patterns:

> That side glance was revealing ... for a fleeting moment I caught the real face behind the mask. It was easier to convince her finally that some unconscious tendency in her forced her to make herself disliked. (K.7)

Psychological 'payoffs' or benefits may also become apparent, which, if left, may deter a patient's progress. An experienced therapist will know the value of following up these kinds of clues:

> She tormented him in a special way by her grotesque anxiety about preserving her chastity. This effective form of vengeance had the secondary purpose of keeping the untrustworthy husband at her side and under her eye. (K.16)

Sometimes the intuition can point to the reality that lies beneath the client's falsely constructed self, as in K.8a in which the client's hypocrisy is revealed:

> It sounded false to me; it was as if a pianist had touched a wrong key. Would you, in casual everyday conversation, say, 'It contradicts my trend to simplicity'? In this case it revealed a hypocritical attitude of the patient, who liked to think of himself as very unpretentious.

It can be uncomfortable for a person to be faced with the truth about him- or herself and the therapist must judge the timing of such an intervention carefully. Nevertheless confrontation of defences can put the client in touch with real feelings and lead to important insight.

The therapist may make associations that reveal the meaning of a dream, which in turn can help the client towards self-understanding. In the example below, R. has made a link between the client's sideways glances noticed in the consulting room and the walking on air from the dream.

> There were many sideways glances, as if checking me out. He told me a dream in which he was walking on air. I then had the chance to say, 'You seem unsure of where you stand.' He admitted this was an ongoing theme for him in relationships. (R.18)

This gives insight about his behaviour and also about how he relates to others.

Category 5: Client's response

How the intuition is received by the client is the subject of this category. It concerns immediate reactions and responses, and is dependent upon use of the intuition by the therapist in the session. As can be seen from Figure 10.5 the reaction may be positive, negative, mixed or undetectable.

The material signifies that the client's response is not always positive. It seems, therefore, that intuitions need to be applied with care and perhaps sometimes not at all. In two cases, the client failed to turn up at the next session, although this was expected by the therapist and an aspect of

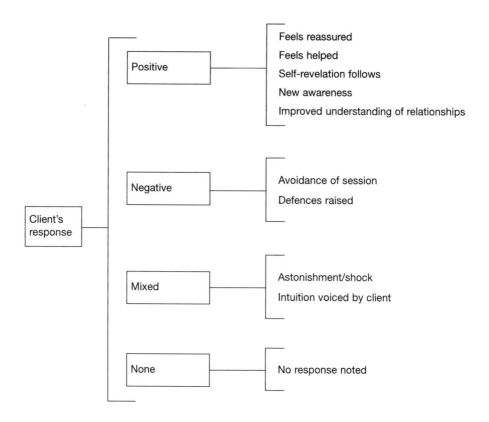

Figure 10.5 Client's response to therapist's intuition.

the intuition itself. In another case, defences were actually raised, indicating that the client was not ready to hear the intuitive intervention:

> She wanted to dodge the issue, apparently, and indulged in much long, boring chat. (R.14)

Shock or astonishment were also reported in response to the intuition, although after recovery from the immediate impact the result was in fact positive.

> The patient jumped up and looked at me as if I were a ghost. (K.19)

Moreover, it is notable that the client's response in ten cases is not stated on the forms, which indicates that therapists are not always able to assess this, or else there appeared to be no immediate response at all.

At other times, individuals felt helped or reassured, as in R.17 quoted under category 2, although this was explicitly stated only twice. On the other occasions, reassurance has been inferred from the client's behaviour, such as noticing a reduction in anxiety.

Positive reactions do nevertheless predominate (32 entries) and include the client's involvement in the progress of the therapy in terms of revealing more about him- or herself and feeling sufficiently trusting and confident to do this. This sub-category (self-revelation) contained the most numerous entries at 12.

> During the session he revealed that most of his worries are about other people not performing and thereby letting him down. Somehow I had picked this up from my own [reported] anxiety at letting him down as a therapist. (R.4)

The client may also show eagerness to increase awareness by agreeing or volunteering to watch out for a particular behaviour in the future outside of sessions:

> Seen as an opportunity to learn something, so he'll watch out for the smile in the future. (R.2)

Equally, self-help procedures may be put in place. Where there has been an increase in understanding of relationships, the client may be willing to practise new ways of behaving when with others:

> He realized then that he could change the dynamic between himself and his wife by saying, for example, 'I feel ignored', rather than an aggressive retort: 'Be like that then!' (R.5)

Unconscious communication cannot be over-estimated and of course this travels in both directions. In two cases, the therapist became aware that the client had picked up her intuition even though it had not been stated:

> I realize that she's really bent on having revenge on her husband, but her words tell me that she lacks support, so I suggest that she form her own support group with peers. She tells me that my suggestion is background to her feelings and I'm aware of her reproof. (R.19)

Category 6: Perceived outcome

Where this has been assessed by the therapist, the data indicate that, on the whole (26 entries), intuitive interventions lead to positive progress in the therapy in terms of increased self-understanding, a reduction in symptoms, or more effective management of life (see Figure 10.6). Alternatively, it may increase the therapist's comprehension of the case or improve the therapeutic relationship. However, it has to be stressed that these are the perceptions of the therapists only and they have not been checked with clients. In a number of cases, namely nine, the result of the

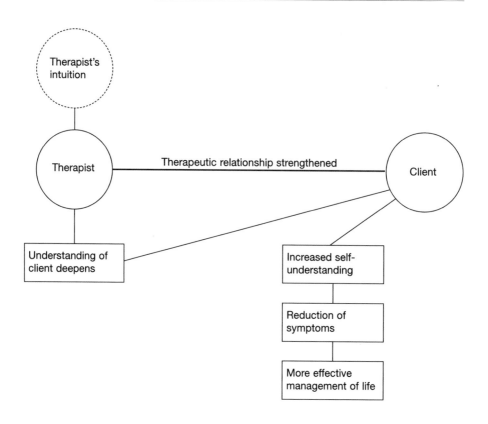

Figure 10.6 Perceived outcome.

intuition is not stated.

As was demonstrated under category 4, some intuitions may help the client and others may assist the therapist, but generally a therapeutic intuition appears to be of most value to the client. An increase in self-understanding is the most frequent result with 14 entries. The individual can better appreciate why problem behaviours persist and what lies behind the neurotic symptoms, because links have been made to unconscious motivations. Further progress may have been made beyond this self-understanding to an actual reduction in symptoms, and the client acknowledges this in some cases, as in K.20:

> Some months after this, her analysis came to a satisfactory end; her chief symptoms had virtually disappeared. A few months later she wrote that she was pregnant and happy at the prospect of motherhood.

He or she may also have developed better coping strategies, like the former prisoner who finds a way of rebuilding her life:

> She had lost all hope she said and she couldn't believe I had arrived when
> I did. She has since entered a rehab and for the first time in 16 years is try-
> ing to get her life back. (N.1)

Such improvements may well have been supported by a strengthening of
the therapeutic alliance, mostly due to empathic and sensitive responses
of the therapist, concerning, for example, timing and pacing and meeting
other unspoken needs. As a result the client feels sufficiently confident to
reveal more difficult experiences, never previously expressed:

> She valued my 'consistency' and the fact that I'd allowed her space and time
> to build trust, which was very important to her. This resulted in the gradual
> revealing of very difficult experiences, which she had never voiced before.
> (R.11)

Intuitive understanding of the patient may also be crucial to the future
progress of the work and it is clear from the diary pages that some cases
could not be comprehended by consulting text books or relying on theory, each individual being unique. K.14 specifically makes this point:

> What was the unconscious meaning of the senseless doings with the cham-
> bermaid? Where did I get the idea that the real text ... could only be recog-
> nized by a reversal? Certainly not from remembering the reading of analyt-
> ic books or attending lectures or seminars.

The therapist must therefore often rely on intuition.

Category 7: Validation

Literature concerning the subjective certainty and degree of accuracy of
an intuition has already been reviewed in earlier chapters. Assagioli
(1974/1984) had recommended using reason to check an intuition,
because subjective feelings of certainty cannot imply objective correctness. His assumption seems to have been that an intuition may be
believed in too readily, but this is not supported by the diary study.
Indeed, there are two examples which demonstrate that the intuition was
initially disbelieved and rejected. C.'s assertion in the focus group that an
intuition 'has a sort of a "yes" to it', can be taken as an example of Jung's
declaration that the phenomenon carries an intrinsic certainty and conviction. Yet subjective feelings of certainty are not taken to imply veracity
according to the diaries, but rather as a marker that the intuitive process
is present. The three entries concerning a sense of certainty have therefore been listed under category 2 (the Form) rather than category 7
(Validation). Indeed, it is notable that feelings of confidence in an intuition are mentioned so few times.

Material from the diary pages demonstrates that therapists use six different ways of validating an intuition (see Figure 10.7)[3]. A client may spontaneously corroborate an intuition if it is reported, by declaring agreement:

> During a visualization, she resisted the invitation to walk in her imagination up a hillside. Something was getting in the way, but I didn't know what. The image of a magic carpet came into my head, so I suggested that she step on to it. Afterwards she told me that the carpet felt good. (R.1)

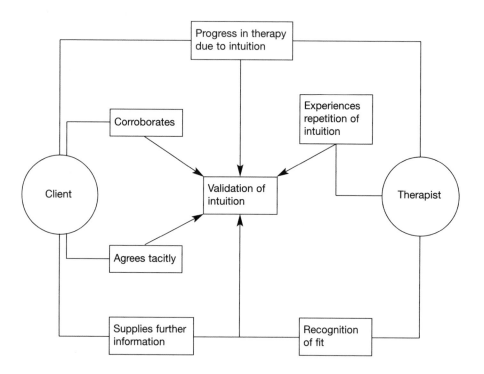

Figure 10.7 Ways in which intuition is validated.

Equally, a therapist may deliberately check the intuitive information with the client, as in M.2:

> My client said she agreed with me and decided to hold her anxiety and wait for her friend to make the next move.

The therapist may not immediately reveal the intuition, but wait until more information is forthcoming which will affirm its accuracy or otherwise, as demonstrated by K.22:

Added memories emerged in her analysis later on and confirmed the conviction that the events had indeed taken the course suggested by my reconstruction.

At other times links may be made to new material with which the intuition fits:

In these short minutes the thoughts occurred that later on fitted together like parts of a jigsaw puzzle to make the essence of the interpretation. (K.I)

Presentiments may also be corroborated by their repetition, until they can no longer be ignored. The therapist may then feel sufficiently confident to bring the intuitive knowledge directly into the session. K.22 reports:

When the analyst listens very attentively to his inner response, he will realize that ... his hunches do not deceive him. As in this case, a sudden flash confirms that the first impression ... was in essence correct.

When the client responds positively to the intuition and progress is made, then its correctness is implied, as in the case from R.12:

She arrived wearing dark glasses and a question arose, 'What is it that she finds unacceptable in herself?' I did not offer this observation directly ... but steered the work on to Gestalt with her inner Child. It emerged that this Child was full of self-loathing.

Where the timing and pacing of sessions is concerned, the therapist may rely on the client to give feedback on their appropriateness and may allow space for this during a review. If nothing is said, then tacit agreement can sometimes be construed:

'Knowing' how far away to hold the spider [in this cognitive-behavioural work]. Judging how much she could take so as not to frighten her. I feel sure she will tell me if I go too quickly. (R.9)

Means of validating intuitions were not specifically asked for on the diary forms, but they are nevertheless evident in most cases. This seems to imply that therapists are aware of the importance of this process and generally careful before introducing intuitive material into sessions, although mistakes may sometimes be made which result in a negative response from the client (see category 5). It is notable that psychotherapists in this study are all very experienced professionals and their caution is in accord with Oskamp's findings of 1963, which indicated that clinical experience decreases confidence in the making of clinical judgements. As Tony Bastick had noted under property 9 of his theory (1982, p. 25), the intuition is not always correct. Yet, in the clinical context, the diary pages indicate that most therapist intuitions are accurate and helpful.

Frequency of intuitions

Notable during this research has been the difficulty expressed by participants in identifying an intuitive moment. Taking the data alone, frequency of distinguishable intuitions appears to be relatively scant, averaging about one in every seven hours of counselling.[2] The main reason for this can be ascribed to the unconscious processing involved and the obscurity of steps whereby conclusions are reached.

In marked contrast to this was P.'s assertion, 'I use it all the time.' He evidently means by this the holding of an intuitive attitude during sessions, whereby he is hypersensitive to clues from the client concerning nonverbal communications and aspects of behaviour which are not currently within the individual's awareness. This points to a crucial feature that has emerged during this investigation, that theory and intuition are incompatible. Evidence put forward indicates that it is not feasible to use logical deductive thought processes at the same time as intuition; the therapist has to opt for either one or the other at any given moment, taking the appropriate attitude. Reik does not see them as mutually exclusive, but rather that they exist on different levels. He does admit, though, that their two realms must be separate, so that the one does not disturb the other (1948/1975, p. 25). It is possible that dominant thinkers may receive fewer intuitions than other types, as their tendency will be towards the deductive mode.

Although recordable intuitions do not appear to be numerous, nevertheless, as can be seen from this study, their impact can be considerable in terms of helping to create a good working alliance, moving the work forward, and offering important information to the therapist and insight to the client.

The question of validity

An assessment is made here as to how far this study can be considered to be valid and reliable, and to what degree the findings can be generalized to the psychotherapy profession as a whole.

Great care has been taken during the process of analysis to ensure that the account is grounded in the data. Units of meaning are taken directly from the diary pages and quotations given to illustrate the findings. The main categories were determined largely by the purpose of the study in the form of questions asked at the outset about the nature of intuitions within a clinical context and what happens as a result of their appearance. The sub-categories, however, were formed solely from the data presented. The indications are, therefore, that face validity is good.

Triangulation was incorporated into the study by taking the material from three different sources. Categorization was made across the full range of material, and subcategories created from all informants. However, the majority of records came from Reik's case material (24) and from mine as researcher (19) rather than from the group of therapists (10). It could be argued that both Reik and I have a particular interest in intuition and are therefore biased and atypical. This is not borne out by existing research, which indicates that most psychotherapists favour intuition (Myers and McCaulley, 1985, pp. 73, 75).

Wherever possible, reference has been made to existing authorities, which are discussed in detail in the earlier chapters of the book, and also to the findings of the focus group. The lack of empirical material to refer to has already been commented upon, which reduces the reliability of some theorists. The various strands of the argument have therefore had to rely to a certain extent on the weight of the evidence put forward. Sometimes the findings of the study do not support views previously expressed, but this may be because those opinions were too subjective. This particularly relates to what happens within the clinical setting. Where the nature of intuition is concerned, agreement can more often be found. Construct validity can therefore only be claimed in part, but this is due to the originality of this study.

It is difficult to say whether replication would produce precisely the same results, and therefore the findings have to be taken as a general guide only. Much depends on the awareness of the therapists and their ability to notice an intuition when it is present and their willingness to record it. It may be that some intuitions do not reach consciousness and therefore cannot be described. There is also the question of how typical the participants are of the profession as a whole in terms of personality type and also theoretical orientation. Intuitive feelers (NFs) appear to dominate the counselling profession (Myers and Myers, 1980/1993, p. 151), yet the chosen sample is marginally more thinking orientated. As already mentioned, this may account for the apparently few entries under 'empathic response'. It is possible, therefore, that different personality types could produce differing results in some categories.

The theoretical orientation of participants favoured psychodynamic and/or psychoanalytic approaches, with some input from psychosynthesis, Gestalt and integrative methods. The psychodynamic emphasis is reflected in the profession in some areas, although an integrative approach is currently becoming more prevalent. Some caution needs to be exercised in generalizing the results to the wider population of psychotherapists and further research is recommended in this area.

Considered within the overall context of psychotherapy research, one of the most important contributions made by this study, in addition to the actual findings, is the provision of a detailed framework for the classification of intuitions as they occur within the clinical setting.

Notes

1. The rationale for arriving at Reik's type as an INTP included the consideration of his approach to *Listening with the Third Ear* (1948/1975), his style and its content. Writing about psychological material is an intellectual pursuit (T – thinking preference), which is largely solitary (I – introverted). The subject is discussed from the perspective of Reik's own inner experience (I). The *New York Times* says of Reik on the cover of the publication that he 'really does possess the "third ear" – the name he gives to the intuitive sensibility' (N – intuition). Reik stresses the importance of the imagination and creativity (p. 22), a sign of preference for the intuitive (N). He does not easily accept others' rules and ideas, in this case Freud's (N). He notes that his American colleagues are mainly interested in the practical applications of psychoanalysis, thus favouring the sensing function (S), whereas his own curiosity lies in the creation of theory and revelation of meaning (p. xi) (N). Yet, since he has chosen to show these aspects to the world, his intuition is likely to be extraverted (E). The general style of writing is somewhat rambling and spontaneous, rather than tightly structured, giving the impression of a preference for the perceiving function (P) over judging (J). According to type dynamics, it would be his perceiving, rather than judging, function that is turned towards the outside world, supporting the view that his intuition is extraverted. However, his overall preference appears to be for introversion. This therefore suggests that his dominant function is introverted thinking, with extraverted intuition as his auxiliary. The type of INTP is thus formed.

2. One participant (M.) stated afterwards that if she had realized that regulators, denoting turn-taking and pacing, were picked up intuitively, then her recorded number of intuitions would have been more numerous.

3. A further method, that of trial empathy, was recommended by Kohut. See Chapter 7.

CHAPTER 11

Can intuition be taught?

When working on the diary study, I had a sense of excitement as the findings emerged. Here at last was genuine empirical material, taken from working practice, which threw real light on the form of intuition in therapy, how it is employed and what happens as a result. Could this now be utilized in training? The next step was to examine existing teaching procedures regarding intuition, with the aim of discovering what particular contribution my research might make. The most straightforward way of acquiring this information was to consult as many colleges as possible, representing a variety of methodological approaches. My sense was that intuition as a theoretical subject is not taught in the majority of psychotherapy and counselling institutions and I decided to set this as a hypothesis.

The training questionnaire

In addition, there were specific outstanding questions I wanted to ask relating to the ways in which intuition features in counsellor training, if at all. I wanted to know whether the nature of intuition was explained to students and whether its application in clinical practice was studied. A further query was whether trainees were actively encouraged to be more intuitive, and, if so, how. If not, then did this mean that their practice might in some way be limited? I was also curious to discover what the relationship could be between a particular methodological approach in counselling or psychotherapy and the ways in which intuition, or aspects of it, are taught.

The research methodology

The most efficient means of obtaining the required information within the limited period of time available was to send out a carefully designed questionnaire. A specimen was therefore drawn up, in line with recommendations made by Oppenheim (1966/1992). This consisted of twenty questions which were divided into seven parts, each of which related to a particular topic, as follows: nonverbal and unconscious communications; creativity and the use of symbolism and metaphor; enhancement of intuitive characteristics; consultation with a secondary self; the transpersonal; relationship to time; the teaching of intuition. Answers were in a 'yes/no' format, and if in the affirmative, approximate numbers of hours were requested where relevant. Additionally, participants were invited to make comments and give further information within certain categories, and extra space was allowed for this purpose. The format as a whole was therefore semi-structured, with the aim of collecting qualitative as well as quantitative material. Initially respondents were asked, as an open question, what they understood by the term 'intuition'. Finally, they were asked to describe their experience of completing the questionnaire. (See Appendix E).

A small pilot study, involving three colleagues, was set up to test the effectiveness of the questionnaire. As a result of the feedback obtained, several adjustments and additions were made. In particular it was recommended that the questions specifically asking about the teaching of intuition should be positioned at the end, rather than the beginning, as it was thought that the participants would have a better grasp of the multifarious nature of the phenomenon as a result of the completion of the questionnaire.

In order to compare findings of this study with other sources, college brochures were requested by e-mail from those who returned the questionnaire, and 12 responded. Of these, only eight were sufficiently detailed to be usable. Therefore further brochures were requested, in particular from schools of psychoanalysis and Gestalt, because they were not represented in the main study, and four were received. A number of trainees was also consulted, as a check against the written comments on the questionnaire. Finally, the study was sent to an independent, experienced tutor, for assessment and feedback.

The participants

These were taken from the *Training in Counselling and Psychotherapy Directory* (BACP, 2003) and were not random, but were limited, to provide some uniformity, to those institutions in the United Kingdom with fully accredited courses. These totalled 100 universities and further education colleges as well as private institutions. To ensure representation from different theoretical approaches, the following were included: integrative, person-centred, psychodynamic, psychoanalytic, humanistic, existential, transactional analysis, Gestalt, transpersonal and cognitive behavioural therapy. A covering letter, personally addressed to the training director or senior lecturer, was attached to each questionnaire, which gave some information about the proposed book and the purpose of the research. There were 27 replies, of which four felt unable to complete the questionnaire, either because the course was being discontinued or because there was a lack of resources. There were thus 23 completed questionnaires of the 100 mailed out, among which the above theoretical models were included, with the exception of Gestalt and psychoanalysis. This was a satisfactory response for a study of this nature (Sanders and Liptrot, 1994, p. 94).

The analysis

Each completed questionnaire was coded firstly with a letter to denote the theoretical approach (e.g. P for person-centred), then a number, followed by 'm' or 'w' to distinguish between responses from men or women if stated, or 'n' if not. The resulting code would thus be, for example, P5m.

Responses were then analysed section by section through the formation of categories, as guided by the research questions, and in line with the recommendations of Glaser and Strauss (1967) for discovering theory grounded in the data. The combination of some small categories was found to be necessary to form larger ones, and adjustments to conceptual labels were made. Any relationships between categories were noted. I then searched for the meaning that lay behind the responses as a whole within each section. Additionally, quantitative analyses were made of the structured aspects of the questionnaire.

Findings

My intention through the questions in Part A was to discover whether nonverbal and/or unconscious communications were studied during training, and, if so, how, which aspects and to what extent. All except one replied in the affirmative as far as nonverbal communication was concerned, but only six (26 per cent) indicated that it was taught directly, in terms of, for example, body language or energy shifts, and hours devoted to such teaching ranged from four to 25 over a three-year course. Others indicated that it was integrated, mainly into counselling practice or skills work, and to a lesser extent as part of counter-transference or within supervision, but hours were unquantifiable. When compared with answers to question 4, concerning subliminal perception, a more technical term, it was clear from the mostly negative responses that this is not taught from a psychological or sociological perspective, and no reference was made to the extensive experimental literature. Indeed, one respondent was unsure of the meaning of the term.

Counter-transference did feature in many courses at 65 per cent (15), and where it did not this was predictable, since the context was person-centred (or favoured this bias) or CBT, theoretical approaches which do not include the concept. There was, however, a surprisingly low relationship between answers to 1b (topics covered within the study of nonverbal communication) and 2 (counter-transference). Only four of the 15 respondents (three psychodynamic and one transpersonal) seemed to consider that counter-transference concerned nonverbal communication. This was puzzling.

Nineteen of the 23 institutes included advanced empathy in their training (83 per cent). Two that did not were both psychodynamic, and the two others were unsure of the meaning. Where hours were given, these ranged widely from one to 100, or the subject was otherwise integrated into various aspects of the course.

There was a wholly positive response to question 5a, asking whether students learn to work with 'hunches' or 'gut feelings', but only eight (35 per cent) specifically mentioned listening to oneself, as for instance in focusing, or in some way attending to one's own body or feeling responses. Interestingly, one mentioned suspension of thoughts (integrative). The others mostly indicated that such feelings were explored in supervision or viewed in the context of psychodynamic theory.

The intention with the 12 sub-questions in part B was to discover to what extent trainings incorporated allological modes of operating, with the exploration of imagery and symbolism, including dreams and the collective unconscious, and creative approaches through drawing, poetry, sandplay, music and drama. Thirty per cent replied in the affirmative to all or all but one of the questions, 26 per cent to seven to ten questions, and 44 per cent to half or less. The transpersonal therapies featured high in this section, followed by humanistic therapies. As far as person-centred trainings were concerned, responses were very varied, and much seemed to depend on the personal inclinations of the teachers or student choice. Psychodynamic approaches lay in the low to middle range offering modest opportunities for 'right-brained' ways of working.

Part C aimed first of all to find out how much students were encouraged to develop their self-awareness and understanding through personal therapy and/or group process. Eighteen of the 23 stated that personal therapy was a requirement of the course or of BACP accreditation and all of these also emphasized group process. At 78 per cent, the impression given is that the majority of training advisors consider that at least some personal development is important. Hours, however, varied greatly, from ten to 200 for personal therapy and two to 200 for group process.

Secondly, it was hoped that responses to the remainder of part C would indicate whether or not there was opportunity within trainings for developing certain characteristics that have been shown to be manifestations of the intuitive type of personality, such as emotional sensitivity, the seeing of patterns and relationships, imaginative, creative and lateral thinking, a non-judgemental frame of mind, the lack of dogmatism and the questioning of theory. Of these ten questions, 83 per cent answered 'yes' to nine or all, and the remainder to six or less. Hours generally could not be quantified as they were not specifically dedicated to such topics, but comments suggested that opportunities arose during skills training, within supervision and group process, or recommended optional courses.

There was a positive response in all but two cases to the concept of some kind of secondary, inner self that could be consulted. The most commonly used term was 'internal supervisor' (14), while two (both transpersonal) employed 'Wise Being', another (person-centred) 'felt-sense', and the remainder no particular word or phrase. The impression here was that students are generally encouraged to reflect on their practice, but that the thinking mode constitutes a certain proportion of this, in line with Casement's description of the technique (1985/1990). Readers are referred again to Chapter 8.

Sixty-one per cent claimed to include the transpersonal in their courses. However, since most gave no hours, it has to be supposed that particular modules are not generally devoted to this subject except in the small proportion of courses which feature spiritual aspects. Just 39 per cent replied 'yes' to the study of peak experiences, but most of these (excepting two transpersonal institutes) merely touched on the subject. As far as meditation was concerned, only 30 per cent replied in the affirmative, and, excepting transpersonal trainings, hours over three years ranged from just three to 20. None of the psychodynamic courses offered meditation to students. This important route to intuitive knowledge therefore appears to be omitted from the majority of syllabuses. Half of the respondents indicated that their students were taught how to work constructively with spirituality/mysticism, but hours given by the non-transpersonal trainings were very low (two to four), apart from one integrative course which had a religious dimension (60).

Some respondents seemed to be perplexed as to why I needed to know whether their courses emphasized the past, present or future. As has been suggested in Chapter 4, intuitive types tend to be future-orientated, and are excited by possibilities. None of the respondents emphasized the future over the present or past, although 52 per cent gave it equivalent prominence. Thirty per cent of trainings did not lay any emphasis on the future at all.

Part G asked whether the course covered the theory of intuition, and whether students were specifically encouraged to develop this function. Fifty-two per cent did not teach intuition from a theoretical perspective and of these, more than half thought that they did not encourage their students to develop their intuition either. Orientations here were a mixture of person-centred, psychodynamic, integrative and CBT. Of the 48 per cent who asserted that they did teach the subject theoretically, less than half were able to quote hours (three to 20), of which one was an optional module. The rest seemed to think that it was in some way integrated into the course. No hours were quoted as regards development of intuition, apart from one transpersonal training which allowed 60 hours. When asked how such development was fostered, answers were too diverse for meaningful classification, apart from a group of eight, which had to do with the processing of personal responses through attention to the body or emotions.

The penultimate question enquired whether the institute would favour the inclusion of the study of intuition into the syllabus. Of those who implied in part G that they taught intuition theoretically, only two (both transpersonal) stated appropriately 'already do'. A further three, having claimed the teaching of intuition, expressed here either doubt that the institute would favour it (two) or that it would not (one). Does this mean that it is being taught secretly, or that it is not in fact already being taught and that the wrong reply was indicated in part G? The latter seems more probable. Of those who did not already teach intuition (52 per cent), half thought that the college would favour its inclusion in the syllabus. Twenty-two per cent of the total thought that the study of intuition would not be wanted: person-centred, humanistic, CBT (one response each) and psychodynamic (two).

Overall, there were no observable differences between male and female responses.

Discussion

Most striking were the enthusiastic reactions to the research from respondents, expressed either in a covering note, or on the questionnaire itself. In nine cases good wishes or good luck were sent, eight participants felt excited or encouraged or that their awareness had increased through involvement with the research, five found it interesting and four wanted to be helpful, while three were eager for more. Equally, frustration, mainly with the difficulty of quantifying aspects of intuition, was stated 13 times, but this had been anticipated. Three people apologized for being too busy to give the questionnaire full attention, while four seemed anxious (for example about misunderstanding some questions) and one appeared to be cynical about the possibility of transforming the research into usable material. Sixteen were willing to be interviewed further if necessary.

As was evident from my research forming the background to Chapter 6, nonverbal communication takes precedence over verbal whenever people are together. I was therefore curious as to whether this balance was reflected in trainings. How much of any course was devoted to unspoken messages, and how much importance was attached to them? The most obvious way in which these are transmitted is through body language and one would therefore assume that psychotherapy and counselling trainings would cover this subject in some detail. Moreover, extensive psychological research literature exists, which would form a very useful background to its study. Of the 23 respondents, only six were able to quote hours devoted to nonverbal communication in terms of body language, at an average of 10 per course. Among the brochures, only one offered a specific module on verbal and nonverbal communication. This is a remarkably low figure for such an important subject, particularly bearing in mind the research quoted in Chapter 6, which suggests that psychotherapists are no better than any one else in picking up body language cues (Dittman et al., 1965). However, most respondents indicated that it was covered in counselling practice or skills work or in supervision, but that hours were not quantifiable. This gave the impression that its inclusion was somewhat arbitrary. There was no reference at all to psychological studies in this area. On the other hand, some respondents added a comment along the lines that they understood the significance of covert messages, for example: 'We take as given that communication is subtle, and mainly nonverbal' (H1w).

It should be noted that it is extremely difficult to cover this subject effectively in supervision, as the client is not present, and the supervisee is unlikely to be able to report blind spots or what has otherwise been missed. Some respondents mentioned work with audio tapes, video and interpersonal process recall[1], all of which offer scope for identifying hidden messages, through factors such as vocal quality, pacing of language, breathing, energy levels, body movements and facial expressions of the client, combined with therapist's reactions. Sessions recorded on video also provide an opportunity to study the therapist's intuitive responses, in terms of tactful timing of interventions, employment of regulators to denote turn-taking, and other factors such as the unconscious matching of postures, all of which may affect the working alliance. Further analysis may expose missed cues, or the general tendency to watch facial expressions rather than other body movements. Therapists need to be alert to the interactional field and the part that they play in this.

As we have also seen from Chapter 6, there are various ways in which therapists can unwittingly make mistakes in interpretation, due to factors such as differences in cultural background, social class or dissimulating display rules. Trainees need to learn about such pitfalls. It is safer to explore details observed directly with the client to identify idiosyncratic meanings, along the lines practised by Gestalt therapists. Movements, tone of voice, facial expressions, energy levels and so on are reflected back without interpretation. The client may be invited to exaggerate the element to discover what lies behind it, or may be asked to portray the opposite. It is notable that two respondents to the questionnaire included the teaching of Gestalt as a route to understanding body language. Indeed, therapists from other orientations have much to learn from this approach.

Seventeen per cent (mainly psychodynamic) stated that nonverbal communication was studied via counter-transference. Since these respondents did not mention other ways in which it might be examined, one has to suppose that the teaching of this subject is confined to that theoretical model in some cases. In counter-transference, we use ourselves as sensitive instruments and focus on our responses to give information about the client's covert messages, many of which may be unconscious. While this is indeed a very useful method whereby certain covert messages may be received and understood, and the intuitive process made more evident, it is by no means comprehensive. As we have seen from the research in chapter 10, many of the cues and prompts are non-subjective, involving direct observation. Moreover, intuition is global and several factors may have to be combined to produce useful knowledge. Trainees may or may not be naturally observant or sensitive to covert communications. This can depend on upbringing and personality preferences. Children raised by unpredictable or moody adults may learn to read unspoken messages as a matter of survival and adjust their behaviour to avoid any impending conflict. Types who have the sensing function in dominant position may be excellent at noticing details, whereas those with it in the inferior position may observe very little. Moreover, how are such communications to be classified? It is extremely helpful to trainees to be able to attach elements observed to a secure framework. This provides the basis for cognitive understanding. A well-researched model already exists within communication psychology, as outlined in Chapter 6. Having words to describe the different types of messages expressed nonverbally by clients assists greatly in comprehending and explaining what is going on.

Advanced empathy, according to the respondents, is taught in 83 per cent of colleges, and this would therefore appear to be the main method whereby clients' hidden or scarcely sensed meanings are searched for and reflected back in a tactful and non-threatening way, as described by Egan (1975/1994). Of the total, only 30 per cent gave hours, while the rest implied that it was integrated into the course in some way. Of those who did quote hours, most remarkable was the wide difference in emphasis given to this aspect of therapy, either a cursory one hour, or in-depth 100. It seems that some students will only touch on how to look for covert messages, while others will have a great deal of practice. The subtler aspects of clients' process may well be overlooked by some trainees therefore. While this may not be so crucial for very short-term, goal-orientated counselling, particularly if cognitive-behavioural techniques predominate, it will certainly affect the quality of long-term psychotherapy.

The next question asked whether subliminal perception was taught. Almost 70 per cent answered 'no', and of those who replied in the affirmative, none gave hours. From the research described in Chapter 6 concerning 'micros', it would appear to be wise to include in the syllabus at least something about messages which are too fleeting to be taken in consciously, especially as these sometimes leak true feelings which are otherwise masked and may be at variance with the words spoken. Experience of working with people seemed to enhance sensitivity to such momentary expressions, and this should perhaps be taken into account when assessing applicants for entry on to courses. Equally, voluntary work with people, even if not directly involving counselling, might usefully be encouraged during training.

Most noticeable as regards the working with 'hunches' or 'gut feelings' is the wide divergence of opinion as to how students might learn to do this. Responses could be divided into two over-arching categories: those who focused on the internal processes of the trainee (listening to oneself, creativity, self-development); and those who thought that such learning was incorporated into some external medium (through supervision, in skills training or counselling practice). Supervisors are indeed sometimes presented with a 'hunch' or 'gut feeling' about a client, a strong sense of something, but without the supervisee being able to clarify it, or pinpoint the origin of the impression. Understanding the nature of the intuitive process can be very helpful in unravelling the elements that have created such an impression. As has been noted elsewhere in the book, these can sometimes be traced in retrospect. 'Irrational' techniques, such as are used in Gestalt therapy, rather than thought-based processes are most suitable for this kind of retrieval. For example, the supervisee can be invited to evoke the client in imagination to re-create the therapy situation, sense again what it is like to be together, re-observe what occurs, describe in detail what is seen and so on. Alternatively, drawing or sandplay can be similarly helpful. Hidden communications may be revealed, and the supervisor can then make recommendations as to whether or not to reflect these back to the client, and if so, how and when.

Trainees themselves need to learn how to work with an intuition, by, for example, evoking an image for it and using visualization to explore it in depth, along the lines practised by psychosynthesis therapists. One student describes how she became aware of a churning sensation in her stomach as she listened to a client suffering from depression. By allowing her attention to dwell on that physical sensation, an image of a vicious electric eel was evoked. As later became clear, this was representative of her client's repressed pain and anger, which she had intuitively picked up (Baillie, 2003, p. 12). Focusing, as described by Gendlin (1978/1981), is also a fruitful way of making sense of one's own intuitive responses. Judging by answers in the questionnaire, only around one-third of courses specifically encourage this type of inner work.

As far as Part B was concerned, covering non-cognitive approaches, responses were very varied and depended both on the theoretical orientation of the course as well as the interests of individual teachers. While half the colleges offered adequate or excellent resources for the development of nonverbal and creative approaches to the work, 44 per cent appeared to provide only limited opportunities to students. The transpersonal therapies, in particular psychosynthesis, offered the best possibilities for enhancing these aspects of the intuitive. Study of the brochures was particularly revealing. One such institute (A21w) gives prominence to creativity within the context of 'going beyond the either/or thinking of our rational minds ... to a realm where unifying ideas and principles exist'. This is seen to be an important aspect of personality integration, because too much emphasis on the rational can cut us off from our originality. Psychosynthesis sees creativity as closely allied to the intuitive within a spiritual context and it is therefore a fundamental aspect of the training. Specific modules focus on the imagination, dreamwork and the creative process which take the trainee towards 'synthetic thinking and beyond the scientific paradigm'. The term 'synthetic thinking' is equivalent to 'global processing' used by psychologists, in which all the elements are brought together and synthesized to form a complete whole. As Chapter 3 demonstrated, this is basic to the intuitive process. Moreover, the emphasis is on experiential rather than theoretical learning, using meditation, visualization and artwork. Group work may include drama and ritual to access unconscious dynamics. A basic assumption is that effective therapists need to be intuitive craftspeople and this type of training emphasizes means by which the faculty of intuition can be enhanced.

Apart from transpersonal approaches such as this one, the study suggests that characteristics indicative of the intuitive type do not seem to be intentionally developed in counselling and psychotherapy courses, but respondents considered that there was scope within the training in a general way. Most emphasized personal development, but, according to the brochures, this was mainly linked to the importance of understanding one's own process so that it should not interfere with that of the client. This, of course, is of crucial importance, but personal development can also productively include enhancement of one's intuitive faculty, as recommended for example by Myers and Kirby (1994, p. 35). Students can be encouraged to become aware of inner images and develop these and to use metaphor and analogy within counselling practice and supervision. Symbolism, as is well known, is the language of the unconscious, and is central to depth work. Personal journals can include poetic writing, and reflections on characters encountered in films or books. Ability to see patterns and relationships can be enhanced by visits to art galleries. These, like those within the client's story, can be set within the bigger picture of, for example, the social, political or cultural contexts. Lateral thinking and the making of novel connections can be developed through the collection of puns and jokes. All such methods create a valuable resource for making those links that can lead to intuitive understanding. Indeed, the personal journal offers particular opportunity for trainees to record how they are developing their intuition. Additionally, attention needs to be given to personal evaluation systems, and possibilities looked at that do not involve received theory or dogma.

Psychotherapy is a complex subject and there is always competition for time on any course. Through extra-curricular activities such as these, intuitive characteristics can be enhanced without taking up too much training time. Tutors, however, do need to initiate and monitor such work and provide information regarding the nature of intuition, so that trainees fully understand the purpose of such activities.

As regards personal therapy, 30 per cent of respondents recommended 30 hours or less, that is, below the BACP minimum requirement of 40 hours. Many professionals would agree that this is insufficient from the point of view of developing self-knowledge and awareness, let alone intuition, especially in cases where hours were 15 or below (26 per cent). Person-centred trainings featured in this low category, but when asked why, the main response was that trainees should pursue personal therapy only if there was a real need. One respondent commented that most in fact do. In contrast, the same proportion of colleges set a high value on personal therapy, at 100 hours or more. Reasons provided in brochures included the ability to contain strong emotions and the need to work through personal issues, which may otherwise limit the counsellor's effectiveness. However, personal therapy also offers a rich learning environment. When investigating the role of intuition in personal development, Patrick and Claudette McDonald emphasized the importance of being able to listen to one's inner voice (1993, p. 8), which, they suggest, can best be learnt within the context of individual psychotherapy. Conversations with trainees revealed that many valued this reflective process as a foundation for being able to tune in to intuition. In order to capture fleeting feelings or sensings, the individual needs to have considerable practice in staying with such moments and allowing them to expand, so that they can be identified. This requires an easy familiarity with one's own process and a freedom from fear as to what may be discovered. Having the confidence to remain with uncertainty and to operate from a small amount of information, were listed in Chapter 4 as beneficial features. People with low self-esteem are unlikely to be able to make the best use of their intuitions, as their tendency will be to belittle any understanding that emanates from the self. Personal therapy can greatly assist in elevating feelings of self-worth and increasing confidence, and hence trust in one's own intuitions.

Psychoanalyst Sanford Shapiro, writing from the perspective of Self Psychology, discusses the therapist's authenticity and the advantages of maintaining a non-defensive presence (1995, p. 75). Only if a counsellor has worked through personal defences can he or she be free to follow intuitive urges about whether to be self-revealing, whether to stay with the client's experience, or maybe to confront. He points out that if an analyst goes against intuition and follows a theory or a supervisor's idea instead, and thereby makes a mistake, the result can be disruption or even chaos, especially if the therapist loses confidence and the atmosphere in the consulting room changes from one of trust and safety to one of apprehension and insecurity.

Hours devoted to group process indicated that person-centred trainings feature in the middle to high range, thereby allowing time for personal awareness and development in this way, but with the emphasis on the building of relationships and interpersonal skills. There would be a real opportunity within this setting for participants to monitor their own defensive processes and to test out hunches or gut feelings with other interactants. Here again, this needs to be specifically facilitated by tutors.

As far as peak and plateau experiences are concerned, Abraham Maslow's work describes the transformational effect that such encounters can have (1970/1976) (see again Chapter 9). Moreover they are allied to emotional and mental health and the feeling that life is rewarding and meaningful. If therapists repress or minimize their own sublime experiences, then they are in no position to assist others in realizing this aspect of themselves. This is such a central part of Maslow's writing, that its omission from some supposedly humanistic trainings is curious. In response to the questionnaire, none of the courses with this bias taught peak experiences, apart, maybe, from a mention in passing. One might well ask whether those who construct such syllabuses have repressed their own capacity for such experiences. Surely they should form a key part of such courses, especially as engagement with them is a known gateway to psychological health.

The transpersonal trainings make a direct link between intuition and spirituality, although, according to the brochures, this is explained in different ways. One features continuous awareness and meditation as the prime routes to the 'Core' or enlightened mind. The opening to the truth of a given state, and of how the past is held within the present, allows a 'natural arising of wisdom' (A23n), which might well be otherwise referred to as intuition. This approach emphasizes sensitivity to arising experiences both in the self and the client. A deep kind of empathy is taught in the form of 'resonance', and images, dreams, the symbolic and the archetypal are all explored through visualization, subtle felt senses and feeling tones and transformational meditation practices. It is taken as given that we are dealing with a mind–body complex and that everything is interconnected, such a philosophy being based on Buddhist psychology. It is evident from reading the brochure that this approach is intuitive rather than analytical, highlighting the whole rather than cause and effect.

The psychosynthesis course already mentioned (A21w), in addition to featuring the imagination and creativity as ways beyond linear, analytic thinking, also incorporates the teaching of reflective and receptive meditation. As already discussed in Chapter 9, this is an important channel through which intuitive material can be accessed. Meditation can be learnt by anyone and is, moreover, invaluable in stilling the mental chatter of a therapist and inducing a relaxed and open state, prior to the arrival of a client. As we have seen, any kind of anxiety is anathema to intuition. Unfortunately, the majority of courses do not include such techniques. When asked the more general question of whether students were taught how to work constructively with spirituality or mysticism, it was clear that half are not. This is a concern, bearing in mind that this can be a powerful aspect of human experience, very well documented in the literature (James 1902/1982; Tart 1975/1992). Equally, less than half of the colleges consulted emphasize the future, of what a person may become; in this there lies hope. Are some institutes unwittingly closing off paths towards a real sense of purpose and a more rewarding life? Is there a generalized repression of the sublime, endemic in our culture and reflected in psychotherapy and counselling trainings? Sensing a client's potential, when clues may be scattered or insubstantial, may require intuition of a high order. James Hillman writes about having a nose for this kind of material, the ability to smell it, sniff it out (1990, pp. 61–3). A therapist may have to hold future possibilities for a client, long before the person becomes able to accept them as realizable. This requires faith in both one-self and the client.

Since much of any therapist's work involves emotional material, and since this is mostly transmitted nonverbally (Andersen 1999) and there-fore picked up intuitively, should not all training courses feature the development of this faculty? Yet just over half do not teach the subject the-oretically and almost one-third of the total appear not to incorporate its development either. Moreover, 22 per cent considered that the inclusion of intuition into the syllabus would not be wanted. This undoubtedly reflects Western educational methods, which are based on intellectual, analytical thinking. The real issue, however, is about which training meth-ods give prime importance to the best interests of clients. Of those colleges which claimed that students were encouraged to develop their intuition, there seemed to be some difficulty in stating precisely in what ways. One humanistic respondent (H10w) exclaimed with honesty: 'Can't say how!', but then qualified that with some examples, including reflect-ing, supervision, creative media and teaching exercises. Others mentioned personal work, awareness of own responses, 'irrational listen-ing', IPR[1], tuning in to the client, group relationships, deep empathy, bigger picture, imagery, meditation, transference and counter-transfer-ence, any of which might indeed involve aspects of intuition. The variety and generality of some of these replies seemed to indicate a lack of clari-ty as to the nature of the intuitive process and exactly how it might be enhanced. As for the theory of intuition, just one respondent made the link with the study of cognitive psychology and neuro-science, while another wrote 'R – L brain'. These apart, there were no allusions to the work carried out by psychologists.

Perhaps it is significant that 30 per cent of participants omitted to state what they understood by the term 'intuition', and two individuals offered excuses for failing to reply. No doubt many were very busy and short of time, but if this was the case, then the indication is that a proportion of trainers do not have a definition of intuition at their fingertips. The mean-ings that were given were diverse, so that little consistency in comprehension was evident. Just four distinct categories emerged: a source for knowing or understanding (mentioned by 39 per cent); not cog-nitive or not rational (22 per cent); unconscious access, perception or learning (also 22 per cent); instinctive (13 per cent). Other aspects were given only once or twice, such as gut feeling, hunch, sixth sense, body sense, felt-sense, tuning in, suddenness, surprise word or image, collective unconscious, shadow or field phenomena, nonverbal, like counter-trans-ference, can be lost, can't be taught, can be developed. While any one of these describe a particular aspect of intuition, none of the responses cap-tures its multifarious nature. The lack of homogeneity among training colleges as to the meaning of intuition, perhaps explains in part the difficulty that professional practitioners had in describing their experiences of it during the focus group that forms the background to Chapter 5.

The question of validity

It has to be remembered that there may be a certain degree of self-selection among the respondents who returned the questionnaire. In other words it would be most likely to attract people who are already interested in the subject, particularly bearing in mind that it takes effort and time to complete it. On the other hand this possibility needs to be weighed against the fact that 22 per cent thought that there would be no place for the study of intuition in their courses. This implies no special attraction to the subject matter, at least by the college authorities.

How credible are the data? It has been noted that some questionnaires were completed in haste, that there was some inconsistency in responses and not all questions received replies. In contrast, many respondents had obviously taken considerable care and time over their replies, and used the extra space on the reverse of pages to add further comments. These factors had to be taken into account when assessing results.

How representative of approaches to counselling and psychotherapy training was the sample? A selection was made that was deemed to be typical of available trainings across the United Kingdom. Because it was limited to BACP accredited courses or equivalent, some modes of training were not represented, such as creative arts therapy and process oriented therapy. Such models may have more to say concerning intuition, and research along these lines would be welcome. The majority of courses emphasized a humanistic philosophical orientation, although five of the colleges were psychodynamic. Nevertheless, the responses covered a reasonable range of the most popular methods. In addition to the questionnaire, brochures were studied and conversations were held with students and colleagues by way of comparison. Results could therefore be generalized to a certain degree, but with some caution. The study would be simple to replicate and there would therefore be no difficulty in testing reliability.

Conclusion

So was my hypothesis confirmed? I was pleasantly surprised that more institutes than I had imagined claimed to teach intuition theoretically as well as practically. My hypothesis was tentatively confirmed, however, to the extent that just over half did not. However, it was noted that there were some inconsistencies in several replies, and the suspicion that some respondents encircled 'yes' to the teaching of intuition, when in fact they meant 'no'. Moreover, since many answers were sketchy or non-existent as regards the nature of the phenomenon, I found it difficult to be persuaded that the subject was in fact being taught theoretically in these instances. These results should also be compared with responses of the focus group participants: only 28 per cent could recall intuition featuring in their courses.

My overall impression was that intuition is generally discussed only when there is an appropriate opportunity or when it happens to occur spontaneously, in for example skills practice or supervision. Moreover, it was left to that particular teacher to explain intuitive processes if he or she so wished. Rarely were specific hours or modules devoted to its teaching. The outstanding exceptions within this study were the transpersonal approaches and Gestalt.

So, bearing in mind the importance of intuition in relation to nonverbal communications, what can we learn and what is best for our clients? I would like to recommend a greater cross-fertilization of ideas and methods. Indeed, this is already happening with the growth in popularity of integrative approaches. Just as the therapeutic relationship is a binding factor across all theories, so is intuition. It can be studied within any counselling or psychotherapy context. Yet tutors often teach in the way that they were taught, and so that particular model is passed on from one generation to the next, with little reference to other models. Indeed, many training establishments will only offer teaching posts to their own graduates. It is rather like training students in an art such as acting or ballet, in which they might learn the Stanislavski method or the Cecchetti style. The problem with this is exclusivity or even fossilization.

We all have much to learn from each other. For example, the psychodynamic teaching of counter-transference demonstrates an important aspect of the intuitive process, with the introspective practice of tracking our thoughts, feelings and sensations, all those subtle reactions to our clients and what they may be indicating. Equally, we can benefit from Gestalt awareness exercises, to become much more observant and willing to explore what the client is saying through body language and other nonverbal signals. (See Chapter 12.) The transpersonal approaches offer meditation to settle distracting thoughts and visualization to contact unconscious messages or to tap into inner wisdom, while creative arts demonstrate how much can be expressed and communicated without the use of words or analytic thought. These are well-tried methods which already exist, and which, when combined with personal awareness and development through one-to-one therapy and group work, can all aid in the cultivation of intuition. Additionally, psychotherapists and psychologists need to set up a dialogue and become familiar with each other's latest research. The literature within communication psychology and related areas such as implicit learning is now extensive, and it is folly to ignore it.

While there is still much to be discovered, many unconscious processes are now well understood and, to answer the question posed by the title of this chapter, yes, the nature of intuition can be explained and taught to a considerable extent, and the faculty can certainly be consciously developed by individuals.

Note

1. Interpersonal Process Recall (IPR) was evolved by Kagan et al. (1963) for the teaching of counselling skills, although it has since been used for therapy process research. A video or audio tape is made of a session. Within a few hours of this the counsellor (or client) responds to a structured set of questions concerning his or her experience at various points on the tape. The participant can also stop the tape at will and explore the subjective thoughts and feelings that occurred at the time.

CHAPTER 12

Ways forward

In describing the experience of writing this book to a colleague, I was aware of the enormous difficulty in trying to grasp something that seemed ineffable. At the outset of the project, it had felt like a maze, but at this stage I could best resort to the analogy of a long mountain trek. I had started out with energy and enthusiasm, with just the first hill in view. As I rounded its top, however, an apparently endless terrain revealed itself, which seemed quite overwhelming. Sometimes there would be a downward slope when I could gather a little speed, or a gently undulating plateau where I could wander along with ease, but all too often it was a question of trudging up steep inclines. Then a mist would come down and it was impossible to see my way forward, so I would be forced to stop and wait a while until it cleared. At other times I would lose my way in a dense forest, and after unwittingly going round in circles I would eventually find a clear exit. At long last the culminating peak came into view and all that remained was the final push. Nearing the top, I could look back and survey the land I had explored, much of which lay clearly in view, although I was aware of the dips that remained obscured. At least I had a good working knowledge now of the ground covered, on which other journeys could be based.

It has seemed paradoxical to use logic and analysis and the medium of words through which to express my discoveries about a process that operates predominantly without these. No doubt it is this tension, that of thinking versus intuition, which has contributed to the feeling of an uphill struggle. Yet some, at least, of this book has been intuitive, such as the making of choices concerning structure, the rhythm and flow of the language, and when to add in accounts from my own practice. While a great deal of material has been collected together, and much sense made of it, I am all too aware that this research is incomplete, and will remain so until more information is available concerning unconscious processes. It is to be hoped nevertheless that it makes a useful contribution to the understanding of those subtle interactions that occur whenever two or more people meet, as in psychotherapy.

Practical applications in training

So the question now is: What best use can be made of the information gathered here for the benefit of therapeutic practice? In teaching the theory of intuition, one might well start where I did, by asking why it has been so neglected and why it is so little understood. Reasons put forward here have included its association with the paranormal, the cultural pre-eminence of rationalism in the West, how behaviourism dominated psychology for a large part of the twentieth century, how psychoanalysis wanted to be recognized as a science and, more generally, denigration of feminine intuition and people's fear of the unconscious. Moreover, which of these reasons still apply and what others might there be?

Attention must of course be focused on the multi-faceted nature of intuition. As we have discovered, this is a perceptive process occurring largely out of awareness, that combines both internal and external cues to produce some new understanding, knowledge or creativity. This arrives in consciousness as a complete entity and may be marked by suddenness and a subjective feeling of certainty. It is an ability which is partly innate and partly acquired through experience. Here we have the basis of a working definition as applied to therapy. Further discussion during training can centre around the type of clues that may contribute to an intuition, and how those from the client and surrounding environment may combine with the therapist's emotional and bodily responses, subjective imagery, past memories and professional experiences to produce the new understanding. Although there are strong links with the transpersonal, I would like to emphasize the importance of demystifying intuition and explaining the process in straightforward terms. Quite simply, it is the other main way in which we use our minds: either we think logically and rationally, step by step in a linear way, looking at cause and effect, and employing language to communicate the process; or else we allow our unconscious to do the work, combining impressions, images, body responses, thought-fragments and feelings, until a whole, meaningful form reaches consciousness and we say to ourselves, 'Yes, that's it!' In the training situation, experiences of intuition can be collected together, aspects of its nature discussed and then the findings can be compared with those in this book. It needs to be remembered that at least 65 per cent of interactions between people are nonverbal and therefore picked up intuitively. A good balance must therefore be struck between intellectual work and the development of intuition, if trainees are to become well-rounded practitioners.

While the respondents to the training questionnaire indicated that aspects of the intuitive process were looked at in a general way, I would like to suggest that such work could be more specifically allied to intuition. The focus group, described in Chapter 5, revealed that professional therapists believed that they had not been taught about intuition, apart from two individuals who had received a transpersonal training. This is at odds with the perception of many counselling teachers consulted, that they are offering experience and understanding of the phenomenon through skills practice and supervision. The apparent gulf in communication between teachers and students about underlying unconscious processes when two people meet needs to be addressed. Equally, students have to take responsibility for developing their own intuition through personal therapy and awareness work, as do graduates as part of their ongoing professional development. After all, a successful therapeutic relationship is built largely on the sensitive use of intuition and research has shown that it is the relationship that heals over and above any theoretical model (Clarkson, 1995).

There is an interesting parallel here between the ways in which intuition is enhanced and further acquired through the early relationships between the child and carers and the process within training and supervision as described by respondents to the questionnaire. In each case this kind of nonverbal know-how is attained by imitation, feedback and experience. Small children do not have the cognitive ability to comprehend the processes involved, and indeed it is not necessary that they should. Adults, on the other hand, do, and a good grasp of how intuition functions is of great help to its development.

Cultivating intuitive qualities

It does seem that some people are more intuitive than others and characteristics of the intuitive type of person have been set out. The profile that emerges gives an indication of how the faculty might be cultivated within individuals and the reader is referred again to Chapter 4. Creative tutors will no doubt invent exercises for students, which will enhance qualities such as emotional sensitivity, imaginative use of symbolism, ability to make novel connections and the confidence to derive meaning from a small amount of information. They will also encourage avoidance of dogma and help students to construct an inner locus of authority. A sense of fun and creativity will no doubt evolve through such exercises. Some suggestions have already been made in the previous chapter, including the keeping of an intuition journal, and some more are offered here.

A technique described by Assagioli employs evocative words to help bring a particular quality into a person's life (1974/1984, pp. 76–9). He makes the point that words are capable of arousing corresponding emotions, ideas and activities. So if, for example, a student wishes to bring more humour into her life, she can begin by giving attention to the word. She can then write it on a card and place it where it will be seen every day. After relaxing, she can meditate on it and allow images to emerge. These can form the basis of a colourful poster which she can create and hang on the wall. A further step is to 'feel' the word, identify with it and consciously adopt the posture and movements that it inspires. The more this kind of focused attention is given to the quality, the more it will become a part of her life. She can, of course, also seek the companionship of humorous people and find ways in which she herself can express the fun part of her nature.

Freedom from dogma may require looking at the internal dynamics, in which some kind of inner critic or judge is laying down the law and persuading the student or supervisee to follow the prescribed theory rather than a gut feeling. Subpersonality work can be most revealing in this context. The student can be invited to write a list of all the internal 'shoulds' and 'oughts' and then an image can be summoned up to represent the part of the personality that gives such instructions. The individual then steps into the subpersonality with full awareness and speaks from this position to its opposite. Positions are swapped and the other replies, and so on. This kind of Gestalt dialogue may help the person become more aware of how much this subpersonality is in control and therefore preventing her from accessing her more intuitive aspects. This is just one example demonstrating the importance of personal therapy and awareness work. Only by understanding and accepting the controlling aspects of oneself can the choice be made to release any suppressed creativity. John Rowan writes lucidly about subpersonalities and his two books provide a rich resource for such work (1990 and 1993a).

Another technique recommended by Assagioli is to 'act as if' you already possessed the desired state or quality (1974/1984, pp. 79–83). Experimental psychology has demonstrated that performing the actions and expressions of a particular state in turn induces the concordant mood in us. Perhaps the student would benefit from being more confident. First, it is useful to study confident people and notice their general posture and how they behave in different situations. Starting with trusted friends, the person can practise adopting that more assertive way of holding herself, moving and speaking until it begins to feel natural. During this process the confident mood will automatically match the actions until the student can claim it as her own. Other ways of building confidence are described in detail in Chapter 2 of my book *Your Mind's Eye* (Charles, 2000). Thinking well of oneself and one's judgement encourages the practitioner to build trust in her intuition. While theories can be helpful in providing a framework for understanding others, the psychodynamics of any case are invariably idiosyncratic. Therapists will often need to draw on intuition in making assessments and building hypotheses, especially at the outset of the work, when little information concerning the client is available. This aptitude points towards possibilities, what the future course of the work might be.

Members of the focus group agreed that having confidence in one's intuition, in a balanced way, was essential, otherwise information and insight from this source would most likely be disregarded. Trusting one's intuition allows it to flourish. Regular affirmation of one's intuitive ability is therefore needed and just noticing it in the first instance gives it credibility. Keeping an intuition journal has already been recommended. Simply spending five minutes at the end of the day, reviewing when intellect has dominated and when intuition has been followed will help to bring the process into consciousness. Watch out for everyday intuitions, how much you have operated from innate know-how, instinctively, rather than thinking things through. When with other people, look out for those unspoken messages which convey so much. What exactly helps to smooth along your social interactions? Bring into awareness the ways in which you may be unconsciously matching each other's movements. What does this express? How do you know when to speak and when not to? Learn to perceive those tiny signals. Have you had a faint hunch about something, but not followed it through? Perhaps you could pursue that now.

At a deeper level, regular meditation and paying attention to that still, small voice within, especially when the way forward is uncertain, gives acknowledgement to the inner guide. Becoming acquainted with this internal wisdom and perhaps giving it an identity, as suggested in Chapter 8, helps to build self-reliance, a significant characteristic of the intuitive type. This, of course, in no way replaces professional supervision. Remember also that intuition can arrive unexpectedly, especially when you are relaxed. So make sure that you have plenty of 'chill-out' time. My best and most creative ideas usually arrive when I am pottering in the garden. One's mind needs rest and refreshment, just as much as the body. Remember that anxiety has a blocking effect, so keep those stress levels as low as possible. You may have to be patient because intuition can never be forced. Much incubation time may be necessary before it is able to communicate with you.

Ask yourself what type of intuitions you normally have. Do they appear when you are looking out for them, or do they take you by surprise? What form do they generally have: an image, thought, feeling or bodily sensation? Do they come in a flash, or do they emerge gradually as part of a reverie? Is there much detail in evidence or is it just a general feeling of a pattern or perhaps a vague notion? What messages from the unconscious do dreams give you? Do you use intuition to help validate something you have worked out logically? How much do you rely on intuition in everyday situations? Naturally intuitive people enjoy playing with vague hunches or gut feelings, allowing them to grow and develop until a sense of what is needed becomes clearer. The more you can become familiar with your own intuition, the more you will encourage it and feel able to turn to it for guidance and inspiration.

The language of the unconscious is metaphor, analogy and imagery. Some exercises for learning to use the mind in these ways and developing an existing facility can be great fun and very creative. Try describing yourself in terms of something else, for example a plant, a tree or an animal, an aeroplane or a book. You can also lighten a session by inviting a client to do this type of exercise; it can be very revealing. Then suggest a drawing of the image and explore the meanings. Practise animating your everyday language with analogies. My husband, who is intrigued by puns and witticisms, is a fine example of a lateral thinker. When asked to come up with some analogies, he immediately suggested: 'as thin as a vegan's cookbook' or 'as fat as a stockbroker's wallet'! Poetry, of course, is replete with imagery and is a valuable resource for stimulating the imagination. Students can be encouraged both to discover poetry that speaks to them, and also to write their own. Visual analogy has often contributed to insight. Freud, by his own admission, conceived the idea of the sublimation of instincts, not initially through logical thought, but by seeing a cartoon in a humorous magazine. The first picture showed a small girl herding a flock of goslings with a stick, while the second depicted her later in life as a governess similarly herding a group of young ladies with a parasol (Sachs, 1946, p. 98).

A feeling for pattern, shape and colour and how these relate can be deliberately enhanced by studying books on art and by visiting galleries. However, cursory attention is not enough. Select a painting that attracts you in some way and spend time contemplating it in depth. What colours has the artist chosen and why? How do they contribute to the overall mood? What shapes dominate the picture and how have they been arranged? Examine the strokes of the brush and notice how the colour has been applied? What does this tell you about the artist? Look for the smallest details and consider what they contribute. Why has this picture spoken to you? Are you identifying with it, or projecting a part of yourself or some memory into it? If so, close your eyes, and become fully aware of what you might be adding to the painting from your own memory store. Make a conscious effort to clear that and then open your eyes and look at the painting again with clear vision. Now step away and take in the work as a whole. What message does it give you?

Tony Bastick emphasizes that emotional sensitivity and variability are pivotal to the intuitive process (1982). However, self-knowledge and self-acceptance are fundamental to feeling at ease with feelings. How willing are you to monitor all the passing moods in yourself, and how many would you rather not acknowledge? Your intuition may be telling you something about yourself or someone else, which you would prefer not to know. In this case you are likely to discount it. Long-term in-depth personal therapy substantially reduces the fear of encountering unpalatable aspects of oneself or others.

It is a common experience to meet a person who reminds you of someone from the past. Feelings and associations are likely to be evoked which are connected with that first person, but they may well cloud your judgement of the new individual, leading you to make all kinds of incorrect assumptions. Intuition cannot function in such an atmosphere; it can only operate when perception is clear. Remember also that we tend to project on to others whatever we would rather not claim as our own, whether that be dark, negative material, or strongly positive. These are just some straightforward examples of why self-awareness is so crucial to the effective functioning of intuition.

Chapter 7 described in some detail the links between empathy and intuition, and the suggestion was made that this kind of emotional sensitivity could be developed. In their book on person-centred counselling, Mearns and Thorne make the point that therapists need to broaden their experience of the world and of different social groups, if they are to be able to empathize with people who come from backgrounds other than their own (1988/1999, p. 28). Suppose that a counsellor is endeavouring to assist a bachelor client who is struggling to make sense of a difficult business situation, yet she herself has no such experience, having spent most of her adult life as housewife and mother. Each has gained a specialized knowledge of the world, which is poles apart from the other. How then might she use her imagination to step into his shoes? While it may be quite impracticable for such a counsellor to gain the required understanding first-hand, she can nevertheless greatly broaden her experience through the reading of novels and the studying of drama. Mearns and Thorne state: 'a good case could be made for requiring counsellors in training to make in-depth studies of some of the world's greatest creative writers. The counsellor who never reads a novel, or who never opens a book of poetry is neglecting an important resource for empathic development.' I wholeheartedly endorse such a viewpoint, not just for enrichment of the imagination and of empathy, but also of intuition. The same authors also highlight the importance of self-acceptance. Counsellors cannot give of themselves empathically if they are feeling deeply troubled and vulnerable and need to defend themselves and keep others at a distance.

Empathy can be further developed by extending the metaphor exercise suggested above, and imaginatively stepping into an object, animal or person. What is it really like when you take on the posture, movements, expressions of that object or being? Write about the experience of becoming, say, a horse. Then choose a person and describe, from the inside, what happens when you step into those other shoes.

The ability to articulate intuitively acquired material may pose a difficulty for some therapists. According to MBTI research, the majority of counsellors are intuitive feelers (NFs), leaving thinking in the tertiary or inferior position (Myers and McCaulley 1985, p. 257). It seems important, therefore, that NF therapists foster their thinking mode to support their intuitive function. This leads to the point that being aware of one's own type preferences can be very helpful in alerting practitioners to personal weaknesses and prejudices, as well as possible unconscious collusion with the client where the two personalities happen to be similar (see Chapter 4). Both Jungian typology and the Myers-Briggs Type Indicator maintain that type influences individual perceptions and judgements and the suggestion is that dominant intuitives are at a distinct advantage, especially in the gathering of covert messages. It is all the more remarkable, therefore, that therapists do not fare any better than the general population in making certain clinical assessments. Students need to become fluent at translating intuitive impressions into communicable language.

Another obstacle is the difficulty many people have in distinguishing thoughts from feelings. I have been struck by how often I may ask a client what he or she is feeling and the person will respond with a thought. If appropriate, I may gently explain the difference. On occasion this has happened with supervisees of considerable professional experience. Becoming familiar with emotional language and having ready descriptions for bodily responses all assist in bringing aspects of intuition into conscious awareness. From time to time, stop for a moment and check in with yourself. What faint feelings are there and what body responses? Exaggerate the responses. Think of an analogy by asking what these are like and then allow an image to develop. What is your intuition saying? As I sit here typing, the sun is streaming through the skylight and I am aware of a longing to go outside. This is at odds with a need to press on and finish the chapter. My body is responding with a slight tension in my chest and I have the image of a small pebble there. As I focus on it in my mind's eye, it changes into a pink-speckled egg. My body becomes increasingly restless and, as I shift and stretch, I have the vision of a bird in a large, wooden cage. There is a sense of something being born, but also a need to escape and fly. Indeed, the door of the cage is open. My intuition is reminding me to keep a good balance between work and play and not to fall into the old pattern of causing myself too much stress. I hear the message: it is time to shut the computer down!

Gestalt awareness exercises

Paradoxically, people who are naturally intuitive often do not notice details, because their attention is focused on the overall picture. Moreover, since they have a tendency to be future-orientated, they are often not sufficiently alert to actualities. The classic Gestalt exercises in current awareness, described in Perls, Hefferline and Goodman (1951/1973) can be very helpful in bringing such individuals more fully into the present. The first is apparently extremely simple and involves making statements about current experience, such as 'Now I am aware that ...' or 'At this very moment I ...' or 'Here I ...' The authors emphasize that the present means at this very instant, and not at an earlier time during the day or what you expect to happen in a few moments. So, for example, I may say, 'Now I am sitting on a chair. I am aware that the chair is hard. On my desk I see a stapler. Now I notice how red it is. At this very moment I see how the light falls across it. Now I am aware that it has a patterned texture on its surface ...' and so on. The experiment is repeated, remembering to include 'now', 'here' and 'I am aware that ...' but this time noticing any resistances, which may take the form of boredom, annoyance or anxiety. How do you prevent yourself from experiencing the fullness of each moment? What I immediately learnt from this experiment was my wish to speculate, for example about the designer of the stapler. Many people spend most of their lives in a semi-trance or daydream, which has the effect of drawing a veil over the present.

Another experiment involves the relationship between figure and ground. The task is to focus attention on any object, say a table. Watch how it becomes clearer as the objects behind fade into the background. Then listen to a sound and notice how it relates to other sounds. Do the same with a physical sensation, and as you attend to it be aware how other sensations recede. A similar exercise can be incorporated into counselling practice. In this, you listen only to the sound of the 'client's' voice, allowing the content to fade out of awareness. Describe the voice in detail, whether it is high or low, soft or loud, muffled or clear and so on. Then become aware what effect the sound has on you in emotional terms. Are you irritated because it is a strain to listen to, or are you lulled by its soothing timbre? Turn your attention towards the voice again and consider what emotional background has produced this particular tonal quality. Exercises such as these increase direct contact with the environment, and the effect of practising them heightens interest in whatever is occurring.

The next stage is to experience oneself as a living and dynamic part of the environment, and to track current interactions, so that everything, both external and internal is included in the awareness. These might be wishes, 'shoulds', how you are drawn to the past or future, as well as direct observations. To return to my desk-top, by way of example: 'I now notice that I want to speculate about the designer of the stapler, but feel I ought to draw my attention back to the desk-top. Here I see the shapes and bright colours of the pens, pencils and 'post-its' and I now feel intrigued. I am aware that my mind wants to wander off to modern art. I have an urge to fiddle with the shapes and colours to produce a picture, but I stop myself. I am aware of wanting to recall a visit to Tate Modern and I feel again, now, the excitement I then had. The sound of a car passes below my window. It intrudes and I feel annoyed ....'

Important for psychotherapy is the ability to trace subtle feeling-tones in oneself, in the other person, and in the space between. Because we have learnt to switch off emotions on account of past painful experiences and the fear of repeating them, many of us have lost touch with the continuity of feeling responses. It has been much safer for us to go into 'neutral' mode. The task here is to recapture the fresh vision of childhood and the emotional openness that we once had. Take a walk outside and allow yourself to become conscious of the ongoing flow of your responses, however faint they may be. What does the weather evoke in you in terms of mood or body response? Be aware of the fresh air against your skin. How do your feet feel today? What happens as this or that person passes by? What are your responses to plants and trees? Continue with this for at least twenty minutes. The more you repeat this exercise, wherever you are or whatever you are doing, the more you will cultivate your sensitivity – and hence your intuition.

Philip Goldberg in his book *The Intuitive Edge* recommends 'absorption sessions', with the aim of increasing the opportunities for the making of connections. In this, you decide on a locale, preferably a place you would not normally venture into, and then go and investigate it. You act like a sponge, soaking up all the new experiences with an attitude of relaxed alertness (1985, p. 167). When there, allow yourself to be spontaneous and do something out of the ordinary.

Becoming more sensitive, alert and aware and the ability to notice the minutest of details, without the blinding influences of defensive mechanisms, are all crucial to intuition. As you continue with the awareness exercises, so you will become more alive and responsive.

Intuition in professional practice

In looking back over the several years during which I have been researching and writing up this project, I am conscious of how my own practice has changed as my intuition has awakened. Firstly, it is no longer difficult to explain what intuition is. Those early days when I was struggling to grasp at something which seemed inexplicable, have long since gone by. There is no more groping or fumbling for the right words, the phrases which are sufficiently adequate to explain such a complex phenomenon. As my understanding has grown, so has my awe of the vast scope and creative power of the human mind. I now know I can allow mine to do whatever it needs to, with minimal interference from myself. Equally, I can use my intellect and direct my thoughts at will.

The study of Jung and other prominent writers was utterly absorbing and deeply enriching, whether or not I agreed with them! I have been able to incorporate many of Jung's theories concerning type into my counselling in a practical way. This has helped me to be much more accepting of how other personalities operate. For example, the opposite of my type is probably ESFP, an extraverted senser, gregarious and practical. Such an individual hates structure, can easily become distracted and will find it difficult to set goals. I may therefore struggle to keep such a client on track. Rather than impose my way of operating, though, I can more effectively tune in to him or her by working very much in the moment and appreciating that the individual will respond best to practical suggestions.

Realizing that I am a dominant intuitive supported by thinking, has encouraged me to focus on my inferior function, that of sensing. Working through the awareness exercises described above has opened my eyes to all sorts of details and feeling-tones which I might otherwise have missed when sitting with a client. So much came to the fore that had simply passed me by previously, the tiny indications, half-made gestures, faint aromas or sounds, intakes of breath, and so on, all laden with meaning. That inner alertness, the tracking of my own responses during sessions, offers a wealth of possibilities for the progress of the work. Little hunches or obscure gut feelings are now taken notice of and allowed to grow, until their significance becomes plain.

Knowing that my type preference is for intuition gives me greater confidence in it. If the problems brought to me seem impossibly complex, I am now able to view the apparent confusion as a resource, out of which something new and creative will develop. I am reminded of the poet Keats and his words concerning what he described as 'negative capability'. Clearly he was writing from experience when he described that quality of 'being in uncertainties, mysteries, doubts, without any irritable reaching after facts and reason' (in Goldberg 1985, p. 157). If I myself have difficulty in seeing the way forward for a particular individual, rather than feeling worried about my seeming incompetence, I will trust that, after sleeping on it for a few nights and allowing for the necessary incubation period, a sense of the next step will be there. What is needed is to wait patiently.

As I worked on releasing my own intuition, I was vividly reminded of the ways in which, earlier in life, I had been obliged to shut down my natural sensitivity and perceptiveness. It was too painful to see so much. Now, however, I was reopening myself to experience. This was far from easy and I needed to put in place some kind of psychological protection. One helpful technique was to take a few moments to meditate before the arrival of a particularly distressed client, and, in my imagination, to shine a light on each of us: for myself, it was to calm any arising anxiety and as a reminder that I could come to no harm; and for the client it represented whatever I sensed the individual most needed at that time. Sometimes I would visualize myself in a kind of protective transparent bubble. While I could perceive whatever was there, it gave me a feeling of safety, affirming to myself that no dark or destructive elements could penetrate the bubble's surface. Techniques such as these gave me the freedom to open myself to the experience of the session, whatever that might be.

Setting up the three studies was both challenging and energizing. If I was to make a truly original contribution to the subject, for the benefit of the profession, then it would stem from these. I knew that the gap in knowledge needed to be filled, which was due to the lack of empirical material relating directly to the counselling situation. In addition to the valuable information supplied by my colleagues in the focus group and diary study, most illuminating was the tracking of my own work with regard to intuition. I was being obliged to become fully aware of barely conscious processes that previously I had taken for granted. In watching out for intuitions and logging them, I was able to be of greater service to my clients, through incorporating them into sessions as appropriate, particularly where the comprehension of nonverbal messages was concerned. Moreover, after studying communication psychology, I had access to a ready-made vocabulary with which such transmissions could be described.

In analyzing the data from the diary study, the realization grew that here was a vehicle whereby we could understand what the arising intuitions consisted of. It was now possible to set out with greater precision how professionals employ the phenomenon within the clinical setting. While some of the results were in line with existing theory, others refuted certain long-held beliefs. Moreover, completely new pieces of information emerged, in particular how therapists actually go about validating intuitions. Having this list at my disposal meant that I could consciously choose to use one or more of the methods to check the intuitions. Employing the intellect for this purpose was by no means the only way of doing this.

Previously, I had largely relied on inference when making assessments and building hypotheses regarding clients. After reading in the experimental literature that intuitive judgements fare no worse than logical ones, I decided to use both methods side by side. This meant that I could compare one with the other and build a firmer foundation for the work. I might therefore look at the psychodynamics of a case, be aware of the process of cause and effect and at the same time take into account the subjective, overall impression given to me.

Meditation and visualization have become regular features in my practice and I often consult with my inner source of wisdom whenever the flow of the work seems stuck. This appears to me as an old jackdaw with a beautiful shiny grey head, who sits on my left shoulder and croaks his messages into my ear. There is something here for me about the image of a bird able to soar above whatever is happening and thereby see everything from a different perspective. Often he is able to supply me with an overview of a client's case, particularly if I am feeling overwhelmed by the amount of material presented. Meditation also helps me to empty out preconceptions and intrusive thoughts to achieve an inner calm, so that I can be more fully available for the client and able to welcome the unexpected. This state is characterized by an aliveness, in which everything is seen in sharper focus. Attention may be panoramic, sweeping over the landscape of a session to gather in an overall impression, yet at the same time picking up the minutiae of the client's body language. Simultaneously, I am keenly attuned to my own internal images, whispers and kinaesthetic responses. Experience has taught me that it is in this mode that intuitions are most likely to arise.

Despite the relatively few identifiable intuitions supplied by participants in the diary study, there are in fact multifarious ways in which we may use the function both during and in between sessions. In total, it constitutes the psychological understanding that theory does not supply. As we have seen, many such intuitions are extremely hard to capture as they occur mostly out of current awareness. It may be helpful, nevertheless, to offer a summary of the possible usages within therapeutic practice. This is not intended to be comprehensive, but it will at least serve as a basis for further thought and discussion.

Uses of intuition in professional practice

Initial assessment

- Understanding the significance of first impressions.
- A guide as to the hidden meaning of presenting symptoms.
- Sensing what questions to ask and when.
- Forming hypotheses from clues gathered.
- As an aid to diagnosis.

Establishing and maintaining a good working relationship

- Being in tune with the client.
- Picking up the signals for a comfortable rapport.
- Using tactful timing and intervention: sensing the 'psychological moment' for offering an insight or possible interpretation.
- When to stay silent.
- Establishing trust.

The therapeutic task

- Selecting treatment options.
- Aid to deciding on the next step.
- Picking out the most salient features from the client's story and knowing what to pursue.
- Knowing which techniques might be helpful and when, such as drawing or visualization.
- When to give caring support, in what manner and how much.
- Guidance as to how safe it is to explore deep terrain.
- Whether to offer practical suggestions and when.
- How best to affirm the client to build self-esteem.
- Sensing when to challenge and how, so as not to threaten or cause anxiety.
- Having a feel for what lies in potential for the client.
- Whether to take the client beyond the mundane and into the transpersonal domain.

Apprehending the psychodynamics of the case

- Counter-transference reactions: information arising from the monitoring of one's own body responses, feelings, thoughts or images.
- Apprehending client's unspoken feelings and thoughts through picking up nonverbal signals.
- Perception of character structure via body posture.
- Knowing when the Inner Child, Critical Parent or other subpersonality is present.
- Identifying resistances and defences.
- Impressions of past important experiences.
- Perception of unconscious motivations (perhaps in contrast to conscious ones) that compel the client to act in this or that way.
- Awareness of absence of usual behaviours and the significance of this.
- A feel for repetitive patterns.
- How the pieces of the 'puzzle' fit together.
- Perception of client's life 'script'.

Deepening the understanding of the client's process

- Making sense of small communications through linking.
- Making connections to produce psychological insight into the case.
- Picking up covert messages through tone of voice and other nonverbal signals, which may hold deep meaning.
- Seeing the significance in casual remarks and apparently unimportant data.
- Grasping hidden psychical data from involuntary scanning.
- Instinctive understanding of client's behaviour.
- Spontaneous analogy with other cases or literary figures to provide deeper understanding.
- Access to other ideas and possibilities through use of wit and puns.
- Aid to discovering the meaning of symbols, dreams or guided fantasies.

Enabling client insight

- Spelling out the emotional undertones.
- Perceiving what the client unconsciously 'asks for' in terms of relationship.
- Picking up meaningful deceptions, whether conscious or unconscious.
- Ability to verbalize for the client what he or she has not yet grasped, whether positive or negative.

Verification

- Having a feel for genuine intuitive material.
- Spontaneous linking of ideas arising from the unconscious with previous knowledge or experience.
- Knowing what to check out with the client and when.

Conclusion

In surveying the research forming the background to this book, it is clear that the conditions of therapy are ideal for intuition. The information is complex, apparently absent or limited, and the time for the making of judgements within sessions is frequently short. Nonverbal messages may often be more important than verbal ones in giving vital clues concerning a client's difficulties. We have seen that subliminal global processing is particularly well suited to this situation. The conclusion reached is that intuition plays a very significant role within psychotherapy and contributes to positive outcome for the client. It is a real concern, therefore, that a substantial proportion of practitioners consulted had no memory of intuition being specifically included in their training. On the other hand, many tutors felt that it was incorporated, but in a general way. Now that we have to hand, in the form of this volume, a clear description of the nature of intuition and the various forms it takes in psychotherapy, it is to be hoped that the subject can be more intentionally included in training.

The making of connections has appeared as fundamental throughout the literature and from the first two studies, but there is a difference in emphasis between transpersonal approaches and those models that do not include a spiritual element. Jung and Assagioli and other transpersonal practitioners are most likely to focus on meditation to increase the possibility of significant links being made and an intuition surfacing to consciousness. While there was evidence from the focus group that some therapists employ this practice by meditating on the client, it was clear from both this and the diary study that this approach was considerably less common than the spontaneous forming of associations between the presenting problem and, for example, background information concerning the patient, previous professional experience with similar cases or personal life history. Richness of associations can be deliberately enhanced, as we have seen, in part through reading, and Jung's chosen areas of study were mythology and comparative religion. These appear to be of less significance to contemporary practitioners than they were in the earlier part of the twentieth century. Indeed, no examples occurred in the two studies mentioned of mythological or primordial images, which take such a prominent place in Jung's psychology. There were, however, several instances of bisociation with well-known figures from literature and the arts. In addition to personal maturity and experience of working with people, a recommendation is therefore made to develop an interest in the humanities.

Therapists who wish to cultivate their intuitive function further are well advised to follow Jung's example in working with the active imagination. He fostered within himself an open, non-judgemental attitude, incorporating play and artistic creation into his life. Equally, he encouraged patients to work with painting and other media, whereby intuitive messages could be received via the images evoked. He made the source of his inner promptings more real by personifying it in the figure of Philemon. Through such creative and imaginative approaches, divergent thinking can be fostered.

Holism has been central to the discussion, but here there has been a disparity of opinion as to its role in the intuitive process. That a content is presented whole and complete is not disputed, but disagreement has centred around the involvement of sensation. It has been seen that a strong theme in Jung's typology is that of the opposition of the psychological functions, yet central to Tony Bastick's theory is the interactive feedback nature of the intuitive process (1982). This investigation has found the opposing of sensation with intuition to be problematic, since both experimental psychologists and the participants of the first two studies have demonstrated that bodily and affective states are involved in intuition. Concern has been expressed that research has shown trained clinicians to be poor at picking up the details of body-language cues. In addition to developing intuition, therefore, therapists need to become more aware of the sensing function.

A strong theme within this enquiry has been that of spirituality. Psychotherapists in the focus group regarded the intuitive process in part as 'transcendent'. It could be that intuition is sometimes experienced as mystical simply because people do not know how to explain it. It has also become apparent that it has the quality of being 'given' in that, as one participant put it, one cannot decide to have an intuition. Certain individuals have interpreted this as 'God given'. Whereas the evidence indicates that an intuition does indeed occur spontaneously, the diary study demonstrated that at least some of the steps central to the process could be traced retrospectively. It is therefore concluded that many intuitions are of the everyday sort, but that some may be subjectively experienced as mystical in character. The impact of intuitive knowledge is not always positive. The research revealed that intuition may sometimes be repressed from fear of confronting unconscious contents, or in the case of professional practice, from anxiety concerning loss of control. Similarly, extraordinary or 'peak' experiences may be repressed and a pathology of the sublime was therefore deemed to be relevant. Jung believed that most of his patients' problems centred on a lack of spirituality. While this view is considered to be extreme, nevertheless therapists need to be open to transcendent experiences in order to be able to encourage these in their clients where appropriate.

Inexactness and confusion as regards the form in which intuition appears has been pointed out in a number of writings, especially Jung's, which indicate that it is neither sense perception, nor feeling, nor intellectual inference, but that it may also appear in these forms (CW 6, para. 770). Explanations as to how it might otherwise appear and the lack of empirical material to back up such claims have been noticeable. This void is filled by the diary study, which gives precise examples of 13 different ways in which intuition manifests itself within the clinical setting. The three mentioned by Jung do feature, in particular feeling responses on the part of the therapist.

Based on the material assembled in this book, the following recommendations for the development of intuition can now be summarized. These fall into two main categories: the first concerns the enhancement of the process in everyday life to increase awareness of it; and the second refers specifically to the context of counselling and psychotherapy.

Ways to develop intuition in general

- Challenge assumed pre-eminence of the outer, logical way of knowing.
- Observe and practise intuition in everyday life.
- Value divergent thinking.
- Develop self-awareness, especially of any subconscious blocks to a particular emotion.
- Take notice of your inner wisdom. Consider evoking a symbol to represent this.
- Learn to trust intuitions by checking them out.
- Overcome any fear of intuition and open up to the unconscious.
- Keep anxiety levels low with regular relaxation, both mental and physical. Create good support systems.
- Take an interest in the arts: drama, literature, music and painting.
- Cultivate the imagination and use it to develop empathy and emotional sensitivity.
- Develop heightened sensory awareness.
- Be open to the transpersonal; allow in peak or mystical experiences.
- Be spontaneous, adaptable and original.

Enhancement of intuition in clinical practice

- Meditate before the arrival of a client, to rid the mind of intrusive thoughts and to be more 'centred'.
- Develop an internal supervisor which is non-judgemental.
- Build a good background knowledge of each client.
- Take notice of the quality of the therapeutic relationship. Be sensitive to 'regulators'.
- Develop an accord with the client, so that external links can be made with one's internal process.
- Oscillate between feelings with the client and thinking about the individual.
- Be sensitive to the client's unspoken needs.
- Be clear about the source of one's own feelings and sensations during the session.
- Be willing to work in non-cognitive ways, such as drawing, modelling, movement, drama.
- Incorporate the poetic and metaphoric into sessions. Welcome dreams. Ask for images; offer them.
- Introduce play and humour.
- Take time to ruminate between sessions.
- Dwell upon details until meanings become clear.
- Be prepared to tolerate ambiguity and vagueness during the incubation period.

- Look below the surface for covert messages and be willing to hear the client's narrative as metaphor.
- Take notice of impressions and 'hunches' and the minutiae of experience.
- Heed images and picture fragments, however fleeting.
- Use free association to make connections.
- Allow clues, background information and the problem to come into relationship.
- Be willing to experiment with novel ideas and associations and to pursue contradictory trains of thought.
- Be flexible and open to deep subjective idiosyncratic meanings.
- Use theory as a guide only and avoid dogmatism.
- Explore shifts in consciousness: a focused awareness, or seeing the whole picture.
- Become more future-orientated and work with potential.
- Be alert to repression of the sublime.
- Be modest and cautious in making judgements and interpretations.
- Validate intuitions by checking with the client or waiting until more information is forthcoming.
- Do not assume that your client is intuitive. Practical assistance may be best.

* * * *

Finally, I would like to end with a quotation from *Hamlet* (V. ii), which aptly depicts the elusive nature of intuition. It can never be summoned to order, but a state of heightened awareness, being ready for it, allows its entry:

> If it be now, 'tis not to come; if it be not to come, it will be now;
>
> if it be not now, yet it will come: the readiness is all.

Appendices

Appendix A

C: Well, I think that may point to how we can develop intuition ...

G: Yep.

C: You know, in getting more competent we may start to be more relaxed, or let go, and that allows for expansion..

G: Yes.

C: That would give my sense of it.

R: Right. And, and you mentioned the word 'abstract', 'holistic and abstract' ...

C: Mm.

R: In what sense?

C: Mm, well, em, the ... you know, I make a distinction between the rational and concrete and arriving at things in a linear process, a, a causal effect, and the way that intuition comes is, em, in symbols or images to me, or, or kind of insights which aren't causal, it's sort of [snaps fingers] it's just there.

R: So it's not logical, it's not about cause and effect, is that what you're saying?

C: It's almost, it's almost the antidote to that, I mean you can arrive at the same conclusion as cause and effect, but intuition is as distinctly different from that as it could be in a way. It, like, comes to you bbmm.

R: So there's something instantaneous about it.

C: Yes.

R: I see some heads nodding here. L., would you agree with that?

L: Yes, bec... I was thinking that, em, I don't know what intuition is, but, em, what I feel about it is that I can't decide to have an intuition.

R: No, no.

L: It kind of feels like it happens to me.

R: In a sense it's given to you, it, it happens to you?

L: It comes, it comes.

R: So that's a particular quality that it has...

Appendix B

Card 5	**SPEED OF PROCESSING**
G: 1.19	Quick decisions possible because of therapist's skill in picking up the clues.
C: 3.23	Information suddenly becomes available.
C: 5.14	Immediacy: 'it's just there'. Snapping of fingers to describe this. No apparent cause.
R & C: 5.19-20	Agreement that the process is instantaneous.
L: 6.24	A coming together of the ingredients 'all of a sudden'.
M: 8.15	'You get there very quickly', but you cannot explain how you worked it out.
M: 9.21-3	Suddenness commented upon: 'suddenly it comes to you'.
M: 9.25	Described as a very quick process.
G: 18.22	The word 'flash' indicating speed: an intuitive flash to say something.
L: 20.18	Experienced as 'completely spontaneous'.
G: 23.19	'Intuitive flashes' referred to.
G: 23.23	An 'enlightened flash'.
M: 27.16-17	Grasping something very quickly.
G: 28.1-2	Concerning the experience of following intuitive flashes in a session.
B: 35.10	Intuition as 'immediate recognition'.
A & M: 35.23-5	Thought to be immediate when located in time.
M: 35.26	'A now thing.'
M: 36.2	Outside time, because of the psyche.
C: 36.3	Involves the past, present and future.
L: 36.4	Immediate.
M: 37.19	It suddenly came in, as a 'blinding flash'.
R & A: 38.6-8	The blinding flash was considered to be the moment of intuition, which occurred after a dream.

Links with:	Card 3. Skill in picking up clues.
	Card 4. Holistic, coming together suddenly.
	Card 6. Psychic ability, if outside time.
	Card 9. Cause and effect not evident.

Definition:	Information suddenly becoming available by a process which cannot be explained.

Appendix C

Date of record   Date of intuition

Session no.   Tape-recorded?   Yes   No
(state if during or between sessions)

Client's initials   Age   Gender   Ethnic origin

Describe what happened

What prompted the intuition?

What form did it take?

Your response

Application in session

Client's response

Outcome   Date

Further comments

Your initials

Appendix D

INSTRUCTIONS FOR KEEPING THE DIARY

This is a phenomenological enquiry into the nature of intuition as experienced by the therapist within a clinical context. In other words, I am interested in your subjective experiences (not the client's).

Entries are needed for one month.

It might be easiest to use your usual note-making time to include a record in the diary. Alternatively speak on to a tape, but follow the same format. Ideally this should be directly after the session, or at least the same day. If you forget or are short of time, do it later anyway, but give the date to indicate the time lapse. Also record any moments of intuition that occur concerning a client between sessions.

There is no need to identify the client by name, but initials, age, gender and ethnic origin are helpful. (The initials don't have to be the real ones, but please keep them the same for each client.)

Describe what happened in your own words. The form it takes may be an image, body sense, thoughts, feelings etc. Include your own reaction to this. Say whether you decide to act on it there and then, or whether you keep it in mind for later. The outcome may be immediate or long-term; include time span by adding date if you fill this in later.

Frequency

I need to know the proportion of sessions affected by intuition, eg 1 in 5. Please work this out at the end of the month. If a moment of intuition occurs either between or during sessions, mark 'N' by the client's name in your appointments diary. Add up the total number of sessions, then divide by the number affected by intuition. If none occurs, I need to know this too.

Tape recording

If you feel able to tape-record sessions, please keep the moments of intuition for me to analyse, indicating position on tape. Your tapes will be returned and confidentiality will be respected.

THANK YOU FOR YOUR VALUABLE ASSISTANCE WITH THIS RESEARCH.

Appendix E

TRAINING QUESTIONNAIRE
Intuition in Psychotherapy and Counselling

Name of institute:

Qualification offered:

Core theoretical model:

Total number of training hours:

Instructions:
Please circle 'yes' or 'no' as appropriate. If your answer is 'yes', state the approximate number of hours devoted to this course. If hours are not quantifiable, use the space overleaf to explain how the topic is included. Give further information where indicated and continue on the back of the page if necessary. Feel free to add any further comments.

Would you like your institute to be   Yes   No
acknowledged in the book?
(Please note that individual responses will be coded for analysis and will remain anonymous.)

What do you understand by the term 'intuition'?

_____

_____

Part A

1a. Does the study of nonverbal   Yes   No   Hours_____
    communication form a part of your
    training course?

1b. If 'yes', please state topics covered.

_____

_____

2. Do you offer a course on counter-
   transference?   Yes   No   Hours_____

3. Do you teach advanced empathy?   Yes   No   Hours_____

4. Is subliminal perception included   Yes   No   Hours_____
   in your course?

5a. Do your students learn how to   Yes   No   Hours_____
    work with hunches or 'gut feelings'?

5b. If 'yes' to 5a, please indicate how

_____

_____

Comments on part A

_____

_____

_____

_____

_____

Part B

6.   Does your institute's training cover any of the following?

6a.   Interpretation of dreams   Yes   No   Hours_____

6b.   Guided visualization   Yes   No   Hours_____

6c.   Archetypes and the collective   Yes   No   Hours_____
      unconscious

6d.   Psychodrama/role play   Yes   No   Hours_____

6e.   Art therapy/therapeutic drawing   Yes   No   Hours_____

6f.   Gestalt dialogue/voice dialogues   Yes   No   Hours_____

6g. Symbolism and the use of metaphor and analogy	Yes	No	Hours_____
6h. The use of narrative	Yes	No	Hours_____
6i. The use of poetry	Yes	No	Hours_____
6j. The use of humour	Yes	No	Hours_____
6k. Music therapy/the use of music	Yes	No	Hours_____
6l. Sandplay	Yes	No	Hours_____

Comments on 6

_____

_____

_____

_____

_____

Part C

7.	Is personal therapy a requirement of students?	Yes	No	Hours_____
8.	Is group process featured in your training?	Yes	No	Hours_____

9. Does your training specifically encourage any of the following?

9a.	Free-floating attention	Yes	No	Hours_____
9b.	An open, non-judgemental frame of mind	Yes	No	Hours_____
9c.	A relaxed atmosphere in sessions	Yes	No	Hours_____
9d.	Emotional sensitivity	Yes	No	Hours_____

9e.	The seeing of patterns and relationships	Yes	No	Hours_____
9f.	Consideration of the whole, the bigger picture	Yes	No	Hours_____
9g.	Imagination	Yes	No	Hours_____
9h.	Creativity	Yes	No	Hours_____
9i.	Lateral thinking	Yes	No	Hours_____
9j.	The criticism/questioning of theory	Yes	No	Hours_____

If you have answered 'yes' to any of the above under 9, please indicate the process whereby this is achieved

_____

_____

_____

_____

_____

Part D

10a. Are your students taught how to   Yes   No   Hours_____
      develop and consult their own inner
      wisdom, in the form of, for example,
      an 'internal supervisor', 'wise being'
      or 'secondary self'?

10b. If 'yes', state term used

_____

Part E

11.	Does your training course cover the transpersonal?	Yes	No	Hours_____
12.	Are students trained in the use of meditation?	Yes	No	Hours_____

13. Are students encouraged to   Yes   No   Hours____
    contemplate on sessions?

14. Does your course include   Yes   No   Hours____
    the study of peak experiences?

15. Are your students taught how   Yes   No   Hours____
    to work constructively with
    spirituality/mysticism?

Part F

16. Does your core model emphasize one of the following?

16a. Past   Yes   No

16b. Present   Yes   No

16c. Future   Yes   No

Part G

17. Does your course cover the subject   Yes   No   Hours____
    of intuition from a theoretical
    perspective?

18a. Does your training specifically   Yes   No   Hours____
    encourage students to develop
    their intuition?

18b. If so, please say how.

_____

_____

_____

_____

19. Would your institution favour   Yes   No   Hours____
    the inclusion of the study of
    intuition into your syllabus?

20. Please describe your experience of completing this questionnaire

_____
_____
_____
_____
_____

Further comments:

_____
_____
_____
_____
_____
_____
_____
_____
_____

As a follow-up to this questionnaire, would you be willing to be interviewed by phone, or personally, for less than $\frac{1}{2}$ hour?   Yes   No

THANK YOU for taking the time to answer these important questions.

References

Allport GW (1965) Pattern and Growth in Personality. New York: Holt, Rinehart & Winston.

Andersen PA (1999) Nonverbal Communication: Forms and Functions. California: Mayfield.

Assagioli R (1965/1975) Psychosynthesis. Wellingborough: Turnstone Press.

Assagioli R (1974/1984) The Act of Will. Wellingborough: Turnstone Press.

Audi R (ed.) (1995) The Cambridge Dictionary of Philosophy. Cambridge University Press.

Baillie KL (2003) Beyond the Rational: Using and Developing Intuition in Therapeutic Practice. Unpublished dissertation. London: Psychosynthesis & Education Trust.

Baldwin M (ed.) (2000) The Use of the Self in Therapy. New York: The Haworth Press.

Barrett-Lennard GT (1965) Significant aspects of a helping relationship. Canada's Mental Health, Sup. 47(13): 1–5.

Bastick T (1982) Intuition: How We Think and Act. Chichester: Wiley.

Bateman A, Holmes J (1995) Introduction to Psychoanalysis. London: Routledge.

Beier E, Young D (1984) The Silent Language of Psychotherapy. New York: Aldine.

Beres D, Arlow MD (1974) Fantasy and identification in empathy. Psychoanalytic Quarterly 43: 26–50.

Berger DM (1987) Clinical Empathy. Northvale, New Jersey: Jason Aronson.

Bergson H (1913/1954) Creative Evolution. Transl. A Mitchell. London: Macmillan.

Berne E (1966) Principles of Group Treatment. New York: Grove Press.

Berne E (1977) Intuition and Ego States: The Origins of Transactional Analysis. San Francisco: Harper & Row.

Bion WR (1967) Second Thoughts: Selected Papers on Psychoanalysis. London: Karnac Books.

Birdwhistell RL (1970) Kinesics and Context. Philadelphia: University of Pennsylvania Press.

Blanco IM (1975) The Unconscious as Infinite Sets. London: Duckworth.

Board R (1958) Intuition in the methodology of psychoanalysis. Psychiatry 21: 233–9.

Boehme J (1622/1958) On the Divine Intuition. In: Six Theosophic Points and Other Writings: 163–208. Intr. by N Berdyaev. Michigan: University of Michigan Press.

Bornstein RF, Pittman TS (eds) (1992) Perception without Awareness: Cognitive, Clinical and Social Perspectives. New York: Guilford Press.

Bowers KS et al. (University of Waterloo, Canada) (1990) Intuition in the context of discovery. Cognitive Psychology 21(1): 72–110.

Breul K (1909) A German and English Dictionary. London: Cassell & Co.

British Association for Counselling and Psychotherapy (2003) Training in Counselling and Psychotherapy Directory (19th edn). Rugby: BACP.

Brown DE (University of Illinois) (1993) Refocusing core intuitions: a concretizing role for analogy in conceptual change. Journal of Research in Science Teaching 30(10): 1273–90.

Burgoon M, Callister M, Hunsaker FG (1994) Patients who deceive: an empirical investigation of patient-physician communication. Journal of Language and Social Psychology 13: 443–68.

Capra F (1975) The Tao of Physics. Colorado: Shambala.

Casement P (1985/1990) On Learning From the Patient. London: Routledge.

Charles R (2000) Your Mind's Eye. London: Piatkus[1].

Chodorow J (ed.) (1997) Jung on Active Imagination: Key Readings. London: Routledge.

Clark FV (1973) Exploring intuition: prospects and possibilities. Journal of Transpersonal Psychology 3: 156–69.

Clarkson P (1989) Gestalt Counselling in Action. London: Sage.

Clarkson P (1995) The Therapeutic Relationship. London: Whurr.

Claxton G (1997) Hare Brain, Tortoise Mind: Why Intelligence Increases When You Think Less. London: Fourth Estate Ltd.

Cohen D (1978) Psychologists on psychology. Journal of National Association of Teachers in Further and Higher Education 2:18.

Comte A (1830–42) Cours de philosophie positive. Paris: Bachelier, Everat.

Croce B (1901/1953) Aesthetic: As Science of Expression and General Linguistic. Transl. D Ainslie. London: Peter Owen.

Darwin C (1859/1968) The Origin of Species. London: Penguin Books.

Darwin C (1872) Expression of the Emotions in Man and Animals. London: Murray.

Davis-Floyd R, Arvidson PS (eds) (1997) Intuition, the Inside Story: Interdisciplinary Perspectives. New York: Routledge.

Desoille R (1945) Introduction à une Psychothérapie Rationelle. Paris.

Dey I (1993) Qualitative Data Analysis: A User-Friendly Guide for Social Scientists. London & New York: Routledge.

DiTiberio JK (1977) The strength of sensing-intuition preference on the MBTI as related to empathic discrimination of overt or covert feeling messages of others. PhD, Michigan State University, Dissertation Abstracts International 37, 5599A.

Dittman AT, Parloff MB, Boomer DS (1965) Facial and bodily expression: a study of receptivity of emotional cues. Psychiatry 28(3): 239–44.

Dodds ER (1951) The Greeks and the Irrational. Berkeley: University of California Press.

Drever J (1952) A Dictionary of Psychology. Harmondsworth: Penguin.

Dymond R (1948) A preliminary investigation of the relationship of insight and empathy, Journal of Consulting Psychology 12: 228-33.

Dymond R (1949) A scale for the measurement of empathic ability. Journal of Consulting Psychology 13: 127–33.

Dymond R (1953) Can clinicians predict individual behavior? Journal of Personality, 22: 151–61.

Egan G (1975/1994) The Skilled Helper: A Problem-Management Approach to Helping. Pacific Grove, California: Brooks/Cole.

Einstein A (1945) Letter to Jacques Hadamard. In Hadamard (1945) (op.cit): 142–3.

Eisenbud J (1946) Telepathy and problems of psychoanalysis. Psychoanalytic Quarterly 15: 32–87.

Ekman P (1975) Unmasking the Face. New Jersey: Prentice-Hall.

Ekman P, Friesen WV (1969) The repertoire of nonverbal behavior: categories, origins, usage and coding. Semiotica 1(1): 49–98.

Ekman P, Friesen WV (1972) Hand movements. Journal of Communication 22: 353–74.

Ekman P, Friesen WV (1986) A new pancultural facial expression of emotion. Motivation and Emotion 10: 159–68.

Elkins D (1995) Psychotherapy and spirituality: toward a theory of the soul. Journal of Humanistic Psychology 35(2): 78–98.

Ellenberger HF (1970) The Discovery of the Unconscious. New York: Basic Books.

Etchegoyen H (1991) The Fundamentals of Psychoanalytic Technique. London: Karnac.

Eysenck HJ (1952) The Scientific Study of Personality. London: Routledge & Kegan Paul.

Eysenck HJ (1965) Fact and Fiction in Psychology. Harmondsworth: Penguin.

Fenichel O (1945) Psychoanalytic Theory of the Neuroses. New York: Norton.

Fenichel O (1953) Identification. In: Collected Papers, 1st series: 97–112. New York: Norton.

Ferenczi S (1928/1955) Child analysis in the analysis of adults. In M. Balint (ed.), Final Contributions to the Problems and Methods of Psychoanalysis: 126–42. New York: Basic Books.

Ferrucci P (1982/1995) What We May Be: The Visions and Techniques of Psychosynthesis. London: Thorsons/HarperCollins.

Fichte JG (1802) Grundlage der gesammten Wissenschafstlehre. Leipzig: Mayer & Muller.

Fordham M (1957) New Developments in Analytical Psychology. London: Routledge & Kegan Paul.

Fordham M (1969) Children as Individuals. London: Hodder & Stoughton.

Frankl G (1994) Exploring the Unconscious: New Pathways in Depth Analysis. London: Open Gate Press.

Freud S (1899/1953) The Interpretation of Dreams, SE IV, Vol. 1. Transl. J Strachey. London: The Hogarth Press.

Freud S (1901/1960) The Psychopathology of Everyday Life, SE VI. Transl. J Strachey. London: The Hogarth Press.

Freud S (1905) Fragment of an Analysis of a Case of Hysteria, SE VII: 3–122. Transl. J Strachey. London: The Hogarth Press.

Freud S (1905/1960) Jokes and their Relationship to the Unconscious, SE VIII. Transl. J Strachey. London: The Hogarth Press.

Freud S (1912/1958) Recommendations to physicians practising psycho-analysis, SE XII: 109–20. Transl. J Strachey. London: The Hogarth Press.

Freud S (1913/1958) On beginning the treatment, SE XII: 121–43. Transl. J Strachey. London: The Hogarth Press.

Freud S (1913/1958) The disposition to obsessional neurosis: a contribution to the choice of neurosis, SE XII: 313–26. Transl. J Strachey. London: The Hogarth Press.

Freud S (1914/1959) The Moses of Michelangelo. In Collected Papers IV: 257–87. Transl. J Riviere. New York: Basic Books.

Freud S (1921/1955) Group Psychology, SE XVIII: 65–143. Transl. J Strachey. London: The Hogarth Press.

Freud S (1933–1964). New Introductory Lectures on Psycho-analysis and Other Works, SE XXII. Transl. J Strachey. London: The Hogarth Press.

Freud S (1933/1964) Revision of the theory of dreams, SE XXII: 7–30. Transl. J Strachey. London: The Hogarth Press.

Freud S (1940) An Outline of Psycho-Analysis, SE XXIII. Transl. J Strachey. London: The Hogarth Press.

Frick RC (1970) A Study of Intuition and Inference. Georgia: Atlanta University, School of Education.

Fulcher R (2002) The Role of Intuition in Psychotherapy. MPhil thesis. London University: Goldsmiths College.

Gendlin ET (1978/1981) Focusing. New York: Bantam.

Gendlin ET (1996) Focusing-Oriented Psychotherapy: A Manual of the Experiential Method. New York: The Guilford Press.

Ghiselin B (ed.) (1952) The Creative Process. New York: Mentor/The New American Library.

Gilbey T (transl.) (1951) Saint Thomas Aquinas (1225?–1274): Philosophical Texts. Oxford: Oxford University Press.

Glaser BG, Strauss A (1967) The Discovery of Grounded Theory. Chicago: Aldine.

Glover E (1950) Freud or Jung. London: Allen & Unwin.

Goldberg P (1985) The Intuitive Edge: Understanding and Developing Intuition. Wellingborough: Turnstone Press.

Goleman D (1996) Emotional Intelligence. London: Bloomsbury.

Graham T, Ickes W (1997) When women's intuition isn't greater than men's. In W Ickes (ed.), Empathic Accuracy. New York: Guilford.

Green E, Green A (1977) Beyond Biofeedback. New York: Delacorte Press.

Greenson RR (1960) Empathy and its vicissitudes. International Journal of Psycho-analysis 41: 418–24.

Grof S (1993) The Holotropic Mind: The Three Levels of Human Consciousness and How They Shape Our Lives. New York: HarperCollins.

Gross H (1918) Criminal Psychology. Transl. HM Kallen. Boston: Little, Brown.

Guiora AZ (1965) On clinical diagnosis and prediction. Psychological Reports 17: 779–84.

Guiora AZ, Bolin RK, Dutton CE et al. (1965) Intuition: a preliminary statement. Psychiatric Quarterly Supplement 39(1): 110–22.

Hadamard J (1945) The Psychology of Invention in the Mathematical Field: 142–3. New York: Dover.

Haftman W (1954) The Mind and Work of Paul Klee. London: Faber & Faber.

Haggard EA, Isaacs KS (1966) Micromomentary facial expressions as indicators of ego mechanisms in psychotherapy. In LA Gottschalk, AH Auerbach (eds), Methods of Research in Psychotherapy. New York: Appleton-Century-Crofts.

Hall JA (1984) Nonverbal Sex Differences: Communication, Accuracy and Expressive Styles. Baltimore, MD: Johns Hopkins University Press.

Hart T (2000) Deep empathy. In T Hart, PL Nelson, K Puhakka (eds), Transpersonal Knowing: Exploring the Horizon of Consciousness: 253–68. New York: State University of New York Press.

Hathaway SR (1955) Clinical intuition and inferential accuracy. Journal of Personality, 24: 223–50.

Hedges P (1993) Understanding Your Personality with Myers-Briggs and More. London: Sheldon Press.

Heimann P (1950) On counter-transference. International Journal of Psychoanalysis 31: 81–4.

Hillman J (1975) Revisioning Psychology. New York: Harper & Row.

Hillman J (1990) The Essential James Hillman: A Blue Fire. Intr. and ed. T Moore. London: Routledge.

Housman AE (1933) The Name and Nature of Poetry. Cambridge: Cambridge University Press.

James W (1902/1982) The Varieties of Religious Experiences. Harmondsworth: Penguin.

Jung CG (1902/1970) On the psychology and pathology of so-called occult phenomena. In CW 1, Psychiatric Studies, 2nd edn. Transl. RFC Hull. London: Routledge & Kegan Paul.

Jung CG (1913/1961) The theory of psychoanalysis. In Freud and Psychoanalysis, CW 4: 83–226. Transl. RFC Hull. London: Routledge & Kegan Paul.

Jung CG (1921) Psychologische Typen. Zurich: Rascher Verlag.

Jung CG (1923/1971) Psychological Types, CW 6. Transl. HG Baynes, rev. RFC Hull. London: Routledge.

Jung CG (1929) Problems of modern psychotherapy. In CW 16: 53–75. Transl. RFC Hull. London: Routledge & Kegan Paul.

Jung CG (1933/1961) Modern Man in Search of a Soul. Transl. WS Dell, CF Baynes. London: Routledge & Kegan Paul.

Jung CG (1941/1966) Paracelsus the Physician. In CW 15: 13–30. Transl. RFC Hull. London: Routledge & Kegan Paul.

Jung CG (1963/1995) Memories, Dreams and Reflections. Ed. A Jaffé, transl. R Winston, C Winston. London: Fontana.

Jung CG (1984/1995) Dream Analysis (Part I): Notes of the Seminar Given in 1928–1930. Ed. W McGuire. London: Routledge.

Kagan N, Krathwohl DR, Miller R (1963) Stimulated recall in therapy using videotape – a case study. Journal of Counseling Psychology 10: 237–43.

Kant I (1798/1974) Anthropology from a Pragmatic Point of View. Transl. VL Dowdell. Carbondale: Southern Illinois University Press.

Keirsey D, Bates M (1978/1984) Please Understand Me: Character and Temperament Types. California: Prometheus Nemesis/Oxford: Oxford Psychologists Press.

Klinnert MD, Campos JJ, Sorce JF et al. (1983) Emotions as behavioral regulators: social referencing in infancy. In R Plutchik, H Kellerman (eds), Emotion: Theory, Research and Experience, Vol. 2: 57–86. New York: Academic Press.

Koestler A (1964/1989). The Act of Creation. London: Arkana/Penguin Group.

Köhler W (1929). Gestalt Psychology. New York: Liveright.

Kohut H (1959) Introspection, empathy and psychoanalysis: an examination between the mode of observation and theory. Journal of American Psychological Association 7: 459–83.

Kohut H (1971) The Analysis of the Self. A Systematic Approach to the Psychoanalytic Treatment of Narcissistic Personality Disorders. New York: International Universities Press.

Kohut H (1977) The Restoration of the Self. New York: International Universities Press.

Kohut H (1980) Reflections. In A Goldberg (ed.), Advances in Self Psychology, New York: International Universities Press.

Kris E (1939) On inspiration: preliminary notes on emotional conditions in creative states. International Journal of Psycho-analysis, 20: 377–89.

Krueger RA (1994) Focus Groups: A Practical Guide for Applied Research. 2nd edn. California: Sage.

Langs RJ (1973a) The patient's view of the therapist: reality or fantasy. International Journal of Psychoanalytic Psychotherapy 2: 411–31.

Langs RJ (1973b) The Technique of Psychoanalytic Psychotherapy, Vol. 1. New York: Jason Aronson.

Langs RJ (1974) The Technique of Psychoanalytic Psychotherapy, Vol. 2. New York: Jason Aronson.

Langs RJ (1978) The Listening Process. New York: Aronson.

Lattimore R (transl.) (1965) The Odyssey of Homer. New York: HarperPerennial.

Leibniz GW von (1765/1981) Of ideas. In P Remnant, J Bennett (transl.), New Essays Concerning Human Understanding, Book II. Cambridge: Cambridge University Press.

Leuner H (1984) Guided Affective Imagery: Mental Imagery in Short-term Psychotherapy. New York: Thieme-Stratton Inc.

Levin LS (1978) Jungian personality variables of psychotherapists of five different theoretical orientations. PhD, Georgia State University. Dissertation Abstracts International 39: 40428–38.

Lévy-Bruhl L (1910/1966) How Natives Think. LA Clare (transl.). New York: Washington Square Press.

Lieberman MD (2000) Intuition: a social cognitive neuroscience approach. Psychological Bulletin 126(1): 109–37.

Livingston Smith D (1989) An interview with Robert Langs. Changes 7(4): 117–21.

Livingston Smith D (1991) Hidden Conversations: An Introduction to Communicative Psychoanalysis. London and New York: Tavistock/Routledge.

Locke J (1689/1997) An Essay Concerning Human Understanding. R Woolhouse (ed.). Harmondsworth: Penguin Books.

Lomas P (1987) The Limits of Interpretation. London: Penguin Books.

Lomas P (1994) Cultivating Intuition. London: Penguin Books.

Lorenz KZ (1951) The role of Gestalt perception in animal and human behaviour. In LL White (ed.), Symposium on Aspects of Form. London: Lund Humphries.

Lowen A (1975) Bioenergetics. London: Penguin Books.

McCosh Rev. J (1882) Intuitions of the Mind, Inductively Investigated. 3rd edn. London: Macmillan.

McDonald P, McDonald C (1993) The role of intuition in personal development. Human Development 14(3): 5–9.

Mahrer AR (1993) Transformational psychotherapy sessions. Journal of Humanistic Psychology 33(2): 30–7.

Maine B (1933) Elgar: His Life and Works, Vol. I. London: G. Bell & Sons.

Maslow A (1970/1976) Religions, Values and Peak-Experiences. London: Penguin.

Mearns D, Thorne B (1988/1999) Person-centred Counselling in Action. London: Sage Publications.

Mehrabian A, Ferris SR (1967) Inference of attitudes from nonverbal communication in two channels. Journal of Consulting Psychology 31: 248–52.

Mendelsohn GP, Geller MH (1963) Effects of counselor-client similarity on the outcome of counseling. Journal of Counseling Psychology 10(1): 71–7.

Mendelson GP, Geller MH (1967) Similarity, missed sessions, and early termination. Journal of Counseling Psychology 14(3): 210–15.

Moreno JL (1946) Psychodrama. New York: Beacon House.

Mowrer HO (1960) Learning Theory and Behavior. New York: John Wiley.

Myers F (1892) The subliminal consciousness: the mechanism of genius, Proceedings of the SPR, 8: 333-403.

Myers I Briggs (1962) The Myers-Briggs Type Indicator Manual. New Jersey: Educational Testing Service.

Myers I Briggs (1975) The Myers-Briggs Type Indicator. California: Consulting Psychologists Press, Inc.

Myers I Briggs (1987/1994) Introduction to Type: A Guide to Understanding Your Results on the Myers-Briggs Type Indicator (European English version). Oxford: Oxford Psychologists Press.

Myers DG (2002) Intuition: Its Powers and Perils. New Haven: Yale University Press.

Myers KD, Kirby LK (1994) Introduction to Type Dynamics and Development. Oxford: Oxford Psychologists Press.

Myers I Briggs, McCaulley MH (1985) Manual: A Guide to the Development and Use of the Myers-Briggs Type Indicator. Palo Alto: Consulting Psychologists Press.

Myers I Briggs, Myers PB (1980/1993) Gifts Differing: Understanding Personality Type. California: Consulting Psychologists Press.

Newman LE (1979) Personality types of therapist and client and their use in counseling. Research in Psychological Type 2: 46–55.

Oppenheim AN (1966/1992) Questionnaire Design, Interviewing and Attitude Measurement. London: Pinter.

Oskamp S (1963) The relationship of clinical experience and training methods to several criteria of clinical prediction. Psychological Monographs 76, No. 547.

Pearmain R (1999) What do we mean by developing empathy and intuition? Counselling 2: 45–8.

Perls FS (1973/1976) The Gestalt Approach and Eye Witness to Therapy. New York: Bantam Books.

Perls FS, Hefferline RF, Goodman P (1951/1973) Gestalt Therapy: Excitement and Growth in the Human Personality. Harmondsworth: Pelican.

Peters RS (1952) Brett's History of Psychology. London: Allen & Unwin.

Petitmengin-Peugeot C (1999) The intuitive experience. Journal of Consciousness Studies 6(2–3): 43–77.

Plato (4th c. BC/1954) The Last Days of Socrates. H Tredennick, H Tarrant (transl.). Harmondsworth: Penguin.

Poincaré, Henri (1929/1969) Intuition and logic in mathematics. Mathematics Teacher 62(3): 205–12.

Pollio HR (1974) The Psychology of Symbolic Activity. New York: Addison-Wesley.

Racker H (1968/1982) Transference and Countertransference. London: Maresfield Reprints.

Raskin N (1974) Studies on psychotherapeutic orientation: ideology in practice. AAP Psychotherapy Research Monographs. Florida: American Academy of Psychotherapists.

Reich W (1945) Character Analysis: Principles and Technique for Psychoanalysts in Practice and Training, 2nd edn. Transl. TP Wolfe. New York: Orgone Institute Press.

Reik T (1948/1975) Listening with the Third Ear: The Inner Experience of a Psychoanalyst. New York: Farrar, Straus & Giroux.

Robinson M, Davidson G (eds) (1999) Chambers Twenty-first Century Dictionary. Edinburgh: Chambers Harrap.

Robson C (1993) Real World Research: A Resource for Social Scientists and Practitioner-Researchers. Oxford: Blackwell.

Rogers CR (1959a) A theory of therapy, personality and interpersonal relationships, as developed in the client-centered framework. In S Koch (ed.), Psychology: A Study of a Science, vol. 3: Formulations of the Person and the Social Context. New York: McGraw-Hill.

Rogers CR (1959b) Toward a theory of creativity. In HH Anderson (ed.), Creativity and its Cultivation, 6:80. New York: Harper & Row.

Rogers CR (1961/1967) On Becoming a Person: A Therapist's View of Psychotherapy. London: Constable.

Rogers CR (1980/1995) A Way of Being. New York: Houghton Mifflin.

Rowan J (1990) Subpersonalities: The People Inside Us. London: Routledge.

Rowan J (1993a) Discover Your Subpersonalities: Our Inner World and the People in It. London: Routledge.

Rowan J (1993b) The Transpersonal: Psychotherapy and Counselling. London: Routledge.

Russell B (1946/1961) History of Western Philosophy. London: George Allen & Unwin.

Sabini M (1988) The therapist's inferior function. Journal of Analytical Psychology 33: 373–94.

Sachs H (1946) Master and Friend. London: Imago Publishing Co.

Samuels A (1985) Countertransference, the 'mundus imaginalis' and a research project, Journal of Analytical Psychology 30: 47–71.

Sanctis S de (1928) Intuitions of children. Journal of Genetic Psychology 35: 18–25.

Sanders P, Liptrot D (1994) An Incomplete Guide to Qualitative Research Methods for Counsellors. Manchester: PCCS Books.

Sarbin TR (1941) Clinical psychology – art or science. Psychometrika 6: 391–40.

Scheflen AE (1963) Communication and regulation in psychotherapy. Psychiatry 26(2): 126–36.

Scheflen AE (1972) Body Language and the Social Order: Communication as Behavior Control. Englewood Cliffs, NJ: Prentice-Hall.

Schuster R (1979) Empathy and mindfulness. Journal of Humanistic Psychology 19(1): 71–7.

Shapiro S (1995) Talking with Patients: A Self Psychological View of Creative Intuition and Analytic Discipline. New Jersey: Jason Aronson.

Sheldon WN (1940) The Varieties of Human Physique. New York: Harper.

Sidis B (1898) The Psychology of Suggestion. New York: Appleton.

Siebeck (1880–1884) Geschichte der Psychologie. Gotha.

Simpson JA, Weiner ESC (eds) (1989) The Oxford English Dictionary, Vol. VIII, 2nd edn. Oxford: Clarendon Press.

Singer J, Loomis M (1984) The Singer-Loomis Inventory of Personality (SLIP). Palo Alto: Consulting Psychologists Press.

Skinner BF (1969) Contingencies of Reinforcement. New York: Appleton-Century-Crofts.

Spinoza B de (1677/1933) On the power of the understanding, or of human freedom. In: Philosophy of Spinoza, V: 250–77. Transl. RHM Elwes. New York: Tudor Publishing Co.

Stephenson W (1953) The Study of Behavior. Chicago: University of Chicago Press.

Stern D (1987) The Interpersonal World of the Infant. New York: Basic Books.

Stevens A (1990) On Jung. London: Penguin.

Storr A (1973) Jung. London: Fontana Press.

Strauss A, Corbin J (1998) Basics of Qualitative Research: Techniques and Procedures for Developing Grounded Theory, 2nd edn. California and London: Sage.

Suzuki DT (1959) Zen and Japanese Culture. Princeton, NJ: Princeton University Press.

Taft R (1955) The ability to judge people, Psychological Bulletin 52: 1–28.

Tart CT (1975/1992) Transpersonal Psychologies. London: Routledge & Kegan Paul.

Thorne B (2002a) The Mystical Power of Person-Centred Therapy: Hope beyond Despair. London: Whurr.

Thorne B (2002b) Regulation – a treacherous path? Counselling and Psychotherapy Journal 13(2): 4–5.

Toukmanian SG, Rennie DL (eds) (1992) Psychotherapy Process Research: Paradigmatic and Narrative Approaches. London: Sage.

Valentine CW (1929) The relative reliability of men and women in intuitive judgments of character. British Journal of Psychology 19: 213–38.

Vanaerschot G (1993) Empathy as releasing several micro-processes in the client. In D Brazier (ed.), Beyond Carl Rogers: Towards a Psychotherapy for the 21st Century. London: Constable.

Van der Post L (1975/1989) A Mantis Carol. Harmondsworth: Penguin.

Vaughan FE (1979) Awakening Intuition. New York: Anchor/Doubleday.

Vernon PE (1933) Some characteristics of the good judge of personality. Journal of Social Psychology 4: 42–57.

Watson JB (1924) Behaviorism. New York: Norton.

Westcott MR (1968) Toward a Contemporary Psychology of Intuition. New York: Holt, Rinehart & Winston.

Wheelwright JB, Wheelwright JH, Buehler A (1964) Jungian Type Survey: the Gray-Wheelwright Test Manual. San Francisco: Society of Jungian Analysts of Northern California.

Whitmore D (1991) Psychosynthesis Counselling in Action. London: Sage.

Whyte LL (1962/1967) The Unconscious Before Freud. New York: Basic Books.

Wild KW (1938) Intuition. Cambridge: Cambridge University Press.

Winnicott DW (1971) Playing and Reality. London: Tavistock.

Winnicott DW (1975) Hate in the countertransference. In: Through Paediatrics to Psychoanalysis: 194–203. London: Hogarth Press.

Wippich W (1994) Intuition in the context of implicit memory. Psychological Research 56(2): 104–9.

Note

1. A new edition of this book is to be issued by the author in 2005.

Bibliography

Allport FH (1924) Social Psychology. Cambridge: Riverside Press.

Allport FH, Allport GW (1921) Personality traits: their classification and measurement. Journal of Abnormal and Social Psychology 16: 6–37.

Anderson WT (1990) Reality Is Not What It Used To Be. San Francisco: Harper & Row.

Atkinson T, Claxton G (2000) The Intuitive Practitioner: On the Value of Not Always Knowing What One Is Doing. Buckingham: Open University Press.

Bahm AJ (1960) Types of Intuition. New Mexico: University of New Mexico Press.

Bailey AA (1960) From Intellect to Intuition. New York & London: Lucis.

Bayne R (1995) The Myers-Briggs Type Indicator: A Critical Review and Practical Guide. London: Chapman & Hall.

Bigge ML, Hunt MP (1965) Psychological Foundations of Education. New York: Harper & Row.

Bohm D (1983) Wholeness and the Implicate Order. London: Ark/Routledge & Kegan Paul.

Boring E (1929) A History of Experimental Psychology. New York: Appleton-Century-Crofts.

Bunge M (1962) Intuition and Science. New Jersey: Prentice-Hall.

Buzby DE (1924) The interpretation of facial expression. American Journal of Psychology 35: 602–4.

Claxton G (1994) Noises From the Darkroom: The Science and Mystery of the Mind. London: Aquarian/HarperCollins.

Eagleton T (1990) The Ideology of the Aesthetic. Oxford: Blackwell.

Elliott R, Shapiro DA (1988) Brief structured recall: a more efficient method for studying significant therapy events. British Journal of Medical Psychology 61: 141–53.

Elliott R, Hill CE, Stiles WB et al. (1987) Primary therapist response modes: comparison of six rating systems. Journal of Consulting and Clinical Psychology, 55: 223–8.

Ewing AC (1941) Reason and intuition. Proceedings of the British Academy 55: 67–107.

Eysenck HJ (1957) Sense and Nonsense in Psychology. Harmondsworth: Penguin.

Fange EA von (1961) Implications for School Administration of the Personality Structure of Educational Personnel (PhD). Canada: University of Alberta.

Fordham F (1953/1966) An Introduction to Jung's Psychology. Harmondsworth: Penguin.

Freud S (1909/1955) Analysis of a phobia in a five-year-old boy. SE X: 5–149. Transl. J Strachey. London: The Hogarth Press.

Freud S (1927/1961) The future of an illusion. SE XXI: 5–56. Transl. J Strachey. London: The Hogarth Press.

Furlong D (1996) Develop Your Intuition and Psychic Powers. London: Bloomsbury.

Ghistra D, Nandagopal D, Ramamurthi B et al. (1976) Physiological characterisation of the 'meditative state' during intuitional practice (The Ananda Marga System of Meditation) and its therapeutic value. Medical and Biological Engineering 14 (2): 209–14.

Good DA, Watts FN (1989) Qualitative research. In G Parry, FN Watts (eds), Behavioural and Mental Health Research: A Handbook of Skills and Methods. Hove: Lawrence Erlbaum Associates.

Hannah B (1976) Jung: His Life and Work. New York: Perigee Books.

Harman W, Rheingold H (1984) Higher Creativity. Los Angeles: Holloway House.

Heppner PP, Kiolighan Jr DM, Wampold BE (1992) Research Design in Counseling. California: Brooks/Cole.

Hill CE, O'Grady KE (1985) List of therapist intentions illustrated by a case study and with therapists of varying theoretical orientations. Journal of Counseling Psychology 32: 3–22.

Hillman J (1997) The Soul's Code: In Search of Character and Calling. London: Bantam.

Holstein JA, Gubrium JF (1995) The Active Interview. London and New York: Sage.

Humbert E (1984/1988) C.G. Jung: The Fundamentals of Theory and Practice. Illinois: Chiron Publications.

Inglis B, West R with the Koestler Foundation (1989) The Unknown Guest: The Mystery of Intuition. Hodder & Stoughton.

Jacobi J (1942/1968) The Psychology of C.G. Jung. London: Routledge & Kegan Paul.

Jacobi J (1953) Psychological Reflections. Bollingen Series XXXI. New York: Pantheon.

James W (1907/1978) Pragmatism: A New Name for Some Old Ways of Thinking. Massachusetts: Harvard University Press.

Jarrett J (1988) Jung's theory of functions: some questions. Journal of Analytical Psychology 33: 355–72.

Jordan F (1896) Character as Seen in Body and Parentage. 3rd edn. London: Macmillan.

Jung CG (1912/1956) Symbols of Transformation, CW 5. Transl. RFC Hull. London: Routledge & Kegan Paul.

Jung CG (1929) Paracelsus, in CW 15: 1–12. Transl. RFC Hull. London: Routledge & Kegan Paul.

Jung CG (1936) Psychologische Typologie. Süddeutsche Monatshefte, XXXIII (5): 264–72.

Jung CG (1938/1986) Aspects of the Feminine. Transl. RFC Hull. London: Ark/Routledge.

Jung CG (1946/1954) Psychology of the transference (Die Psychologie der Übertragung). In: The Practice of Psychotherapy, CW 16. London: Routledge & Kegan Paul.

Jung CG (1960/1969) The Structure and Dynamics of the Psyche, CW 8. Transl. RFC Hull. London: Routledge & Kegan Paul.

Jung CG (1990) C.G.Jung: Typologie. Munich: Deutscher Taschenbuch Verlag.

Kagan N, Krathwohl DR, Miller R (1963) Stimulated recall in therapy using video-tape – a case study. Journal of Counseling Psychology 10: 237–43.

Kant I (1781/1902) Kritik der reinen Vernunft. Berlin: Preussische Akademie der Wissenschaft.

Keefe T (1976) Empathy: the critical skill. Social Work 21(1): 10–14.

Kendall E (1998) Myers-Briggs Type Indicator, Manual Supplement, Step 1 (European English ed.). Oxford: Oxford Psychologists Press.

Klein M (1961/1989) Narrative of a Child Analysis. London: Virago.

Klein MH, Mathieu-Coughlan P, Kiesler DJ (1969/1986) The experiencing scales. In LS Greenberg, WM Pinsof (eds), The Psychotherapeutic Process: A Research Handbook. New York: Guilford Press.

Le Shan L (1974/1983) How To Meditate. Wellingborough: Turnstone Press.

McKenna S (transl.) (1926) Plotinus: The Ethical and Other Treatises, Vol. 1. London and Boston: The Medici Society.

McLeod J (1994) Doing Counselling Research. London: Sage.

Maritain J (1977) Creative Intuition in Art and Poetry. Guildford: Princeton University Press.

Maslow AH (1971/1993) The Farther Reaches of Human Nature. London: Penguin/Arkana.

Masson J (1989/1993) Against Therapy. London: HarperCollins.

Myers I Briggs (1976) Report Form for Myers-Briggs Type Indicator. California: Consulting Psychologists Press, Inc.

Nadel L (1996) Sixth Sense. London: Prion.

Naparstek B (1997) Your Sixth Sense. San Francisco: HarperCollins.

Papadopoulos RK (ed.) (1992) Carl Gustav Jung: Critical Assessments, Vols. I–IV. London & New York: Routledge.

Perls FS (1969/1992) Gestalt Therapy Verbatim. New York: The Center for Gestalt Development.

Poincaré H (1913/1946) Mathematical Creation. In GB Halsted (transl.), The Foundations of Science. New York: The Science Press.

Quenk AT (1984) Psychological Types and Psychotherapy. Florida: Center for Applications of Psychological Type.

Reber A (1993) Implicit Learning and Tacit Knowledge: An Essay on the Cognitive Unconscious. Oxford: Oxford University Press.

Rogers CR (1951) Client-Centered Therapy: Its Current Practice, Implications and Theory. London: Constable.

Rycroft C, Gorer G, Storr A et al. (1966/1968) Psychoanalysis Observed. Harmondsworth: Penguin.

Samuels A, Shorter B, Plaut, F. (1986). A Critical Dictionary of Jungian Analysis. London: Routledge.

Sanford A (1983) Models, Mind and Man: Aspects of the Psychology of Understanding, Intuition and Thinking. Glasgow: Pressgang.

Schiller F (1869/1967) On the Aesthetic Education of Man: In a Series of Letters. EM Wilkinson, LA Willoughby (eds and transl.). Oxford: Clarendon Press.

Schopenhauer A (1883/1910) The World as Will and Idea, 7th edn. Transl. RB Haldane, J Kemp. London: Kegan Paul, Trench, Trubner.

Spoto A (1989/1995) Jung's Typology in Perspective. Illinois: Chiron.

Stocks JL (1939) Reason and Intuition. Oxford: Oxford University Press.

Storr A (1972/1991) The Dynamics of Creation. London: Penguin Books.

Sullivan HS (1947) Modern Conceptions of Psychiatry. New York: William Allison White Foundation.

Szalita-Pemow AB (1955) The 'intuitive process' and its relation to work with schizophrenics. Journal of the American Psychoanalytic Association, 3: 7–18.

Taylor E (1992) William James and C.G. Jung. In Papadopoulos (1992) (op.cit.).

Van der Hoop, JH (1939) Conscious Orientation. New York: Harcourt Brace.

Vaughan F (1985/1995) The Inward Arc. Nevada City: Blue Dolphin.

Westcott MR (1964) Empirical studies of intuition. In CW Taylor (ed.), Widening Horizons. New York: John Wiley.

Winnicott DW (1965) The Maturational Process and the Facilitating Environment. London: The Hogarth Press.

Wordsworth W (1807/1950) The Poetical Works of Wordsworth. Ed. T Hutchinson. London: Oxford University Press.

Wundt WM (1862). Beiträge zur Theorie der Sinneswahrnehmung. Leipzig: Wilhelm Engelmann.

Wundt WM (1907) Outlines of Psychology. Transl. CH Judd. 3rd. rev. English edn. Leipzig: Wilhelm Engelmann.

Yontef GM (1979) Gestalt therapy: clinical phenomenology. Gestalt Journal 2(1): 27–45.

Zohar D (1991) The Quantum Self. London: Fontana.

Index

Figures in italics denote tables and diagrams.

241